T0157482

Bristol and the Birth of the Atlantic Economy, 1500–1700

Bristol and the Birth of the Atlantic Economy, 1500–1700

Richard Stone

THE BOYDELL PRESS

First published 2024
The Boydell Press, Woodbridge

ISBN 978 1 83765 053 8

The Boydell Press is an imprint of Boydell & Brewer Ltd
PO Box 9, Woodbridge, Suffolk IP12 3DF, UK
and of Boydell & Brewer Inc.
668 Mt Hope Avenue, Rochester, NY 14620–2731, USA
website: www.boydellandbrewer.com

A CIP catalogue record for this book is available
from the British Library

The publisher has no responsibility for the continued existence or accuracy of URLs for
external or third-party internet websites referred to in this book, and does not guarantee
that any content on such websites is, or will remain, accurate or appropriate

For my family

Contents

Illustrations

Figures

Tables

Acknowledgements

If there is one thing that I have learned during the more than fifteen years I have been working on the project which ultimately became this book, it is quite how generous people are with both their time and their support. It would thus be virtually impossible for me to personally acknowledge everyone who has contributed in some way, and I would almost certainly inadvertently end up leaving people out. So, to everyone who has corresponded with me, read my work, listened to a paper, discussed my research, participated in one of my classes, or helped me in any other way, thank you!

Many of those to whom I am most indebted have been my friends and colleagues at the University of Bristol, spanning the Department of Historical Studies, School of Humanities, Early Modern Studies Research Group, Centre for Black Humanities, Centre for Environmental Humanities, and Bristol Record Society. Evan Jones deserves particular credit for sparking my love of trade history and introducing me to the Port Books, as does Ronald Hutton for fighting my cause at many key moments in my career. Special thanks are also due to my friends and former colleagues Harriett Webster and Andrea Livesey, who at different times in this journey have been invaluable.

For sharing research data and images, as well as numerous conversations about our interrelated research topics, I am deeply grateful to Jonathan Harlow, Peter Taylor, Margaret Condon, and the participants in the Ireland-Bristol Trade in the Sixteenth Century project. Susan Flavin supported me when I was first learning to transcribe the Port Books and has always been my go-to person with questions on Irish trade. Madge Dresser has played a key part in shaping my thoughts on Bristol's relationship with slavery, as well as providing invaluable support and encouragement over the years.

I am deeply grateful to my editor Peter Sowden at Boydell and Brewer, both for suggesting that my work on Bristol would make a good book, and for his endless patience as I have written it. Jess Farr-Cox (the Filthy Comma) has done an excellent job of copy-editing the whole book and provided the index. Helpful suggestions from the anonymous reader(s) at both proposal and final manuscript stage have made this a much stronger work. Finally, historians would never get far without archivists, and the staff at Bristol Archives, The

National Archives, and University of Bristol Special Collections have been endlessly supportive.

By far my biggest debt is to my family: my parents Alan and Christine, my brother James, and my sister-in-law Lara. To them this book is dedicated.

Abbreviations

[year] (e.g. 1604) Book of Rates	Book of Rates for stated year (see Bibliography for full reference)
BRO	Bristol Archives
Enrolled Accounts	TNA PRO E356/28-29 – Enrolled Accounts, 1560–1603
Gloucester Port Books	Adam Matthew Publications/University of Wolverhampton, 'The Gloucester Port Book Database, 1575–1765' (1998)
[year] (e.g. 1492/3) Particular Account	Bristol 'Particular' Customs Account for stated year, EXCEL Dataset (see Bibliography for full reference)
[year] (e.g. 1637/8) Port Book	Bristol King's Remembrancer Port Book for stated year, EXCEL Dataset (see Bibliography for full reference)
Register of Servants to Foreign Plantations	BRO 04220/1-2 Register of Servants to Foreign Plantations. EXCEL Dataset created from: http://www.virtualjamestown.org/indentures/about_indentures.html#Bristol
TNA PRO	The National Archives/Public Record Office
[year] (e.g. 1654/5) Wharfage Book	Wharfage Book of the Society of Merchant Venturers of Bristol, EXCEL Dataset for stated year (see Bibliography for full reference)

Introduction

Let us take, for example, the *Unicorn*. We know that she could carry 130 tons of goods, and that her home port was Bristol. We know that she was under the command of her master James Powell, who had just sailed her back to Bristol from Toulon in France. We also know that between 10 August and 29 August in 1601, she was being loaded with a cargo to be carried to the port of La Rochelle on France's Atlantic coast. We know what this cargo was: 30 tons of lead (in the form of sowes, at eighteen to the ton); 300 goads of cotton cloths in two packs; three woollen broadcloths in one pack and another overlength cloth; and 15 dicker of calf-skins (which were being exported under a licence awarded to someone called Bazans). We know who owned these goods: John Aldworth, John Barker, John Whitsonne, John Webb, Richard Tagg, Christopher Carie, John Fowins and Thomas White, all of whom were from Bristol. Admittedly, due to the tendency of Bristol's Tudor merchants to engage themselves in illicit dealings, there is an element of uncertainty. She may have been carrying rather more leather than was covered by the licence, and she just might have in fact been heading to Spain and concealing this due to the ongoing war. But you'll need to read Chapter 1 to find out all about this. All in all, it's safe to say that we know quite a bit about the *Unicorn*, which is pretty remarkable given that her working life was slap bang in the middle of an era often referred to as 'the Dark Ages in English economic history'.[1] What is even more surprising is that she is not a special ship, but an example chosen more or less at random. We could have looked at hundreds, even thousands of other ships that sailed into and out of Bristol across the sixteenth and seventeenth century in a similar amount of detail. And this was not a meticulous piece of source-linkage, bringing together information from numerous carefully researched documents. All of this information came from just five manuscript pages of one document: the Surveyor's Overseas Port Book for the Port of Bristol, 1600/1.[2] That is essentially what this book is about: using the remarkable detail provided by customs records such as the Port Books to shine a light onto the so-called 'Dark Ages

---

1   F. J. Fisher, 'The Sixteenth and Seventeenth Centuries: The Dark Ages in English Economic History', *Economica*, New Series, 24(93) (1957), pp. 2–18.
2   1600/1 Port Book, ff. 7r, 28v, 29r, 30v, 31v.

in English economic history' and to examine how the day-to-day activities of hundreds of perfectly normal ships such as the *Unicorn* collectively form a set of developments that were to transform the course of history.

An Era of Revolutions

That the sixteenth and seventeenth centuries were, or at least have been thought of as, a 'dark age' in English economic history is unfortunate, as this was also a time when many of the most important developments in the history of the English economy began. Indeed, it might justifiably be called an era of revolutions, or at least of the beginnings of revolutions. Various scholars have attributed to this time and this place (and the activities of England's overseas merchants) the origins of such epoch-making events as the British Empire (and its offspring the United States), the beginning of the Industrial Revolution, and even of the capitalist financial system. Looking at the development of overseas trade in this crucial period through documents as rich in detail as the Port Books thus has the potential to be hugely valuable.

Arguably the first revolution of this era is what Ralph Davis has called the 'Commercial Revolution'. This was the shift of English overseas trade from its medieval pattern, focused almost entirely on sending woollen cloth to ports in the North Sea or along Europe's Atlantic coast, to a modern, globe-spanning trade network exporting a wide range of manufactured goods and re-exports.[3] There is consensus amongst economic historians as to the timing of this Commercial Revolution, with most adopting what might be called the 'three phases' model. According to Davis, 'in the centuries before the Industrial Revolution, English overseas trade went through three waves of expansion, separated by periods of near stagnation'.[4] The first, he argued, occurred between 1475 and 1550, driven by increased European demand for English woollen cloth; the second between 1639 and 1689 as a result of new markets in southern Europe, and the opening up of new trades in tobacco, sugar, and calicoes; and the third in the mid-eighteenth century, fuelled by increases in both production of manufactured goods, and the purchasing power of colonial populations. In probably the most widely cited study of the development of English overseas trade in the century before 1660, Robert Brenner adopted and adapted Davis's 'three phases' model. While Brenner still saw the phases as discontinuous, conducted by separate groups of merchants, he suggested some chronological overlap. For Brenner, the broadcloth-based expansion occurred between 1480 and 1550, with the collapse of the broadcloth trade leading to a period of stagnation between

---

3   R. Davis, *A Commercial Revolution* (London, 1967), p. 1.
4   R. Davis, *English Overseas Trade 1500–1700* (London, 1973), p. 7.

1550 and 1614, and then crisis and decline between 1614 and 1640. He then divided Davis's second phase into two separate developments: the creation of long-distance import- and re-export-driven trades with the Near and Far East between 1550 and 1650; and the rise from the early seventeenth century of the plantation trades in tobacco and sugar.[5]

While historians are relatively agreed on the chronology of the growth of England's overseas trade in the early modern period, there is much less consensus on both the causes and the consequences of this development. There are two major areas of debate: whether the causes of expansion and change were internal or external; and whether the Atlantic economy (and specifically the enslaved labour central to it) caused the Industrial Revolution in Britain. Much of the early scholarship fell under the Whig tradition of historical writing. Arguably following on from the works of Richard Hakluyt's *Principal Navigations*, this traced and celebrated the efforts of England's explorers, founders, and pioneers. It discussed how their dreams of an empire to rival and even surpass that of Spain ultimately came to fruition, at times even leaning towards a teleological sense of inevitability.[6] The history of discovery and colonisation continues to be a lively field, with the most recent studies such as the Cabot Project seeking to add to the often very slim source base for early ventures. This is revealing previously unknown layers of complexity, such as the role of Italian financiers in backing Bristol's late fifteenth-century discovery voyages, and allowing us a more nuanced and detailed insight into the motivations of those involved.[7]

A different body of work has looked beyond innovation and enterprise as drivers in their own right, and considered the underlying economic courses of the evolution of English overseas trade. Much mid-twentieth-century scholarship, typified by historians such as Ralph Davis and F. J. Fisher, explained the shift to new markets through a crisis-centred model.[8] For them, English merchants opened up the new trades which were ultimately to fuel the expansion of the country's overseas trade as a result of the need to find new markets for

---

5   R. Brenner, *Merchants and Revolution: Commercial Change, Political Conflict, and London's Overseas Traders, 1550–1653* (London, 2003), p. xi.
6   A Bristol example in this tradition would be C. MacInnes, *Bristol: A Gateway of Empire* (Bristol, 1939).
7   F. Guidi Bruscoli, 'John Cabot and His Italian Financiers', *Historical Research*, 85 (2012); E. T. Jones and M. M. Condon, *Cabot and Bristol's Age of Discovery* (Bristol, 2016); M. M. Condon and E. T. Jones, 'William Weston: Early Voyager to the New World', *Historical Research*, 91 (November 2018), pp. 628–46.
8   G. D. Ramsay, *English Overseas Trade during the Centuries of Emergence: Studies in Some Modern Origins of the English-Speaking World* (London, 1957), pp. 25–33; B. E. Supple, *Commercial Crisis and Change, 1600–1642: A Study in the Instability of a Mercantile Economy* (Cambridge, 1949), pp. 23–131; and F. J. Fisher, 'London's Export Trade in the Early Seventeenth Century', *Economic History Review*, 2nd ser., III(2) (1950), pp. 151–61; Davis, *Commercial Revolution*, pp. 5–6.

English cloth, replacing those lost with the collapse of the Antwerp entrepôt in the mid-sixteenth century. The crisis-centred explanation has been challenged by Robert Brenner, who highlighted that it was independent social groups of merchants (not the Merchant Adventurers responsible for the declining cloth trade) who pioneered new ventures, and argued that 'the rise of the new trades of the Elizabethan era' was 'based, from the start, on imports'.[9] Brenner has famously argued that the system of capitalism originated with increased competition and market imperatives and efficiency gains in early modern English agriculture.[10] This, he argued, led to greater market dependence rather than subsistence production, and increased purchasing power at all levels of society as a result of efficiency gains in agriculture and manufacturing that made products cheaper. This increased demand for consumer goods, according to Brenner, allowed imports to rise significantly even when the cloth trade was in decline, and spurred merchants to open up new trades, seeking to acquire imported goods more cheaply by going directly to the source of supply.[11]

Many studies of English overseas trade have opted to either begin or end in the mid-seventeenth century. This has the advantage of allowing a closer focus on the factors influencing the development of trade at that point in time, but also means long-term trends can be overlooked. Brenner, for example, concluded his study *Merchants and Revolution* in 1653, while in the most recent substantive study of English overseas trade in this period, Nuala Zahedieh has looked at the relationship between London and the colonies in the period 1660–1700.[12] While paying a great deal of attention to the origins and drivers of early American trade, Brenner thus saw it only in its nascent form and did not have the scope to discuss its longer-term impact. Zahedieh, meanwhile, was able to observe the impact of the colonies on the English economy as a source of both raw materials and manufactured goods, and to show the significance of the Navigation and Staple Acts in creating a protected market in which English merchants were able to thrive. It was not within the scope of her study, however, to look at the longer-term factors that led to the emergence and growth of the colonial trades.

Recent work has begun to shift back to thinking about the people who drove developments in overseas trade. Rather than 'great men' though, the focus now is more cultural, looking at 'great organisations', their formation and function. In a study spanning the period 1000–1800, and taking the whole of Europe as its scope, Sheilagh Ogilvie has examined the role of merchant guilds. Her work has

9   Brenner, *Merchants and Revolution*, p. 5.
10 For more on the 'Brenner Thesis' on the origins of capitalism and resultant debates, see E. Meiksins Wood, *The Origin of Capitalism: A Longer View* (London, 2017), pp. 95–121.
11 Brenner, *Merchants and Revolution*, pp. 39–45.
12 *Ibid.*; N. Zahedieh, *The Capital and the Colonies: London and the Atlantic Economy, 1660–1700* (Cambridge, 2010).

shown that these institutions, which controlled much of the trade of medieval and early modern Europe, were not a positive force for economic development. Instead, they sought to control access to trade, both through formal monopolies and more informal mechanisms, maximising profits for their close-knit membership even to the detriment of the economy more broadly.[13] Notably it was those nations around the North Sea (England and the Netherlands) where guilds were superseded by open-access institutions that proved to be the drivers of economic expansion in the centuries after 1500. Edmond Smith has examined these successor organisations, the merchant companies which drove England's global commercial expansion during the reigns of Elizabeth I and the Stuarts, and the communities of merchants who formed them. For Smith, 'England's economic development was a cultural and social phenomenon as much as an economic one', and it was much more the day-to-day activities of England's mere merchants which drove the rise of England's global networks than either the endeavours of the state or the exploits of adventurers and buccaneers. In particular Smith stressed the importance of collaboration in the economic success of the merchant community. This included both forming a commercial culture with agreed practices and values that kept the wheels of commerce turning smoothly, as well as innovative business models such as the formation of corporations, which allowed them both to pool their capital and to act as a single body in their dealings with others and thus be ready to take advantage of the opportunities which global commerce presented.[14] Misha Ewen has taken this a step further, considering how a wider public beyond the elites contributed to the success of colonial ventures. Her work shines a light on the overlooked role of women and the labouring poor in supporting ventures, both as investors and participants in other ways. It stresses how quickly English society as a whole became tightly invested in colonisation, contributing a great deal to its success.[15]

Moving from the causes to the consequences of the developments of English overseas trade in the sixteenth and seventeenth centuries, the most notable area is the long-running and often heated debate on the relationship between slavery and Britain's Industrial Revolution. This was sparked by the work of Eric Williams, most famously in his 1944 book *Capitalism and Slavery*. In what is now known as the 'Williams Thesis' he argued that profits from the slave trade and the sale of sugar in Britain provided both a significant amount of the capital and the demand for British manufactured goods that kick-started the

---

13   S. Ogilvie, *Institutions and European Trade: Merchants Guilds, 1000–1800* (Cambridge, 2011).
14   E. Smith, *Merchants: The Community That Shaped England's Trade and Empire* (London, 2021), pp. 4–8.
15   M. Ewen, *The Virginia Venture: American Colonisation and English Society, 1580–1660* (Philadelphia, 2022).

Industrial Revolution in the latter years of the eighteenth century.[16] Many of Williams's arguments have been dismissed by subsequent scholars. In particular, he significantly overestimated the profitability of the slave trade itself, and it has been shown that its profits could not have financed industrialisation.[17] Other aspects of Williams's argument, however, have been developed by scholars in the nearly eighty years since *Capitalism and Slavery* was first published. The broader argument that slavery played a significant role in causing the British Industrial Revolution still carries a great deal of weight, particularly when focusing on more dynamic factors rather than straightforward capital accumulation. Joseph Inikori, for example, has argued that an integrated Atlantic economy emerged in the period 1500–1850, and that this was 'a major factor in the development process in Europe'.[18] In particular, Inikori has highlighted the close relationship between the counties in northern England and the Midlands, which were the heartlands of the Industrial Revolution and Atlantic trade, even suggesting that they 'were more tightly linked to the evolving Atlantic economy than to the rest of their respective national economies'.[19] Here he highlights the central role of demand for manufactured products from Africa and the Americas in the eighteenth century in spurring development and innovation in their manufacturing industries.

Similar arguments have been developed by those working on world systems theory, and the question of the 'Great Divergence'. The debate over the Williams Thesis was reignited in the 1980s by Immanuel Wallerstein, whose work on world systems theory (an idea that originates in sociology) suggested that the colonies played a significant part in financing industrial development. Inspired by Braudel's work on the Mediterranean, Wallerstein suggested that a world-system of trade emerged in the early modern period, and due to the interconnected nature of local economies, developments in one place could only be understood by taking into account those elsewhere. According to this model, wealth generated in the 'periphery' (the colonies) became a vital source of capital accumulation for the 'core' (Britain). As a result, industry developed in Britain, while the colonies were left relatively underdeveloped and focused on production of raw materials.[20] Wallerstein's arguments have provoked a great deal of criticism, not least from Patrick O'Brien who argued that the colonies were of peripheral importance to European economic development. In what

---

16   E. Williams, *Capitalism and Slavery* (London, 1964).

17   K. Morgan, *Slavery, Atlantic Trade and the British Economy, 1660–1800* (Cambridge, 2000), pp. 41–8.

18   J. E. Inikori, 'Atlantic Slavery and the Rise of the Capitalist Global Economy', *Current Anthropology*, 61(supplement 22) (2020), pp. 161–3.

19   *Ibid.*, p. 164.

20   I. Wallerstein, *The Modern World-System II: Mercantilism and the Consolidation of the European World-Economy, 1600–1750* (London, 2011).

has become known as the 'small ratios' argument, he suggested that colonial commerce generated funds sufficient to finance just 15 per cent of expenditure during industrial development; that expansion occurred in a wide range of industries that did not rely on colonial imports; and that the colonies accounted for only a small proportion of European economic activity.[21]

Recent work by Kenneth Pomeranz and others has restated the case for the pivotal role of the American and Caribbean colonies in facilitating the development of industrial capitalism in Britain. Pomeranz sought to explain the 'Great Divergence': why, given their similar development hitherto, Europe (and specifically Britain) industrialised in the nineteenth century when Asia did not. While much previous scholarship focused on arguments about what made Britain exceptional, Pomeranz sought to compare developments in Britain to other parts of the world. Rather than asking why the Industrial Revolution occurred in Britain, he instead sought to ask why it did not occur in the Yangtze Delta.[22] His findings showed that the divergence occurred remarkably late, with many parts of Asia achieving similar levels of economic growth and development to Britain, right up to the eve of the Industrial Revolution in 1750.[23] For Pomeranz, Britain kicked on from here into further development (while the Yangtze Delta did not) due to resource barriers. Further growth in societies prior to industrialising Britain was stymied by the lack of fuel and fibre (or, more specifically, the land needed to produce it), which meant they simply could not continue to expand.[24] In the case of Britain, however, the twin discoveries of exploitable, accessible coal, and the 'ghost acres' of a vast 'unpopulated' continent on the other side of the Atlantic, provided huge amounts of both these resources and allowed development to continue unchecked.[25] The importance of the Atlantic economy to English economic development in the pre-Industrial Revolution era has become increasingly widely accepted in recent years. As mentioned, Zahedieh chose to focus her study of London's late seventeenth-century trade purely on the capital's relationship with the colonies.[26] Indeed, even Patrick O'Brien has modified his position to concede that, while it should still not be exaggerated, foreign commerce was 'obviously important' for the British Industrial Revolution.[27] Zahedieh has built on these arguments through her work on the copper industry. Her findings stress the importance

---

21   P. O'Brien, 'European Economic Development: The Contribution of the Periphery', *Economic History Review*, 35(1) (1982), pp. 1–18.
22   K. Pomeranz, *The Great Divergence: China, Europe, and the Making of the Modern World Economy* (Princeton, 2000), p. 8.
23   *Ibid.*, pp. 13–14.
24   *Ibid.*, pp. 209–42.
25   *Ibid.*, pp. 264–85.
26   Zahedieh, *Capital and the Colonies*.
27   Quoted in *ibid.*, p. 5.

of the massively increased colonial market for a wider variety of exported goods, including copper, in driving innovation to increase production and the investment that turned ideas into a reality. As Zahedieh has stated, 'invention is only the first stage in converting a new technology into commercial success', with investment needed to establish production on a commercial scale. Much of this investment came from merchants with Atlantic interests, showing the importance of these new markets to fostering innovation and development in the industrial sector.[28]

While arguments regarding the role of the Atlantic economy in driving the commercial developments that led to the Industrial Revolution in Britain have gained a great deal of traction in recent years, there is still a good deal of ongoing scholarship that focuses on internal causes. The five authors of *British Economic Growth, 1270–1870*, for example, highlight the long-term growth of the British economy in the centuries prior to industrialisation. Their long-run examination of estimates for population, land use and production shows a persistent upward trend in GDP per capita, resulting in a doubling between the mid-fourteenth century and 1700.[29] For them, the transition to modern economic growth that occurred in Britain during the Industrial Revolution 'sprang from processes of structural economic change, commercial speciali-sation, and technological innovation whose origins should be seen as stretching back to the late-medieval period'.[30] This argument might be seen as a return to the 'Commercialisation Thesis' for the origins of modern industrial capitalism; that enough economic growth simply needed to occur before a tip-over into capitalist-type behaviours occurred.[31] Another recent study highlighting factors internal to Britain, however, can be seen as an extension of the 'Brenner Thesis'. The idea that Britain experienced a consumer revolution in the early modern period has been long held, with both increasing variety and increasing amounts of consumer goods becoming common at all levels of society.[32] Jan de Vries, however, has suggested that this was driven not by an increased supply of such goods, but by an increased demand for them. In his words, 'in a specific historical period, in a specific geographical zone a new form of household economic behaviour became increasingly influential, increasing simultaneously the supply of market-oriented production and the demand for a broader but

28   N. Zahedieh, 'Colonies, Copper, and the Market for Inventive Activity in England and Wales, 1680–1730', *The Economic History Review*, 66(3) (2013), p. 818.

29   S. Broadberry, B. M. S. Campbell, A. Klein, M. Overton and B. van Leeuwen, *British Economic Growth, 1270–1870* (Cambridge, 2015).

30   *Ibid.*, pp. 400–1.

31   Meiksins Wood, *Origin of Capitalism*, pp. 11–17.

32   S. Flavin, *Consumption and Material Culture in Sixteenth-Century Ireland: Saffron, Stockings and Silk* (Woodbridge, 2014), pp. 1–3.

not indiscriminate range of consumer goods'.[33] This development, which de Vries labelled the 'Industrious Revolution', occurred over the long eighteenth century between 1650 and 1850 and was 'instrumental in setting the scene for the Industrial Revolution'.[34] For de Vries, this period saw householders in Britain work harder and direct more of their labour towards market-related activities, and the main driver of this industriousness was a new desire to acquire consumer goods.[35]

It is clear, then, both that the period 1500–1700 contained the roots of momentous developments in economic history, and that historians are not agreed on their cause or nature. The core of this disagreement lies in the nature of the so-called 'Dark Ages in English economic history'. With hard evidence in short supply, it is natural that there will be gaps and areas of uncertainty, and disagreement over how to interpret the evidence we do have. Perhaps the best way to resolve these debates, then, is to add more evidence to the discussion, and use it to shine a light on this 'Dark Age'. This book contributes to the ongoing debates on England's early modern economic history in two principal ways. The first is by offering a long duration study based on the most detailed statistical evidence base to date. As the opening example shows, the Port Books and other customs records potentially offer a thorough picture of England's overseas trade in this period. Previous historians have tended to overlook the evidence offered by these detailed customs records, or at least to engage with them only at a surface level, picking out illustrative examples, calculating simple statistics, or focusing on individual years. In large part this is because of the sheer amount of work needed to turn the pages and pages of information in these manuscript volumes into usable data. A late seventeenth-century writer said of processing the Port Books that it 'would require the full-time work of four men to deal with London alone each year'.[36] Although in Ralph Davis's view this probably said more about the inefficiency of the seventeenth-century civil service, he agreed that the task was 'enormous'.[37] More recently, Kenneth Morgan suggested that 'the hundreds of goods and diverse weights and measures listed in the Port Books … almost defy analysis' and that 'given a lifetime in which to conduct an investigation, it would be possible to use these sources for selected years to calculate the volume of Bristol's exports and then to convert quantities into

33   J. de Vries, *The Industrious Revolution: Consumer Behaviour and the Household Economy 1650 to the Present* (Cambridge, 2008), pp. ix–x.
34   *Ibid.*, p. 180.
35   *Ibid.*, p. 122.
36   R. Davis, 'English Foreign Trade, 1660–1700', in W. Minchinton (ed.), *The Growth of English Overseas Trade in the Seventeenth and Eighteenth Centuries* (London, 1969), p. 85.
37   *Ibid.*, p. 85.

prices by using the Book of Rates'.[38] The advent of cheap computer technology has, however, completely transformed the potential of the Port Books. While the process of transcription is still time-consuming, once this is completed, calculations that previously would have taken days can now be performed in seconds. This study is thus able to engage with detailed data spanning two centuries in a way which would have been impossible for previous generations of scholars.

The second main contribution of this book is in offering a detailed examination of the port of Bristol in this crucial period. This is significant because, first, Bristol was, after London, England's second-biggest port in this era, and indeed is often described as the country's 'second city'. Previous studies of English overseas trade in this period have tended to focus almost exclusively on London.[39] There have been studies of Bristol's trade in both the sixteenth and seventeenth centuries, but none based on detailed statistical evidence.[40] It is true that London still accounted for the bulk of English overseas trade in this period, accounting for between two-thirds and three-quarters of activity at the beginning of the seventeenth century.[41] In the century and a half after 1650, however, this pattern broke down, with Atlantic-facing ports such as Bristol, Liverpool and Glasgow expanding significantly and playing a much more significant part in the nation's overseas trade.[42] A study of Bristol as it began to rise to increased prominence is thus significant in its own right. The second reason that a study of Bristol offers a valuable window onto the forces driving the development of overseas trade is the comparatively simple makeup of the port's commercial activities. London traded with the Baltic, the Netherlands, Europe's Atlantic coast, the Mediterranean, Africa, the Americas, and Asia. It is thus difficult to view any one branch of trade in isolation, which has often led to misleading conclusions. In particular, the rise of new branches of trade is often credited to the need to replace lost markets after London's cloth trade with the Netherlands began to decline.[43] Bristol, however, was always focused on the

---

38   K. Morgan, *Bristol and the Atlantic Trade in the Eighteenth Century* (Cambridge, 1993), p. 91.

39   Davis, 'English Foreign Trade, 1660–1700'; Davis, *English Overseas Trade 1500–1700*; Fisher, 'London's Export Trade'; Supple, *Commercial Crisis and Change*; Zahedieh, *Capital and the Colonies*.

40   For example, P. McGrath, *Merchants and Merchandise in Seventeenth-Century Bristol*, Bristol Record Society Vol. 19 (1955); W. B. Stephens, 'Trade Trends at Bristol, 1600–1700', *Transactions of the Bristol and Gloucestershire Archaeological Society* (1974); J. M. Vanes, *The Port of Bristol in the Sixteenth Century*, Bristol Historical Association Pamphlets no. 39 (Bristol, 1977); D. H. Sacks, *The Widening Gate: Bristol and the Atlantic Economy, 1450–1700* (London, 1993).

41   Supple, *Commercial Crisis and Change*, p. 7; Fisher, 'London's Export Trade', p. 152.

42   Ramsay, *English Overseas Trade*, pp. 132–65.

43   Davis, *Commercial Revolution*, pp. 5–6.

Atlantic world. By looking at trade trends in Bristol, it is possible to examine the dynamics of this increasingly important commercial arena in isolation.

The overriding argument of this book is that the dynamics of the Atlantic economy are fundamental to understanding Bristol's, and more broadly England's, commercial development in the sixteenth and seventeenth centuries. The research it presents pushes the impact of Atlantic markets on Bristol's trade back to the mid-sixteenth century, as the flow of New World gold and silver into Spain created a profitable market for English exports, and stimulated interconnected markets along Europe's Atlantic seaboard. As Bristol was never heavily involved in the Netherlands cloth trade, this challenges the idea that innovation in the Commercial Revolution was crisis-led, instead suggesting it was driven primarily by opportunity. When England gained its own American and Caribbean colonies in the mid-seventeenth century, these are shown to have had a rapid and transformative effect on both the scale and nature of Bristol's overseas trade. In little more than two decades the medieval pattern of overseas commerce was revolutionised; trade doubled in size and continued to grow rapidly (peaking in the 1680s), and the new markets came to account for more than 50 per cent of the city's imports. It is argued that the growth of these new trades was driven as much by colonial demand for English exports as it was for imports of colonial cash crops. From as early as the seventeenth century, trade with the Atlantic slavery economy was thus already stimulating growth in manufacturing and industry in both Bristol and its hinterland, providing a market for a diverse range of manufactured goods (from hats and nails to coaches and clay pipes), as well as creating new industries to process and refine the huge amounts of tobacco and sugar that flowed into the city.

The Port City of Bristol

Located on England's western coast at the mouth of the Severn Sea, Bristol is naturally placed for Atlantic trade. Indeed, the very location of the city is based on its potential for trading connections. Its name, 'Brig Stowe' in the original Anglo-Saxon, means 'place by the bridge'. At the meeting point of road, river and maritime transport networks, Bristol is the ideal place for a market. Although in later centuries these features led Bristol to decline as a port, in the early years its high tidal range (the second-highest in the world, in excess of 40 feet) and the high-sided Avon Gorge and six-mile river approach that guarded it from attack by sea were assets. Encircled on three sides by the rivers Frome and Avon, Bristol was also easily defended from land-based attacks.[44] It also sits in the middle of a vast and productive area, accessible along the Severn

---

44   J. W. Sherborne, *The Port of Bristol in the Middle Ages* (Bristol, 1965), p. 1.

(navigable as far up as Shrewsbury) and along the coast. This encompassed both fertile agricultural land and valuable mineral resources, joined as the centuries progressed by substantial manufacturing industries in the Wiltshire cloth belt and later in the Midlands.

Bristol was founded much later than many of England's other significant medieval towns, with the first evidence of permanent settlement in the area dating from some time in the century before the Norman Conquest. From these late beginnings, however, the town grew quickly and was already a flourishing centre for trade by the Domesday Survey in 1086.[45] Lack of surviving documentary evidence means that Bristol's early commercial history will always be somewhat opaque, but it is clear that from its very earliest years, it faced towards the Atlantic. In the eleventh century, Bristol's principal connections were with Viking settlements in Ireland, especially Dublin, and through them with Norway.[46] The exact commodity makeup of this trade is unknown, but it is clear that it included enslaved people bought from all over England.[47] While Bristol's slave trade had largely died out by the twelfth century (perhaps in part due to the abolitionist efforts of St Wulfstan, but also as there simply were no Vikings left to trade with), the city and its overseas commerce continued to expand, described as 'almost the richest of all of the towns in the kingdom'.[48] Ireland still appears to have been the principal focus of trade, with especially strong links between Bristol and Dublin, although there is also some evidence of emerging trade with France.[49] By the thirteenth century the city's trade was developing into its classic medieval pattern, with a major trade in wine emerging, focusing on the Bordelaise region.[50] This was joined in the fourteenth century by a rapidly growing cloth trade.[51] Having not previously been noted as a centre of cloth manufacture, by the middle of the century Bristol had grown to be the most significant cloth-exporting port in the country, with 750 cloths a year, representing 60 per cent of the nation's cloth exports. The 1450s and 1460s then saw a further significant growth in the cloth trade, peaking at over 8,000 cloths in a year compared to just 3,000 from London.[52] Noteworthy too is the first development of significant trade with Portugal, which also received nearly 1,900 cloths from Bristol.[53]

45   M. D. Lobel and E. M. Carus Wilson, 'Bristol', in M. D. Lobel (ed.), *The Atlas of Historic Towns, Volume 2* (London, 1975), p. 3
46   Sherborne, *Port of Bristol*, pp. 2–3.
47   D. Pelteret, 'Slave Raiding and Slave Trading in Early England', *Anglo-Saxon England*, 9 (1981), pp. 112–13.
48   Sherbourne, *Port of Bristol*, p. 3.
49   *Ibid.*, pp. 3–4.
50   *Ibid.*, pp. 7–8.
51   *Ibid.*, pp. 8–9.
52   Lobel and Carus Wilson, 'Bristol', p. 10.
53   Sherbourne, *Port of Bristol*, p. 11.

Bristol's trade in the fifteenth century is perhaps best known for its voyages of 'discovery': John Sturmy's attempts to break into the Mediterranean trade in the 1450s and 1460s and John Cabot's accidental discovery of North America when searching for a maritime route to Asia.[54] The century also witnessed the rise and decline of long-distance trade with Iceland.[55] In the short term, however (as discussed in Chapter 3), these new ventures had limited economic significance and other developments played a greater part in shaping the port's commercial fortunes. From this period on, the availability of more detailed customs records, and better survival of sources generally, means that we can tell the story of Bristol's developing overseas trade in more detail and with more certainty. The city's trade was dealt a severe blow with the loss of Gascony in 1453, which disrupted the symbiotic relationship that had emerged between Bristol and the English ports of the Bordelaise region. Nonetheless, the customs accounts show that trade recovered quickly, reaching its old levels by the 1470s, thanks, in large part, to the rise of a new branch of trade with Castile in the Iberian Peninsula. By the 1490s, this new trade accounted for between two-thirds and three-quarters of Bristol's commerce. In terms of goods, however, trade retained its medieval character, with a strong focus on cloth and wine. Indeed, woollen cloth accounted for as much as 99 per cent of the value of Bristol's exports at this time.[56]

The period covered by this book (the sixteenth and seventeenth centuries) was transformational for Bristol, seeing patterns of trade that had been relatively consistent for centuries completely transformed. Previous studies have characterised the sixteenth century as a period of decline and uncertainty for Bristol, with its cloth trade engrossed by London merchants and its continental markets disrupted.[57] The research presented here, however, challenges these arguments, showing instead that Bristol's trade prospered throughout the century thanks to a diversification of exports, high prices in Spain as a result of the influx of New World bullion, and a buoyant Irish market. Until the Civil War, the pattern of trade was much the same as in previous centuries, with a roughly equal share of Irish, French and Spanish trade and little diversification into new markets. The second half of the seventeenth century, however, saw

---

54 Jones and Condon, *Cabot and Bristol's Age of Discovery*; S. Jenks, *Robert Sturmy's Commercial Expedition to the Mediterranean (1457/8)*, Bristol Record Society Vol. 58 (Bristol, 2006). The term 'discovery' is, of course, a problematic one given that there were people in the Americas long before Cabot or Columbus set foot there.

55 E. M. Carus-Wilson, *Medieval Merchant Venturers* (London, 1967), pp. 98–142.

56 R. Stone, 'Bristol's Overseas Trade in the Later Fifteenth Century: The Evidence of the "Particular" Customs Accounts', in E. T. Jones and R. Stone (eds), *The World of the Newport Medieval Ship: Trade, Politics, and Shipping in the Mid-Fifteenth Century* (Cardiff, 2018), p. 183.

57 Vanes, *The Port of Bristol*, pp. 22–3.

this pattern transformed by the advent of trade with the new English colonies in North America and the Caribbean. That these new trades emerged in this period has long been recognised; however, this book shows for the first time that they developed much faster and much earlier than previously supposed, already accounting for as much as 70 per cent of Bristol's trade by the 1650s. Based on a simple count of shipping, McGrath estimated the growth to be a much slower one, accounting for less than a sixth of Bristol's trade in the 1650s and 1660s, rising to between a quarter and a third in the 1680s.[58] After centuries of dominance, wine was replaced by tobacco and sugar as Bristol's principal imports, and cloth exports were joined by a diverse range of manufactures, metals and agricultural produce. The emergence of these new trades resulted in a considerable expansion of Bristol's overseas commerce and the beginnings of a redevelopment and gentrification of the city that has been dubbed an 'urban renaissance'.[59]

The eighteenth century has often been seen as Bristol's 'Golden Age', with the expansion that began in the late seventeenth century continuing apace, and the city continuing to focus on American markets. By far the most discussed aspect of Bristol's commerce in this period (both in scholarship and in the popular consciousness) is its development into Britain's leading slave-trading port. Having only officially entered the trade in 1698 (see Chapter 6 for a discussion of potential earlier involvement), by the 1720s Bristol was sending out an average of twenty-five slave-trading vessels a year, and by the period 1728–32 this had risen to forty-eight. In the 1730s, the city was responsible for as many as half of all British slave-trading voyages each year.[60] While Bristol was surpassed by Liverpool in the slave trade, it continued to send out as many as twenty-three slave-trading ships per year as late as 1788–92.[61] The transatlantic traffic in enslaved Africans was, however, commercially at least, not the most significant way in which the city benefited from the Atlantic slave economy in the eighteenth century, accounting for just 4–9 per cent of all ships leaving the port.[62] In many respects, the development of Bristol's trade in the eighteenth century was an escalation of the patterns seen since the 1650s, with ever-increasing quantities of tobacco and sugar from the North American colonies and the Caribbean flowing into the port. Following its expansion in the second half of the seventeenth century, the volume of American shipping arriving at Bristol doubled over the course of the eighteenth century, with the

58   McGrath, *Merchants and Merchandise*, p. xxi.
59   M. Dresser, *Slavery Obscured: The Social History of the Slave Trade in Bristol* (Bristol, 2001), pp. 96–128; R. Leech, J. Barry, A. Brown, C. Ferguson and E. Parkinson (eds), *The Bristol Hearth Tax, 1662–1763*, Bristol Record Society Vol. 70 (Bristol, 2018), pp. 55–65.
60   Morgan, *Bristol and the Atlantic Trade*, p. 132.
61   *Ibid.*, p. 133.
62   *Ibid.*, p. 131.

Caribbean accounting for as much as 60 per cent.[63] Walter Minchinton also dubbed Bristol a 'Metropolis of the West' during this period. While it may have been surpassed as a centre for international trade by the northern ports, it had a significant role as a redistribution centre, redistributing goods from across the region and in return supplying the region with colonial produce.[64] Paradoxically, the prosperous eighteenth century also marked the end of Bristol's status as England's second city. By 1800, Bristol was Britain's sixth-largest port, and by 1855, its twelfth-largest.[65] Relative decline did not, however, equate to absolute decline, and in fact Bristol continued to expand as a centre for both trade and industry. Shipping traffic continued to increase, from 103,000 tons in 1791 to 400,600 in 1855, and value of trade too remained high, with average customs duties of £289,635 in the 1750s growing to £1,193,000 in 1856.[66]

The period covered by this book is, then, key for Bristol's commercial history. While the city may have held its greatest national and international significance in the high Middle Ages and the eighteenth century, the sixteenth and seventeenth centuries witnessed some dramatic and crucial transformations. This was the era when Bristol transitioned from its medieval trading pattern, focused around the exchange of cloth and wine along Europe's Atlantic coast, to a modern one that was truly global in scale and involved a diverse range of both import and export goods. It saw the beginnings of both a rise in population, and the development of a broad range of crafts and industries that were to define the modern city. The period also witnessed rising affluence for Bristol's merchants, setting them up for investment in the New World colonies and at home, developing business opportunities in the coming centuries, and the beginnings of the construction of refined homes and civic buildings that characterise much of the modern city. Perhaps most crucially, these years also saw the beginnings of the links to Atlantic slavery, which were key in the following centuries, and are central to the complex ways in which the city engages with its past today.

The Records

The key source for this study is the King's Remembrancer Port Books, now held in the E190 series at the National Archives in Kew. These were detailed records submitted by the customs officers of every port to the Exchequer at the end of

63   *Ibid.*, p. 13.
64   W. Minchinton, 'Bristol, Metropolis of the West in the Eighteenth Century', *Transactions of the Royal Historical Society*, 5th ser., IV (1954).
65   K. Morgan, 'The Economic Development of Bristol, 1700–1850', in M. Dresser and P. Ollerenshaw (eds), *The Making of Modern Bristol* (Bristol, 1996), p. 49.
66   *Ibid.*, p. 56.

every year.[67] With the obvious exception of smuggled goods, every consignment exported from or imported into the country was recorded in these books, along with a wealth of supporting detail, such as the type of commodity, the duty it paid, its weight, number, or volume, and the containers that housed it; the name of the owner, and a varying amount of detail about his (or occasionally her) occupation and nationality. In addition, the books provide the name of the ship, her master, home port, her immediate port of origin or destination, and usually her tonnage. These records were submitted in standard pre-prepared parchment volumes, and were usually fair copies written up later, rather than the original notes taken when the goods passed through the customs house. In each port there were three principal customs officers (along with an array of deputies, clerks and waiters to assist them). The Customer was responsible for actually collecting taxes, recording their payment, and issuing a docket to prove payment; the Controller kept a duplicate set of records to ensure the Customer's honesty; and the Searcher inspected the goods on the ships to ensure nothing was loaded on which duty had not been paid. Every customs officer, from the Customer and Controller down to the Searcher, submitted their own account, so at one time there would have been a huge number of these Port Books.[68] Time, however, has not been kind to what is now the E190 series. Up until 1911 they were stored in sacks in an exposed and weatherbeaten room and thus many were severely affected by damp.[69] Indeed, the National Archives Schedules of Destruction reveal that many of the Port Books were deliberately destroyed as they were not considered valuable.[70] What was once a fine series, therefore, has been reduced to a patchy scattering of examples, many of which are in too

---

67   For the customs service, a 'port' did not mean an individual town or harbour, but rather a broader administrative area. Each of these 'ports' would have a 'head port' where the local customs service was based, smaller 'member ports' which for customs purposes were subject to and included in the accounts of the head port, and 'creeks' where goods could also be legally loaded and unloaded. See N. S. B. Grass, *The Early English Customs System: A Documentary Study of the Institutional and Economic History of the Customs from the Thirteenth to the Sixteenth Century* (Cambridge, 1918), pp. 105–6. In the case of the port of Bristol, until 1575 the port encompassed the River Avon and the Gloucestershire reaches of the River Severn up as far as Worcester. Thereafter, however, Gloucester was made an independent port, responsible for all customs upriver of the ferry crossing between Aust and Beachy. See S. Flavin and E. T. Jones (eds), *Bristol's Trade with Ireland and the Continent: The Exchequer Customs Accounts*, Bristol Record Society Vol. 61 (Bristol, 2011), p. xix.

68   S. Flavin and E. T. Jones, 'Introduction', in S. Flavin and E. T. Jones (eds), *Bristol's Trade with Ireland and the Continent, 1503–1601: The Evidence of the Exchequer Customs Accounts*, Bristol Record Society Vol. 61 (Dublin, 2009), p. xx.

69   R. W. K. Hinton, *The Port Books of Boston 1601–1640*, Lincoln Record Society Vol. 50 (Hereford, 1956), p. xiii.

70   I am grateful to Margaret Condon (formerly of the National Archives) for providing me with this information. Record of the act of destruction has proved hard to track down, but it is also mentioned by Nuala Zahedieh in *Capital and the Colonies*, p. 10.

poor a condition to be used. Nonetheless, the sheer level of detail means that they remain an invaluable resource for the study of early modern English trade.

To conduct this study, detailed data from eleven Port Books spanning the seventeenth century has been entered into Excel spreadsheets, allowing it to be subjected to a wide variety of analysis. These have been supplemented by four late sixteenth-century Port Books that were digitised by the 'Ireland-Bristol Trade in the Sixteenth Century' project, and simple totals have also been extracted from a number of books that were not in good enough condition to yield a full set of data.[71] Data has also been used from the Particular Accounts (the predecessors of the Port Books, which replaced them in 1565). While there are some differences in what they recorded, they are essentially very similar documents, providing a consignment-by-consignment summary of the port's overseas trade. Datasets from nine Particular Accounts provided by the Ireland-Bristol project have been used, spanning the period 1503–64. In addition, a further fourteen Particular Accounts transcribed by the Cabot Project, covering the mid- to late fifteenth century, have also been consulted to provide long-term context and information on Bristol's experimental voyages to the Mediterranean and elsewhere.[72]

The Port Books and Particular Accounts have been supplemented with a number of other sources that shed light on aspects of Bristol's trade not covered by the customs records, or that provide information on trade in the many years for which no Port Books survive. The most important of these is the Wharfage Books, compiled by Bristol's Society of Merchant Venturers. Wharfage was a local tax on ships using the docks at Bristol, but fortunately the Society adopted the model of the Port Books for their record-keeping. It is thus possible to extract a dataset almost as full as that from the Port Books. The Wharfage Books survive in a complete run from 1654 to 1694. While they do not contain any details of exported goods, they cover the crucial period from 1638 to 1662 (the period in which Bristol's American trades emerged), for which no customs records survive.[73] Unfortunately, as the Wharfage tax was based on the volume rather than value of the goods, they are not especially useful as a continuous data series. However, by (laboriously) applying customs valuations from the Books of Rates by hand to the goods for selected years, they can yield a detailed dataset very similar to that from the import Port Books.

For the sixteenth century, Port Books can be supplemented with the more continuous Enrolled Accounts. These were produced by the Exchequer from

71   The 'Ireland-Bristol' project datasets have been published through the University of Bristol's online ROSE repository, and are available at http://www.bris.ac.uk/Depts/History/Ireland/datasets.htm.

72   http://www.bristol.ac.uk/history/research/cabot/publications/

73   S. S. Wilson, *Descriptive List of Exchequer, Queen's Remembrancer, Port Books, Part 1 – 1565 to 1700* (London, 1960).

the Port Books, and provide a summary for each port of the poundage duty collected, along with the number of broadcloths exported and tons of wine imported. They can thus be used to both examine year-to-year fluctuations in trade, and provide data for years from which no Port Books or Particular Accounts survive. Unfortunately, however, the Enrolled Accounts cease in 1604. From 1610 to 1640 another series of continuous data survives in the form of the New Imposition returns.[74] This was an extra duty charged in addition to poundage, which proved controversial as it was directly imposed by the King.[75] These are at best an unreliable measure of trade, and at worst a misleading one. Stephens has calculated that they only applied to a third of Bristol's trade, and deliberately targeted trade in goods that was seen as not in the national interest, such as exports of raw materials or imports of luxuries.[76] A shift in the type of goods traded, say from lead (which paid a high rate of imposition) to cloth (which did not), could thus create the impression of a significant decline in trade when it had in fact remained stable. From 1604 until the beginning of the Wharfage Books in 1654, it is thus necessary to rely entirely on the surviving Port Books for statistical information.

Particular aspects of Bristol's commercial history have been illuminated with a variety of other records. In particular, the Register of Servants to Foreign Plantations allows the rise and decline of the indentured servant trade to be discussed. Customs duties were not payable on exports of people, so the flow of labourers to the New World colonies was not recorded in the Port or Wharfage Books. As these servants were treated as property (bound to serve the owner of their indenture for a fixed period, typically five to seven years), this has usually been treated as a trade alongside the other branches of Bristol's overseas commerce. Fortunately for future historians, to prevent kidnapping, in 1654 the authorities of Bristol instituted a process of record-keeping for all indentured servants being shipped out of the city. These records survive from 1654 to 1686 and provide details of the servant, the date of indenture, sometimes their trade and place of origin, the master they were bound to and his/her occupation, the ship on which they were to travel and its destination.[77] By applying an estimated valuation to each servant, the indentured servant trade can thus be examined directly alongside the commodity trades recorded in the Port Books.

The Burgess Books, which were transcribed in full by the Bristol & Avon Family History Society, list all those given the freedom of Bristol, and thus allowed to practise their trade in the city.[78] Surviving in a continuous run from 1557, these provide the name, date, trade, and details of patronage for all 17,657

74   The National Archives/Public Record Office, E356/28-9.
75   P. Croft, 'Fresh Light on Bate's Case', *The Historical Journal*, 30(3) (1987), p. 523.
76   Stephens, 'Trade Trends at Bristol', p. 158.
77   Register of Servants to Foreign Plantations.
78   Anon., *Index to the Bristol Burgess Books, Volumes 1 to 21: 1557–1995* (Bristol, 2005).

people who were admitted to the freedom of Bristol in the period covered by this volume.[79] The record of trade is the crucial element, as this allows the emergence of new occupations such as tobacco-processing to be traced, as well as the growth in other crafts and industries as a growing overseas market swelled demand.

Another source provides an insight into the origins of goods that were not produced in Bristol: the Coastal Port Books. While goods moving coastwise (including along major river systems) did not pay customs duties, customs officers were nonetheless required to keep a record of all such goods in order to prevent smuggling.[80] Without such record-keeping, it would be all too easy for a merchant to say they were loading goods to take to the next port along the coast, and then 'accidentally' ship them to France. Survival of Bristol's Coastal Port Books from across the sixteenth and seventeenth centuries is, unfortunately, a little patchy, but the records from smaller ports within the region still provide valuable insight into the goods moving to and from Bristol. This book makes use of David Hussey's findings from analysing coastal books from across the Severn Sea region in a notional year of c. 1699.[81] It also provides some fresh analysis of the Gloucester Coastal Port Books transcribed by Hussey's study, providing a longer run of data stretching back into the seventeenth century. These records provide an invaluable insight into where Bristol was sourcing its export goods.[82] While this is primarily a study based around detailed analysis of the Port Books and other records of overseas trade, this range of other sources allows a breadth of understanding, and investigation of how trade impacted on the city of Bristol and its region more broadly.

As noted above, previous studies of English trade and economic development in the early modern period have readily admitted that the lack of available data is a major limiting factor. In part this is due to the paucity and inconsistent survival of records that can yield hard data. While this study is still bound by this limitation to some extent, computer technology has nonetheless made much more data available. For it was not necessarily always the case that trade data did not survive from early modern England, but rather that it survived in forms that were too dense to allow detailed analysis. Few of the sources looked at here have not been considered before, but digitising them has made it possible to analyse them in much greater depth, and also to look at a much greater volume of data than previously, under the time constraints of hand calculation. The position of this study might thus be summed up as 'standing on the shoulders of giants, holding a laptop'.

79   This is the total of burgesses enrolled between 1557 and 1705.
80   D. Hussey, *Coastal and River Trade in Pre-Industrial England: Bristol and Its Region 1680–1730* (Ithaca, 2000), pp. 7–8.
81   *Ibid.*, p. 18.
82   Gloucester Port Books.

Chapter Outline

The structure of this book sits somewhere between a chronological and a thematic account. The first three chapters focus on the markets that, while they characterised medieval Bristol, remained important in this period, namely France, Ireland, the Iberian Peninsula (as well as occasional efforts to break into new markets). While they spill over into the latter seventeenth century, the focus of these chapters is thus predominantly on the sixteenth and early seventeenth centuries. The second half of the book looks at developments from about 1650, when the advent of trade with the New World colonies transformed Bristol's commercial world. The focus is thus on assessing the imports and exports involved in the new American trades, although there is still some overlap with European commercial activity.

Chapter 1 focuses on Bristol's trade with continental Europe, paying particular attention to the second half of the sixteenth century and the first half of the seventeenth. It challenges the long-held view that Bristol was in serious decline as a centre for overseas trade in the late Tudor and early Stuart years, instead presenting evidence of a significant commercial expansion and growth in overseas trade. The root of this prosperity is shown to have been the buoyancy of markets along Europe's Atlantic littoral. The influx of New World bullion into Spain and Portugal drove up prices, meaning that Bristol's merchants were presented with a profitable market for the wide range of cloth, manufactured goods, agricultural and mineral produce that made up the city's exports. The vitality of Atlantic markets is often overlooked in explanations of the development of English trade in the sixteenth and early seventeenth centuries, with explanations instead focusing on the decline of Dutch trade and a desperate search for new markets. These findings thus have broad implications beyond Bristol. Early links to slavery are also highlighted, through the role of enslaved people in the New World in mining the gold and silver that drove up prices on the Iberian Peninsula, but also large numbers of enslaved Africans in major ports such as Sevilla and Lisbon. Bristol is shown to have benefited significantly from slavery more than a century before its own involvement in transatlantic slavery began.

The second chapter focuses on Bristol's trade with Ireland, an area of commerce that has often been overlooked but was equally dynamic in the sixteenth and seventeenth centuries. Although at times hit badly by periods of warfare and restrictive legislation, Bristol's trade with Ireland is shown to have been buoyant in the early seventeenth century. Thanks to both the expansion of settlement into new areas, and the desire of Irish consumers for a wide range of manufactured wares, Bristol's Irish exports grew tenfold in the early Stuart years, making up more than a third of the city's export trade by the 1630s. Far from a 'colonial trade', as has sometimes been suggested, Ireland is shown to have possessed a dynamic and advanced economy of its own. The Bristol customs records show that Ireland possessed a substantial cloth manufacturing industry, significant independent trading connections with continental Europe, and agricultural exports that fed enslaved people on the New World plantations.

While the Iberian, French and Irish trades of the first two chapters had been the focus of Bristol's overseas commerce since the Middle Ages, the period from the mid-fifteenth century onwards saw the city experiment with a wide range of new business opportunities. Chapter 3 examines Bristol's attempts to open new trade routes, which met with very mixed success. Since the writings of Richard Hakluyt in the Elizabethan era, England's colonial endeavours have been written about as a continuous process. The likes of Cabot and Hawkins were held up as pioneers, who sowed the seed that finally took root at Jamestown, and eventually flourished into a global empire. The evidence presented in this chapter, however, supports a very different interpretation. The period from the mid-fifteenth century witnessed several attempts by Bristol merchants to open up new trades with markets in North America, Africa, the Mediterranean, and elsewhere. These were, though, neither desperate attempts to replace lost markets (as has sometimes been suggested) nor part of a grand imperial project. Instead, they were experiments from a point of strength, which were frequently cast aside if they did not quickly deliver the hoped-for profits.

The second half of the book turns to the New World trades that opened up in the second half of the seventeenth century, examining Bristol's commercial relationship with the Caribbean and North American colonies. Chapter 4 tracks the growth of Bristol's New World trade, focusing on imports of tobacco and sugar. The dramatic falls in price of tobacco and sugar turned them from expensive luxuries to items of everyday consumption for most of the population. Having barely featured less than twenty years earlier, by 1654 these two commodities made up 70 per cent of the goods coming into Bristol. The Port Books and Wharfage Books are used to track the continued growth of tobacco and sugar imports, with the value of Bristol's American trades doubling again by the 1670s, before levelling off for the rest of the century. The chapter also looks at the impact on the city beyond its docks, using the trades stated when freemen were enrolled to trace the rise of the tobacco- and sugar-processing industries in Bristol.

Chapters 5 and 6 look at the export side of Bristol's New World trade. Chapter 5 examines the diverse range of goods that were exported from Bristol to North America and the Caribbean. As discussed above, domestically produced exports have tended to be ignored in accounts of the development of overseas trade in the seventeenth century, but were potentially much more significant than previously assumed. This is particularly true given the significance of the New World market for English exports in debates about the role of slavery in driving the Industrial Revolution. The chapter opens by examining the diverse range of goods Bristol was exporting in the second half of the seventeenth century, including extractive and agricultural goods, and a wide range of manufactured goods ranging from cloth and clothing to all manner of metalware. It then considers the sources of the goods Bristol was exporting. The Burgess Books are used to uncover increased employment in a range of crafts and industries in the city, spurred by the growing demand from overseas markets, and the Coastal Port Books shed light on the range of goods brought in from across Bristol's extensive hinterland. Finally, the types of goods sent to each of Bristol's export markets are compared, highlighting the existence of a shared material culture that spanned the American colonies, Ireland, and Europe's Atlantic coast.

Chapter 6 focuses on the trade in labourers, both indentured and enslaved. New analysis of the city's Register of Servants to Foreign Plantations shows that the trade in indentured servants was, in commercial terms at least, less significant than has been assumed. Even at its peak, the servant trade is shown to have made up little more than 10 per cent of Bristol's New World exports. Furthermore, those responsible for the shipments of servants are shown to have been separate from the merchants responsible for Bristol's main overseas business. Instead, the agents were mostly mariners connected to the sea who managed the journeys of only a few servants each. Combined with the high skill level of many of the servants, this seems much more like assisted migration, rather than the outright trade in human beings from Africa for which Bristol is notorious. Conversely, the Atlantic slave trade is shown to have been much more commercially significant to Bristol's early American trade than previously supposed. New evidence shows that Bristol's entry into the slave trade considerably pre-dated the ending of the Royal African Company monopoly in 1698. A number of examples of vessels conducting illegal slave-trading voyages are identified in the customs records, with the earliest dating back to the 1660s. Although hard to detect due to its illicit nature, the evidence suggests a small but regular trade, perhaps involving a few vessels a year. Bristol ships thus potentially carried more than 10,000 Africans to a life of enslavement in the four decades before accounts of the city's involvement in the slave trade normally begin.

Finally, the Technical Appendix explains the methodology used for analysing the Port Books, and the myriad decisions and calculations needed to turn records that were never meant for statistical processing into a usable form. As well as clarifying the approaches of this study, it is hoped that this will lay the groundwork for future analysis of the Port Books.

Overall, this book seeks to re-write our understanding of the development of Bristol, England's second port, in the crucial sixteenth and seventeenth centuries. It shows that, far from being in a state of decline and decay in the sixteenth century, Bristol's trade was in fact expanding rapidly as its exports found a profitable new market due to New World silver raising prices in Spain. In the seventeenth century too, the course of Bristol's commercial history is significantly different from previous understandings. American trade grew much faster and much earlier than previously assumed, accounting for as much as half of the city's imports by the 1650s, and seeing the value of trade more than double. Using these findings from Bristol, this book also seeks to add nuance to how we understand England's overseas trade and economic development in the early modern period. It suggests that the Atlantic economy was driving development much earlier than has been supposed, as far back as the mid-sixteenth century, and furthermore that exports, to markets in the New World and the old, were a much more important factor in overseas trade than previously thought. Finally, it strengthens claims that slavery played a significant part in the development of the English economy that ultimately led to the Industrial Revolution, highlighting both the significant market that the emerging colonies provided to commercialising industry and agriculture in Britain, and the role of slavery in Spain, Portugal and their empires in providing a market for English goods from the sixteenth century onwards.

I

The Rise of the Atlantic Economy

At the very beginning of January 1595, the *Red Lyon* of Haarlem in the Netherlands arrived in Bristol. At 130 tons, she was a mid-sized ship, and over the next fortnight she unloaded her cargo of sweet seck wine. Via a long and risky sea voyage, these barrels of wine had been brought from the port of Sanlúcar de Barrameda in the far south of Spain.[1] Sitting at the mouth of the Guadalquivir River, Sanlúcar was one of the outports of Sevilla, the monopoly port for all of Spain's burgeoning trade in gold, silver, and other valuable goods from the New World. For much of Bristol's trading history this would have been nothing out of the ordinary. After all, Eleanor Carus-Wilson suggested that Bristol exploited its westerly position to ply markets along Europe's Atlantic coast from at least the fifteenth century, with France, Ireland and the Iberian Peninsula accounting for the majority of its trade.[2] It is the date of this voyage from the south of Spain that makes it noteworthy: January 1595 was right in the middle of the Anglo-Spanish War (1585–1604), just seven years after the famous Armada had been repelled. The following year, an English fleet under the command of Robert Devereux, Earl of Essex, sacked the port of Cadiz seventeen miles down the coast from Sanlúcar. That Bristol merchants were happily continuing to trade with a region that their compatriots were shortly to invade perhaps tells us something about the complexities of English attitudes to the war, and that not all Englishmen were fired up with religious and national feeling. Further, it speaks to the prosperity of Spain's trade with England in the latter sixteenth century. Merchants such as Richard Stap and Richard Powell (the owners of the *Red Lyon*'s cargo) and dozens of others like them were prepared to run the gauntlet of privateers, the risk of their goods being seized, and to go against the broader tide of patriotic feeling to keep these commercial connections open. In spite of the state of open warfare, almost £5,000 worth of goods were imported to Bristol from Spain in 1594/5. Spain and its New World wealth had become central to Bristol and the rising tide of prosperity that characterised the city's commerce in the late Tudor and early Stuart years.

1   1594/5 Port Book, ff. 6r–7v.
2   E. M. Carus-Wilson, *Medieval Merchant Venturers* (London, 1967), p. 13.

Although less spectacular than the rise of transatlantic trade in the second half of the seventeenth century, the previous 150 years saw momentous developments in English overseas commerce. The broadcloth trade with the Netherlands, which had been the backbone of England's most important export market since the Middle Ages, first flourished and then, from the mid-sixteenth century, began to crumble.[3] In its place, English merchants began to reach further afield, establishing new trade routes into the Mediterranean and, more pertinent to this chapter, along Europe's Atlantic coast. This period also witnessed the rise to prominence of London, which outstripped the provincial ports to account for as much as 75 per cent of English overseas trade by the close of the sixteenth century.[4]

Generally this period is seen as one of crisis and change, with the travails of overseas commerce leading to economic disruption in England, and merchants forced to seek out new markets to replace those lost in the Low Countries.[5] This chapter challenges existing narratives of the development of both Bristol's and England's overseas trade in the century before 1650. In particular, it argues that the nascent Atlantic economy has been overlooked as an important influence on England's commercial fortunes. Having never traded with the Netherlands, Bristol was insulated from the commercial difficulties faced by London at this time. Rather than a period of stagnation and crisis, Bristol was in fact undergoing considerable commercial expansion in the years leading up to 1650. New evidence from the Port Books shows that Bristol's import and export trades both grew considerably over the course of this century. This expansion was not driven (as previously suggested) by growing demand for exotic luxury goods.[6] Instead it rested on steady demand for minor luxuries such as wine and dried fruit, and a significant market for a wide range of English exports. The influx of New World bullion into Spain led to high prices in the south of the Iberian Peninsula, fuelling the growth of a vibrant economy along Europe's

---

3   R. Davis, *English Overseas Trade, 1500–1700* (London, 1973), pp. 11–19.
4   For estimates of London's share of English overseas trade, see F. J. Fisher, 'London's Export Trade in the Early Seventeenth Century', *Economic History Review*, 2nd ser., III(2) (1950), p. 152; W. B. Stephens, 'The Cloth Exports of the Provincial Ports, 1600–1640', *Economic History Review*, 22 (1969), p. 242.
5   G. D. Ramsay, *English Overseas Trade during the Centuries of Emergence: Studies in Some Modern Origins of the English-Speaking World* (London, 1957); B. E. Supple, *Commercial Crisis and Change, 1600–1642: A Study in the Instability of a Mercantile Economy* (Cambridge, 1949); Fisher, 'London's Export Trade'; R. Brenner, *Merchants and Revolution: Commercial Change, Political Conflict, and London's Overseas Traders, 1550–1653* (London, 2003); A. M. Millard, 'The Import Trade of London, 1600–1640' (unpublished PhD thesis, University of London, 1956); R. Davis, *The Rise of the Atlantic Economies* (London, 1973).
6   D. H. Sacks, *The Widening Gate: Bristol and the Atlantic Economy, 1450–1700* (London, 1993), p. 40.

Atlantic littoral. Bristol benefited not only from direct trade to Spain, but also the commercial prosperity of Portugal, France and Ireland, the other Atlantic-facing nations. These same Atlantic markets, particularly on the Peninsula, also became increasingly important for London's merchants.[7] Thus, rather than a desperate search to replace their dwindling Low Countries trade, it may be that the capital's merchants were drawn by the same commercial opportunities that Bristol was taking advantage of.

This chapter begins by providing a chronological outline of the development of Bristol's trade in the sixteenth and early seventeenth centuries, drawn from the most detailed analysis to date of the surviving customs records and an understanding of the likely impacts of smuggling. It then moves on to look at the nature of Bristol's trade in this period, considering the types of goods involved and the regions with which the city was trading. This reveals a picture of consistency rather than change. Other than a shift from broadcloth to a more diverse range of exports, Bristol is shown to have been trading with the same places and importing the same range of minor luxuries as in previous centuries. Finally, the buoyant market in Spain and Portugal created by the rise of New World trade reflects the links between slavery and Bristol's late sixteenth and early seventeenth-century prosperity.

Bristol's 'Lowest Ebb'?

Nyne hundred houses and above is clerely fallen down, the grasse growyng in the streetes, beyng moche of the residue in great decaye and inhabited with poore people veray like in breve tyme and space.[8] [1530]

Merchauntes heere, being barred of their accustomed trade with Spayne and Portingall, are exceedinglie hindrede and distressed, to the greate decaye and impoverishmen of this cittie, havinge verye small trade for the mayntenaunce of their shippinge.[9] [1597]

This Citty is poore and soe … twoe or three marchantes of London are able to buy all the Inhabitantes of Bristoll out of all their meanes in the world saving their persons.[10] [1619]

---

7   Fisher, 'London's Export Trade', pp. 154–5.
8   J. M. Vanes, *Documents Illustrating the Overseas Trade of Bristol in the Sixteenth Century*, Bristol Record Society Vol. 31 (Bristol, 1979), p. 28.
9   *Ibid.*, p. 37.
10   P. McGrath, *Records Relating to the Society of Merchant Venturers of the City of Bristol in the Seventeenth Century*, Bristol Record Society Vol. 17 (Bristol, 1952), p. 183.

If the above petitions from Bristol's merchants are to be believed, the sixteenth and early seventeenth centuries were dire. Houses were falling down, trade greatly decayed, and merchants were impoverished. Indeed, this period of crisis appears to have spanned the best part of a century. The problem, however, is that they were lying, or at the very least greatly exaggerating their plight. This was the normal formula for petitions to the Crown. The petitioner would outline in great depth the state of and reasons for their woe, and then suggest remedies. Often this was abolition of some irksome duty, or permission to participate in a restricted activity such as a monopoly-protected trade. This, however, was all an elaborate charade. The monarch knew full well that these claims of poverty were a complex fiction, although the demands might be acceded to if there was another reason to curry favour with the merchants.[11]

Some scholars of Bristol's trade in the late sixteenth and early seventeenth centuries have taken a similar line to the merchants' petitions. G. D. Ramsay, for example, described the reigns of Elizabeth I and James I as a 'dark epoch' and 'the lowest ebb in the trade of Bristol', with Bristol having 'slipped out of contact with the major currents of European trade'.[12] Similarly, W. B. Stephens has suggested that Bristol's imports and exports suffered a 'steady decline' from about 1611/12, reaching 'an abysmally low level in the period 1625–9' before a 'partial and hesitant recovery in the 1630s'.[13] Other historians, however, have been more positive about Bristol's commercial welfare under the Tudors and early Stuarts. While Jean Vanes felt that there might have been a crisis of sorts in the mid-sixteenth century, precipitated in large part by the collapse of broadcloth exports, by the end of the century other branches of trade were showing sufficient signs of recovery for her to conclude that Bristol 'could quickly return to something like its former prosperity'.[14] Patrick McGrath argued that this positive story continued into the early decades of the seventeenth century, suggesting that Bristol's trade was expanding at this time, with the 1630s in particular being a period of prosperity.[15] The most detailed study of Bristol's overseas trade in this period is that conducted by D. H. Sacks. Amongst other sources, Sacks examined two Port Books (from 1575/6 and 1624/5). Taking a similar line to Ramsay, Sacks described the sixteenth century as a 'bleak new season in [Bristol's] economic history', with the city's merchants unable to

11   I am grateful to Evan Jones for numerous discussions on the nature and strategy of Bristol's petitions.

12   Ramsay, *English Overseas Trade*, pp. 134–7.

13   W. B. Stephens, 'Trade Trends at Bristol, 1600–1700', *Transactions of the Bristol and Gloucestershire Archaeological Society* (1974), p. 157.

14   J. M. Vanes, *The Port of Bristol in the Sixteenth Century*, Bristol Historical Association Pamphlets no. 39 (Bristol, 1977), pp. 25–6.

15   P. V. McGrath (ed.), *Merchants and Merchandise in Seventeenth-Century Bristol*, Bristol Record Society Vol. 19 (1955), pp. xix–xxi.

compete with their wealthier London counterparts, and thus forced out of the market.[16] While he did observe an increase in customs returns between 1575/6 and 1624/5, Sacks suggested that such apparent growth could be 'only illusory', a result of adjustments to the customs rates, rather than any real growth of trade.[17] The prevailing view has thus remained that Bristol's trade struggled throughout the period between 1500 and 1642.

These disagreements on the subject of the health of Bristol's trade in the late Tudor and early Stuart years are largely a result of the lack of any clear-cut, accessible sources. Previous studies have thus been forced to rely on either unreliable qualitative sources (such as the petitions above), or potentially unreliable sampling of the statistical evidence. By providing a thorough examination of the available quantitative material, this chapter fills this void. Detailed analysis of the Bristol customs records from the late sixteenth and early seventeenth centuries paints a very different picture from the tales of woe presented in the petitions. While there were ups and downs and some difficult periods, generally the sixteenth century was a time of modest prosperity for Bristol's overseas trade. In the early seventeenth century the picture was even brighter, with the customs returns showing a significant expansion in both imports and exports.

Early Tudor Stability

Although England's loss of Gascony in 1453 was a major blow to Bristol's trade, by the end of the fifteenth century the city had largely recovered its commercial prosperity once political relations settled down (although this resurgence was in large part due to a profitable new trading relationship with Castile).[18] Overseas commerce remained healthy throughout the first decade of the sixteenth century. As the Particular Accounts show, in 1550/1 Bristol exported £21,600 worth of goods and imported £14,000 worth. This is remarkably consistent with the £21,000 worth of imports and £13,000 worth of exports seen sixty years earlier in 1492/3 (Figure 1). The more continuous data series provided by the Enrolled Accounts show that such a simple comparison conceals a significant amount of variation from one year to another (Figure 2). Nonetheless, they confirm that Bristol's trade remained reasonably steady throughout the first six decades of Tudor rule. The city admittedly did not share in the broadcloth boom that saw London's trade expand significantly in

16 Sacks, *Widening Gate*, p. 24.
17 *Ibid.*, p. 376.
18 For a more detailed account of the development of Bristol's overseas trade in the latter fifteenth century, see R. Stone, 'Bristol's Overseas Trade in the Later Fifteenth Century: The Evidence of the "Particular" Customs Accounts', in E. T. Jones and R. Stone (eds), *The World of the Newport Medieval Ship: Trade, Politics, and Shipping in the Mid-Fifteenth Century* (Cardiff, 2018), pp. 183–203.

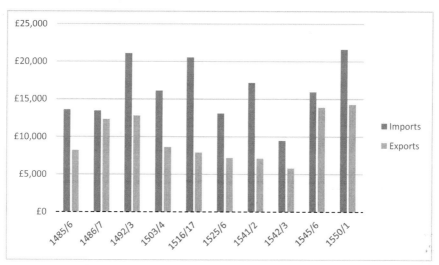

Figure 1. Bristol's trade in the late fifteenth and early sixteenth centuries, as recorded in the Particular Accounts.

Sources: 1485/6 Particular Account; 1486/7 Particular Account; 1492/3 Particular Account; 1503/4 Particular Account; 1516/17 Particular Account; 1525/6 Particular Account; 1541/2 Particular Account; 1542/3 Particular Account; 1545/6 Particular Account; 1550/1 Particular Account. Enrolled Accounts in the early sixteenth century did not distinguish between imports and exports, simply recording tons of wine, cloths of assize, and total poundage paid. Thus, this graph shows a single total for the value of all trade.

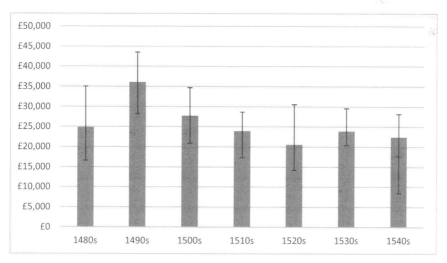

Figure 2. Decade averages for Bristol's trade in the late fifteenth and early sixteenth centuries, as recorded in the Enrolled Accounts, with error bars showing maximum and minimum values for the decade (in pounds sterling).

Source: Enrolled Accounts.

the first half of the sixteenth century.[19] Excluded by the Merchant Adventurers monopoly, Bristol simply did not trade with the Low Countries, which were absorbing ever-growing quantities of English cloth. Indeed, Bristol's broadcloth exports tailed off significantly during this period, falling from an average of 6,700 cloths a year in the 1490s to just 2,300 in the 1540s.[20] Nevertheless, diversification into other types of export goods meant that the city was able to maintain its overall levels of trade. The steady trade of this period is far from the 'bleak new season' that Sacks has suggested Bristol experienced in the early sixteenth century.[21]

Smuggling and the Mid-Century 'Crisis'
According to Vanes, if Bristol did experience a crisis in its overseas trade, it was in the middle of the sixteenth century, as a straight reading of the Bristol customs accounts certainly suggests.[22] Customs figures from the first six decades of the sixteenth century are, unfortunately, not directly comparable with those from the last four, as customs valuations underwent a significant revision in 1558. Once the figures have been adjusted to account for this inflation, however, they suggest a striking drop-off in Bristol's trade (Figure 3).[23] Bristol's recorded trade averaged £20,000 in the 1560s, less than half what it had been (after adjustment of the figures) in the 1540s. Although there was a modest improvement, recorded trade remained similarly low in the 1570s and 1580s.

The customs figures, however, do not account for smuggling, which in the mid-sixteenth century made up a significant percentage of Bristol's trade. As Evan Jones has shown, illicit trade was rife in mid-sixteenth-century Bristol, indulged in by the majority of the city's wealthiest and most successful merchants.[24] This illicit trade focused on two principal sets of commodities. On the export side, grain and leather were smuggled in order to avoid the expense, inconvenience, and risks involved in acquiring licences to trade in these prohibited goods.[25] Very little smuggling occurred on the import side of Bristol's trade, but following the introduction of significant New Imposition duties in 1558 the city's merchants also began to smuggle wine on a significant

19   Davis, *English Overseas Trade*, pp. 11–14.
20   Enrolled Accounts.
21   Sacks, *Widening Gate*, p. 24.
22   Vanes, *The Port of Bristol*, pp. 22–3
23   T. S. Willan has calculated that, on average, the valuations contained in the Book of Rates were roughly doubled in 1558 (T. S. Willan (ed.), *A Tudor Book of Rates* (Manchester, 1962), pp. xxvii–xxviii). To facilitate an effective comparison between pre- and post-1558 figures, therefore, it is necessary to double earlier valuations. See the Technical Appendix for a fuller discussion of customs valuation adjustments.
24   E. T. Jones, *Inside the Illicit Economy: Reconstructing the Smugglers' Trade of Sixteenth Century Bristol* (Farnham, 2012), pp. 104–5.
25   *Ibid.*, pp. 98–111.

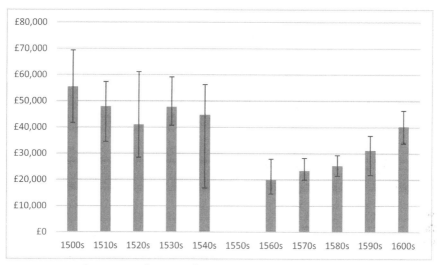

Figure 3. Decade averages for Bristol's sixteenth-century overseas trade, as recorded in the Enrolled Accounts, with error bars showing maximum and minimum values for the decade (in pounds sterling).

Source: Enrolled Accounts.

scale. The 1558 duty increased taxes on French wine to as much as 40 per cent (similar taxes were created for Iberian wines in 1573), eating into merchants' profit margins and thus creating an incentive to trade illicitly.[26] Due to the lack of surviving records, it may never be possible to measure the extent of Bristol's illicit wine trade. That imports fell by more than half following the introduction of the duty, however, hints at the potential scale.[27] For the grain and leather trades, on the other hand, Jones has been able to estimate the likely extent of smuggling by comparing the private ledger of notable Bristol merchant John Smyth with the official customs records. According to his ledger, grain and leather accounted for between a third and half of all of Smyth's exports.[28] The vast majority of this trade was conducted illegally. For example, the accounts for a voyage of Smyth's *Trinity* in 1540 show customs duties to have been paid on just 20 per cent of the grain on board, and none of the leather.[29] While the exact extent of Smyth's unlicensed trade varied from one voyage to the next, it is clear that a significant proportion of his exports were never recorded in the customs accounts.

26   *Ibid.*, p. 193.
27   *Ibid.*, p. 194.
28   *Ibid.*, p. 107.
29   *Ibid.*, pp. 100–3.

Bristol's supposed 'crisis' of the mid-sixteenth century may, therefore, simply be a statistical illusion: a function of the fact that an increasingly large portion of the city's trade was never declared to the customs officers and is thus absent from the records. Even before the 1550s, Bristol's trade was significantly greater than recorded in the customs accounts, with potentially over a third of all exports going unrecorded. Much of the post-1558 drop in recorded trade is also likely to have been caused by a rise in illicit wine imports, rather than a fall-off in trade itself. Wine accounted for 50 to 60 per cent of Bristol's import trade in the first half of the sixteenth century. Therefore, if a significant proportion of this bypassed the customs house in the years after 1558, the apparent impact on Bristol's recorded trade would be dramatic. Unfortunately, by its very nature, the extent of this illicit trade evades quantification. Clearly, however, it was on a significant enough scale that the customs records from the middle years of the sixteenth century are not a reliable witness to the extent of the city's trade. Rather than having experienced a significant commercial decline, it may therefore be the case that Bristol's merchants were simply carrying out a greater percentage of their trade undercover.

The Prosperous War Years (1585–1604)
The last decade of the sixteenth century and the first years of the seventeenth century saw the beginnings of a recovery in Bristol's recorded trade. Allowing for a continuation of illicit trade, this is likely to represent the beginnings of growth, seeing Bristol's commerce surpass levels from the first half of the sixteenth century. Bearing in mind that it coincided with the Anglo-Spanish War, this phase of growth is all the more surprising. Some previous scholars have suggested that the disruption of trade with one of Bristol's principal markets saw the city virtually moribund in the 1580s and 1590s.[30] The absolute opposite was in fact the case, with Bristol's trade expanding despite war with Spain (Figure 4). While recorded exports remained low (almost certainly due to the high proportion of illicit wares involved in Bristol's export trade), imports rose considerably. From an average of just £13,000 in the 1560s, Bristol's recorded imports grew to £22,000 in the 1590s. The first four years of the seventeenth century (the last from which the Enrolled Accounts survive) show this growth to have continued, with an average of £32,500 worth of goods imported per year.

As goods captured as prizes paid normal customs duties, and thus were recorded in the customs accounts alongside regular trade, some of this late-century revival may be a result of the actions of Bristol's privateers. Closer analysis of the surviving Port Books, however, shows that this was not entirely the case (see Figure 5). In 1594/5, at the height of the war, as much as 37 per cent

---

30   Ramsay, *English Overseas Trade*, pp. 136–7; K. Andrews, *Elizabethan Privateering* (Cambridge, 1964), p. 141.

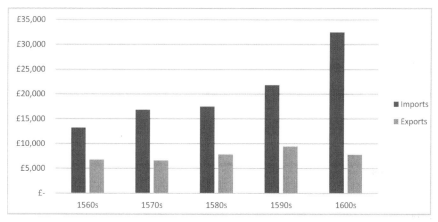

Figure 4. Bristol's Enrolled Accounts, 1560s–1604.

Source: Enrolled Accounts.

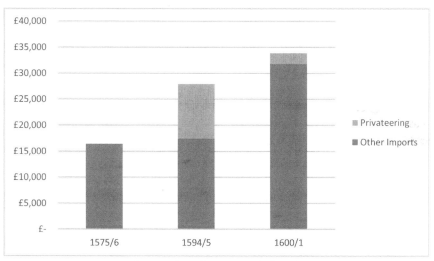

Figure 5. Privateering and normal trade as recorded in the Bristol Port Books, 1575/6–1600/1.

Sources: 1575/6 Port Book; 1594/5 Port Book; 1600/1 Port Book.

of all goods imported into Bristol came from privateers. By 1600/1, however, this had fallen considerably. Little more than £2,000 worth of prize goods came into Bristol, making up just 6 per cent of total imports. Privateering thus certainly played some part in Bristol's success during the early years of the war, but by the end of the war, the city's merchants had turned their attention back to peaceful trade and were prospering as a result. Indeed, by the start of the seventeenth century, Bristol's recorded imports were almost twice what they had been before the outbreak of war. Despite wartime disruption, trade was therefore prospering. Indeed, as a substantial illicit trade is also likely to have continued, Bristol's trade may have been even healthier than these figures suggest.

The New Century: Ongoing Growth

Following the return to peace in 1604, the first four decades of the seventeenth century saw Bristol's overseas trade continue the expansion that had characterised the last years of Elizabeth's reign. Unfortunately, the cessation of the Enrolled Accounts in 1604 means that detailed figures are less readily available to chart this development. We are instead forced to rely on the few surviving Port Books to provide a record of the total extent of Bristol's overseas commerce.[31] While the lack of a continuous data series is less than ideal, the Port Books nonetheless furnish us with a good impression of the continued upward trajectory of Bristol's trade.[32] Imports were up to £45,000 by 1612/13, and had grown further to £50,000 in 1624/5. It was, though, the 1630s which were to see the most spectacular phase of growth in this period, with Bristol's recorded imports soaring to £83,000 in 1637/8. Even accounting for inflation, this took Bristol's trade well beyond the highest levels seen in either the fifteenth or sixteenth centuries.

The early seventeenth-century Port Books show Bristol's exports to have grown at a rate that outstripped the expansion of the city's import trade. From an average of around £7,000 throughout the last four decades of the sixteenth century, declared exports jumped to £28,000 in 1608/9. Rather than representing growth, this sudden increase in exports declared at Bristol may instead

31   W. B. Stephens has attempted to use the New Imposition returns to provide a continuous data series for this period (Stephens, 'Trade Trends at Bristol'). The New Impositions were a series of taxes introduced by the Crown in the early seventeenth century. While the returns on their collection survive in a relatively continuous series, their utility as trade statistics is limited as they only applied to some goods. Indeed, Stephens himself noted that they only represent approximately a third of Bristol's trade. They also did not tax all goods equally, with particularly high duties on luxury imports and raw material exports. A decline in the New Impositions collected could, therefore, merely reflect a shift from trading in highly taxed goods to those with lower tariffs, rather than a fall in trade. Indeed, as the data presented in this chapter reveals, the New Imposition returns could show a decline in trade, even when the more reliable Port Books show it to have been increasing.

32   While unreliable as a measure of trade themselves (as they only applied to a select few commodities and are thus not representative of trade as a whole), the New Imposition returns do give a continuous series of customs figures throughout this period. These show that the years from which Port Books survive were fairly typical of those around them and can thus be taken as representative of trade in those years more generally. For a more detailed discussion of Bristol's New Imposition returns from the early seventeenth century, see Richard Stone, 'The Overseas Trade of Bristol in the Seventeenth Century' (unpublished PhD thesis, University of Bristol, 2012), pp. 48–50.

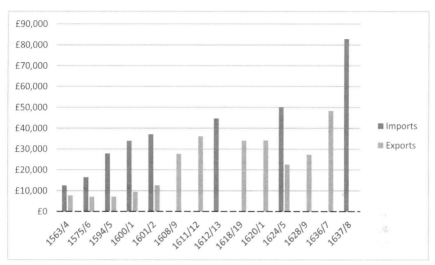

Figure 6. Bristol's overseas trade as recorded in the Port Books, 1563/4–1637/8.

Sources: 1563/4 Port Book; 1575/6 Port Book; 1594/5 Port Book; 1600/1 Port Book; 1601/2 Port Book; 1608/9 Port Book; 1611/12 Port Book; 1612/13 Port Book; 1618/19 Port Book; 1620/1 Port Book; 1624/5 Port Book; 1628/9 Port Book; 1636/7 Port Book; 1637/8 Port Book.

reflect the increasing availability of licences to trade in prohibited goods. John Latimer, for example, records the issuing of a royal licence in 1614 to John Whitson and four other Bristol merchants for the export of 1,000 dickers of tanned calf-skins per annum. The Port Books also often noted the licence under which skins were exported, most frequently that issued to 'Francis Knight and others'.[33] On the other hand, it seems highly unlikely that it would have been possible to entirely conceal a trade of this scale in the years prior to 1600, so it must, at least to an extent, represent genuine growth. After all, the skins exported in 1620/1 (£6,500) were worth the equivalent of almost 92 per cent of Bristol's total recorded exports in 1594/5 (£7,100). While the scale and speed of this increase hints at the likely extent of Bristol's illicit trade in the latter sixteenth century, some at least must have also represented genuine growth. Bristol's export trade was hit briefly by the renewed outbreak of war with Spain in 1625, but generally remained healthy throughout the first four decades of the century. Through the 1610s and 1620s it regularly topped £30,000 in a year, and in the 1630s exports grew further, reaching £48,000 in 1636/7. This confirms the finding from the 1637/8 import account that the 1630s saw a renewed phase of rapid growth for Bristol's overseas trade. Far from being a 'dark epoch' or

33   J. Latimer, *The Annals of Bristol in the Seventeenth Century* (Bristol, 1900), p. 54; TNA PRO E190/1133/1; E190/1134/11; E190/1136/1; E190/1136/3.

'the lowest ebb in the trade of Bristol', the Tudor and early Stuart years were reasonably good for commerce in England's second city. While not matching the prosperity of London's broadcloth boom, the first half of the sixteenth century saw modest, ongoing prosperity for Bristol's merchants. On the surface the customs accounts suggest that the middle years of the sixteenth century witnessed something of a 'crisis', but the significant extent of Bristol's illicit trade would suggest that this was not in fact the case. Despite recurring wars with Spain, the last decades of the sixteenth century and first four of the seventeenth saw a renewed expansion of Bristol's overseas trade. Indeed, on the eve of the Civil War, Bristol was prospering, with both imports and exports expanding rapidly.

The Quest for Luxury Imports?

In the late sixteenth and early seventeenth centuries, Bristol was clearly much more prosperous than previously supposed, raising the question of why this was the case. How was Bristol able to succeed commercially when the rest of the country was undergoing a period of crisis and change? It is here that the Port Books really come into their own. The detailed data that they provide on the goods that the city was both importing and exporting, as well as the regions with which it was trading, allow us to probe the causes of the city's success.

Regional Distribution
When looking at the places with which Bristol was trading, the most remarkable feature of the late sixteenth and early seventeenth century was consistency. Previous scholars have suggested that Bristol diversified its trade in this period, forging connections with an increasingly broad range of markets.[34] The quantitative evidence presented in this chapter, however, does not support this argument. As discussed in more detail in Chapter 3, an assortment of new trades, from the Baltic to the Barbary coast in North Africa, were occasionally recorded in Bristol's customs records in the early seventeenth century. Economically, however, these were relatively insignificant, dwarfed by the scale of the city's existing trades. As it had since the Middle Ages, Bristol's commerce continued to focus along Europe's Atlantic coast.[35] Until the dramatic changes of the 1640s (Chapter 4), Ireland, France and the Iberian Peninsula continued to account for the vast bulk of Bristol's trade. In 1637/8, for example, Bristol imported £29,200 worth of goods from France, £21,500 from Ireland, and £23,200 from the Iberian Peninsula (Figure 7). Less than £9,000 worth of goods came from elsewhere, of which £1,000 worth were from unknown destinations, and £5,500

---

34   Sacks, *Widening Gate*, pp. 41–4; Vanes, *Port of Bristol*, pp. 25–6.
35   Carus-Wilson, *Medieval Merchant Venturers*, p. 13.

from the Atlantic islands (which were basically an extension of the Iberian trade). Although the range of other countries of origin appearing amongst Bristol's imports increased, this is very similar to the pattern of Bristol's trade at the beginning of the sixteenth century. In 1503/4 France (£6,200), Ireland (£3,400) and the Iberian Peninsula (£4,300) collectively made up 91 per cent of Bristol's import trade, exactly the same percentage as in 1637/8.

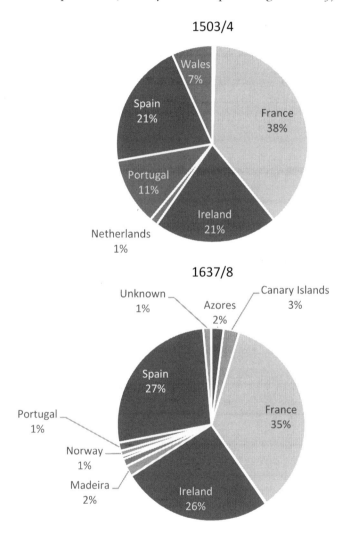

Figure 7. Bristol's imports by country of origin as recorded in the Particular Accounts and Port Books, 1503/4 and 1637/8 (in pounds sterling).

Sources: 1503/4 Particular Account and 1637/8 Port Book.

In the wider context of English trade at this time, such stability perhaps comes as something of a surprise. Work on London shows that its merchants increasingly sought out new markets, in southern Europe as well as further afield, perhaps seeking to replace lost trade with the Netherlands. Bristol, however, which never had commercial connections with the Low Countries, was able to sustain a period of ongoing growth based on its traditional markets. This suggests that much greater credit should be given to the strength of these markets in driving the growth of English trade. The Atlantic economy was not merely a substitute for lost markets for cloth in the Netherlands, but a prosperous economy capable of attracting the attention of English merchants on its own merits. The following section examines the development of trade with France and Spain in greater depth (Ireland is considered in Chapter 2).

Imported Goods

At first glance, examining the makeup of commodities on the import side of its trade does little to explain Bristol's prosperity. As with the markets, a comparison of the types of goods coming into the city on the eve of the Civil War with those brought in a century and a half earlier reveals a remarkable consistency (Figure 8). There may have been minor shifts in the exact balance of commodities, with some declining in importance and others rising, but the broad makeup was much the same. The prosperity of Bristol's import trades was not, as Sacks suggested, driven by a newfound quest for high-value imports.[36] Instead, Bristol's merchants continued to bring back the same mix of minor luxuries and raw materials that they always had. In terms of imports, then, what drove change was not demand for different types of goods, but an increased market for the same types of goods that had always been brought from overseas.

As at the beginning of the period, Bristol's most important import in 1637/8 was wine, which made up half of all goods coming from the continent. Declared wine imports had been through a rough patch in the middle of the sixteenth century (Figure 9). As discussed above, however, this is likely to have been caused by an increase in smuggling, rather than a decline in the volume of trade. By the early seventeenth century, declared imports of wine had largely recovered to their pre-1558 levels. Bearing in mind that the incentive to smuggle remained (albeit slightly reduced by the rising price for wine), it is likely that the real level of trade was higher than these figures suggest. The 1630s saw a further considerable growth of Bristol's wine trade, with the 3,400 tons imported in 1637/8 surpassing anything seen in the latter fifteenth century. Indeed, Bristol's imports of wine on the eve of the Civil War surpassed those prior to the loss of

---

36   Sacks, *Widening Gate*, p. 40.

1503/4

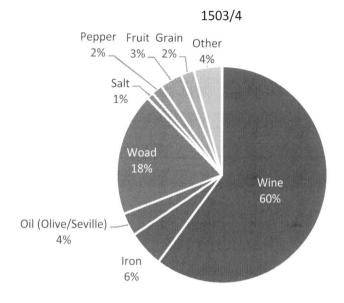

Pepper 2%
Fruit 3%
Grain 2%
Other 4%
Salt 1%
Woad 18%
Wine 60%
Oil (Olive/Seville) 4%
Iron 6%

1637/8

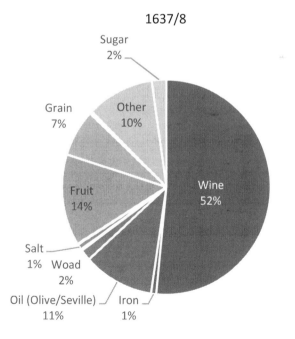

Sugar 2%
Grain 7%
Other 10%
Fruit 14%
Wine 52%
Salt 1%
Woad 2%
Oil (Olive/Seville) 11%
Iron 1%

Figure 8. Makeup of Bristol's imports in 1503/4 and 1637/8 (in pounds sterling).
Sources: 1503/4 Particular Account; 1637/8 Port Book.

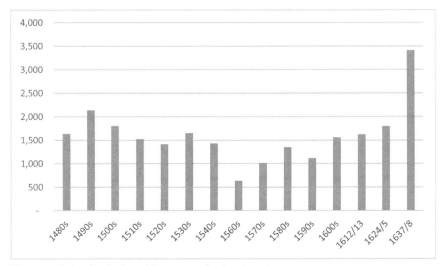

Figure 9. Bristol's declared imports of wine (tons).

Sources: Enrolled Accounts; 1612/13 Port Book; 1624/5 Port Book; 1637/8 Port Book. The figures up to 1604 are decade averages, derived from the Enrolled Accounts. The final three figures are from the Port Books, and represent wine imports in a single year.

Gascony in 1453.[37] This prosperous trade in wine explains the ongoing significance of France (particularly the Bordelaise region) to Bristol's overseas trade.

Of exotic luxury goods such as silks and spices, there is little sign in the Bristol imports. Pepper, which featured to an extent from the late fifteenth century, saw a brief surge in importance in 1575/6 with £3,300 worth being imported. But this proved to be temporary, with only small quantities of pepper featuring in the seventeenth-century accounts. Odd consignments of exotic spices did come into Bristol most years, but the quantities are so small that these should not be accorded any great significance. Susan Flavin has even speculated that luxury goods may instead have been brought overland to Bristol from London.[38] A hint that this was occurring comes from records of goods being sent out of Bristol. These show many types of goods that cannot have originated in England, including some exotic foodstuffs and luxury continental cloths that do not appear amongst Bristol's imports. The most likely explanation is that London merchants could simply access these goods more cheaply

37   Wine imports into Bristol in the decade 1440–50 averaged 2,200 tons per annum, with a peak of 3,075 tons in 1440/1. Source: E. Power and M. M. Postan (eds), *Studies in English Trade in the Fifteenth Century* (London, 1933), pp. 333–5.
38   S. Flavin, 'Consumption and Material Culture in Sixteenth-Century Ireland', *Economic History Review*, 64(4) (November 2011), p. 1164.

than their Bristol counterparts, and thus it was more economic for people from Bristol to purchase them in London rather than overseas. London's trading connections reached further into the Mediterranean than those of Bristol, and thus closer to the sources of supply of many of these wares. The prices they could achieve would thus be lower than those in Bristol's Iberian markets, where costs would have been inflated by passing through the hands of a greater number of middle-men.

More noteworthy than occasional shipments of spices is the increase in Bristol's sugar imports, although these were still well short of the levels achieved in the latter seventeenth century after the growth of the American trades. As much as £4,000 worth of sugar was brought into Bristol in 1620/1, with a more modest £1,300 in 1637/8. Indeed, as early as 1616 Bristol had its own sugar house, a site for processing unrefined brown sugar into its purer white form. This was set up at St. Peters, close to the docks, by Robert Aldworth, one of the city's leading overseas merchants.[39] Too much, however, could easily be made of this growth. Sugar still only made up just over 2 per cent of Bristol's continental imports in 1637/8, the same proportion as in 1485/6. The only other consumer luxury that could perhaps be described as growing in importance was the amount of fruit that Bristol imported. Fruit, predominantly Iberian raisins, had featured amongst Bristol's imports throughout this period, but saw significant growth in the early seventeenth century. By 1637/8 Bristol was importing £8,200 worth of fruit, almost 14 per cent of imports from the continent. While there are some signs of rising consumer demand for imported goods, this cannot, therefore, be seen as the principal driver of the expansion of Bristol's trade in the late sixteenth and early seventeenth centuries. Exotic luxury goods barely featured at all, and even minor luxuries (at 14 per cent of continental imports in 1637/8) were not much more important than they had been a century and a half earlier. Bristol's import trade at this time was still, as it had been for centuries, predominantly concerned with wine.

As well as consumer goods, such as wine and dried fruit, Bristol also imported significant amounts of raw materials, many of which were destined for use in the region's cloth industry. The dyestuff woad had been an important import for Bristol in the late fifteenth century, but the volume tailed off throughout the period as domestic woad production increased (Figure 10). Iron imports from the Asturias region in northern Spain underwent a similar decline. At peak, these had topped a thousand tons a year, forming the staple of Bristol's summer trade, but none was imported in 1620/1, and just 120 tons in 1637/8. Imports of olive oil, on the other hand, saw a significant surge in the early seventeenth century. Perhaps crucially, olive oil could not be produced in England, and was

39   K. Morgan, 'Sugar Refining in Bristol', in K. Bruland and P. O'Brien (eds), *From Family Firms to Corporate Capitalism: Essays in Business and Industrial History in Honour of Peter Mathias* (Oxford, 1998), p. 114.

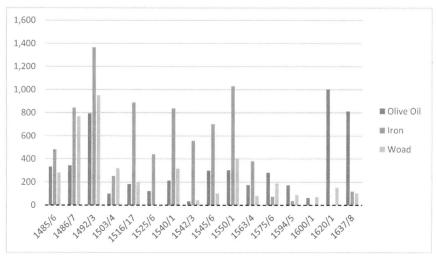

Figure 10. Bristol's imports of olive oil, iron, and woad (tons).

Sources: 1485/6 Particular Account; 1486/7 Particular Account; 1492/3 Particular Account; 1503/4 Particular Account; 1516/17 Particular Account; 1525/6 Particular Account; 1540/1 Particular Account; 1542/3 Particular Account; 1545/6 Particular Account; 1550/1 Particular Account; 1563/4 Port Book; 1575/6 Port Book; 1594/5 Port Book; 1600/1 Port Book; 1620/1 Port Book; 1637/8 Port Book.

also an important ingredient in the manufacture of soap for the cloth industry. Over 800 tons of olive oil was imported in 1637/8 and 1,000 in 1620/1, almost three times typical annual imports in the sixteenth century.

The pattern described above does not fit with D. H. Sacks's characterisation of the development of Bristol's trade in the sixteenth and early seventeenth centuries. Having been forced out of the export trade in broadcloth by the greater buying power of the London merchants, Sacks suggested that Bristol's merchants instead focused on a 'quest for imports'.[40] Highlighting an apparent imbalance between imports and exports, Sacks argued that merchants focused on acquiring high-priced goods, and were forced to cobble together an export cargo or even illegally export bullion in order to do so.[41] While there were some changes on the export side of Bristol's trade, the Port Book figures do not fit with the idea of a 'quest for imports' as the main driver. Instead, it seems that Bristol's merchants continued to trade with their normal markets, and simply brought back increasing quantities of the same types of goods. Two statistical errors made by Sacks also accentuate the gap that he saw between exports and

40   Sacks, *Widening Gate*, pp. 28–32, 40.
41   *Ibid.*, p. 39.

imports. The first of these was to overlook 'hidden exports' that do not appear in the customs records. These include the illicit trade, which could account for both a sizeable percentage and the most profitable element of Bristol's exports.[42] By the latter part of the period there would also be fish from Newfoundland, much of which was shipped straight from the Banks to the Iberian Peninsula and exchanged for Spanish wine and other goods for sale in England.[43] The other error was to over-value wine in relation to other goods involved in Bristol's trade. The wine price adopted by Sacks is more than double that used in this study. As wine accounted for as much as half of all of Bristol's imports, this will have considerably exaggerated the apparent difference between the value of imports and the value of exports in Sacks's figures.[44] Bristol's trade thus would not have been as driven by imports as Sacks suggests.

The Wider Picture

These findings from Bristol also shed new light on the drivers of development in the English import trade more broadly. As F. J. Fisher has shown, the same Iberian markets that formed the backbone of Bristol's success at this time were also becoming increasingly important to London. Indeed, by the eve of the Civil War, the London Port Books show that exports to Spain and the Mediterranean equalled those to the old haunts in Germany and the Low Countries.[45] Figures from Bristol that show the commodity makeup of the Iberian trades thus help to shed light on the dynamics of one of the most important developments in early seventeenth-century English commercial history. That the English import trade was expanding during the first four decades of the seventeenth century, despite the wider travails of overseas commerce, is not a new observation. A. M. Millard, for example, calculated that London's imports grew from £1,000,000 in 1600 to £3,000,000 in 1640.[46] Robert Brenner has attempted to explain this contrast between a moribund export trade and a surging demand for imports.[47] For Brenner, the key lay in the development of the English economy. While

---

42 Jones, *Inside the Illicit Economy*, pp. 215–16.
43 P. E. Pope, *Fish into Wine: The Newfoundland Plantation in the Seventeenth Century* (Chapel Hill, NC, 2004), pp. 79–122.
44 Based on their current wholesale prices, Sacks valued wine at £15 the ton and broadcloth at £8 the cloth, whereas here they are valued at £9 the ton and £4.50 the cloth respectively (*Widening Gate*, p. 38). As is discussed in greater detail in the Technical Appendix, however, the valuations of goods paying poundage were in fact significantly lower than their wholesale prices. This study, therefore, uses valuations of roughly half the wholesale price so that cloth and wine can accurately be compared with other goods. As Bristol no longer shipped significant amounts of broadcloth, but wine was a crucial import commodity, Sacks's valuations therefore over-value the import trade in relation to exports.
45 Fisher, 'London's Export Trade', pp. 154–5.
46 Millard, 'The Import Trade of London', p. 316.
47 Brenner, *Merchants and Revolution*, pp. 39–45.

European economies remained in crisis, a considerable home market was growing in England. This, Brenner argued, was the result of both the shift from subsistence production to market integration, and increased purchasing power at all levels of society due to efficiency gains in both agriculture and industry. For Brenner, while the impacts of the cloth export crisis were severe, they were also geographically limited to cloth-producing areas. In other parts of England, economic prosperity meant a growing demand for imported goods, and in particular for luxuries such as silks and exotic foodstuffs.[48] This chapter does not seek to challenge Brenner's argument that a growing domestic market for imported goods helped to fuel the expansion of English overseas trade in the late sixteenth and early seventeenth centuries. That Bristol's imports underwent a significant expansion without a particularly noteworthy increase in the amount of luxury goods being shipped, however, suggests that this argument may overlook other contributory factors. It is, therefore, well worth examining the commodity makeup of the export side of Bristol's trade to see if overseas demand for English goods played a previously overlooked part in driving growth at this time.

Export-Driven Growth

The Cloth Trade

In the fifteenth century Bristol's exports to the continent were completely dominated by cloth, with this single commodity making up over 98 per cent of all goods sent out on Bristol ships.[49] Cloth still made up 94 per cent of Bristol's continental exports in 1503/4. Broadcloth dominated: this high-quality, heavy woollen fabric formed the backbone of England's exports throughout this period. Indeed, many historians have considered it of such significance that they assess the health of England's export trade purely in terms of number of cloths shipped.[50] The first half of the sixteenth century is usually seen as the heyday of the broadcloth trade, with growing exports to the Low Countries fuelling an expansion of English overseas trade. For Bristol, however, the story was different. As Figure 11 shows, Bristol's broadcloth exports crashed in the early sixteenth century, falling from an average of almost 6,700 cloths per year in the 1490s to just 2,300 in the 1540s. The second half of the century saw them tail away to almost nothing, with an average of just 260 cloths in the first four years of the seventeenth century. This decline in the broadcloth trade led Sacks to describe the sixteenth century as a 'bleak new season in [Bristol's]

48   *Ibid.*, p. 42.
49   Stone, 'Bristol's Overseas Trade', pp. 193–7.
50   See, for example: A. Friis, *Alderman Cockayne's Project and the Cloth Trade: The Commercial Policy of England in Its Main Aspects, 1603–1625* (Copenhagen, 1927), pp. 115–30; Stephens, 'The Cloth Exports', pp. 228–48.

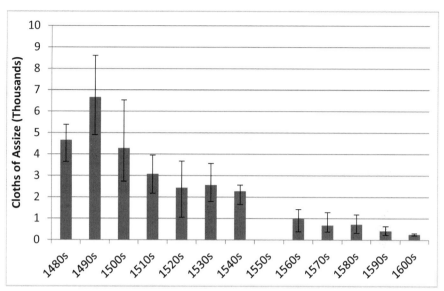

Figure 11. Bristol's broadcloth exports as recorded in the Enrolled Accounts, with error bars showing maximum and minimum values for the decade.

Source: Enrolled Accounts. The error bars indicate the maximum and minimum annual exports recorded in that decade. There are no surviving figures for the 1550s.

economic history'.[51] That this precipitous decline in Bristol's broadcloth trade should occur at the same time as London's trade was continuing to expand was, for Sacks, unsurprising. He saw this as part of a re-orientation of the nation's trade towards the capital, with Bristol's merchants simply unable to compete. In support of this argument, he highlighted contemporary petitions from Bristol merchants, claiming that they were unable to buy sufficient cloth, as Londoners were buying up all that was available, even within Bristol's own clothmaking districts.[52]

While there is no denying that Bristol's broadcloth trade was in terminal decline by the end of the sixteenth century, this does not mean that the city had completely ceased to be a major cloth-exporting centre. Bristol had always exported some other types of cloth, but these underwent a noteworthy increase in the 1540s and 1550s. Exports of fabrics other than broadcloth underwent further significant expansion in the early seventeenth century. By 1618/19 they surpassed exports of the traditional broadcloths, with more than £6,200 worth making up 32 per cent of Bristol's exports to the continent. The

51   Sacks, *Widening Gate*, p. 24.
52   *Ibid.*, pp. 28–32.

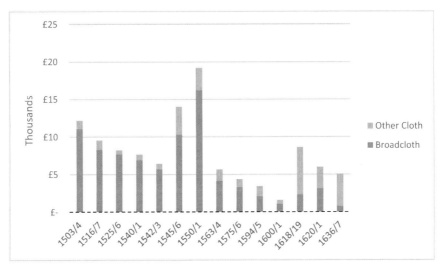

Figure 12. Bristol's continental cloth exports as recorded in the Particular Accounts and Port Books (in pounds sterling).

Sources: 1503/4 Particular Account; 1516/17 Particular Account; 1525/6 Particular Account; 1540/1 Particular Account; 1542/3 Particular Account; 1545/6 Particular Account; 1550/1 Particular Account; 1563/4 Port Book; 1575/6 Port Book; 1594/5 Port Book; 1600/1 Port Book; 1620/1 Port Book; 1636/7 Port Book.

decline of Bristol's cloth trade, therefore, was not as total as the dwindling away to virtually nothing of broadcloth exports would suggest. That there was a significant drop-off is without question, but the rise of trade in new types of cloth meant that, in a good year, such as 1618/19, the value of cloth being shipped through Bristol could come close to that of the halcyon years at the beginning of the sixteenth century. Rather than a substitution for lost sources of broadcloth, this shift to other types of fabric is better thought of as adjusting to exports that better suited the market. These new varieties of cloth, known as the New Draperies, were considerably lighter than the heavy English broadcloth. They were, thus, much more in demand in the warmer climates of the Iberian Peninsula and Mediterranean which had become the main centres of Bristol's trade.[53] Indeed there is even some evidence that the Bristol Corporation deliberately tried to establish a New Drapery manufacturing industry in the city. In 1610 they invited a group of people from Colchester to 'set up the trade of "bayes and says"', paying for their travel expenses, granting them freemen status, and making them loans of £50 each.[54]

53   Fisher, 'London's Export Trade', pp. 157–8.
54   J. Latimer, *The Annals of Bristol in the Seventeenth Century* (Bristol, 1900), pp. 40–1.

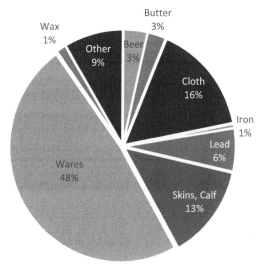

Figure 13. Bristol's exports by commodity as recorded in the 1636/7 Port Book (in pounds sterling).

Source: 1636/7 Port Book.

Agriculture, Extraction, and Manufacturing

While there is no question that Bristol's cloth trade had declined by the beginning of the sixteenth century, this was not of particularly great commercial significance to the city. In place of cloth, Bristol had instead developed a much broader base of exports, leaving it better able to respond to the demands of the market, and less vulnerable to disruption in the event of a crisis of either supply or demand for different types of goods. By the eve of the Civil War, cloth made up little more than a quarter of Bristol's exports to continental Europe (see Figure 13). Rather than relying on cloth, Bristol instead drew on the increasingly prosperous agriculture, manufacturing, and mineral extraction industries in the region. This access to a wide range of goods, combined with the high prices achievable in the Iberian Peninsula, allowed Bristol's export trade to flourish in the first four decades of the seventeenth century, a period when London's exports were struggling.[55]

One of the most important types of commodity amongst Bristol's exports is unfortunately also the most difficult to assess using the customs records. By the early seventeenth century, the Bristol Port Books show the city to have been shipping considerable amounts of agricultural produce. As discussed above, however, agricultural goods were the prime focus of Bristol's substantial illicit trade. The calf-skins, grain, and butter appearing in the customs records may therefore be the tip of the iceberg. In the 1530s and 1540s, grain and leather were crucial to the exports of leading Bristol merchant John Smyth (47 per cent of his exports between 1539 and 1541), and he also smuggled other agricultural

55   Fisher, 'London's Export Trade'.

goods such as peas, beans, tallow and butter.[56] These were the most profitable parts of Smyth's export trade. He made between 50 and 150 per cent gains on grain, and as much as 80 per cent on leather, while he was often forced to sell exports of cloth at a loss.[57] With such substantial profits achievable, it is easy to see why many Bristol merchants risked trading illicitly in grain and leather. While we do not have further detailed records like those relating to Smyth, other evidence suggests that large amounts of agricultural produce continued to be smuggled out of Bristol in the last four decades of the sixteenth century. For example, between 1559 and 1603, 401 informations were submitted to the Exchequer concerning Bristol merchants smuggling leather and foodstuffs.[58] In the early seventeenth century, the much greater availability of licences for leather export resulted in a significant rise in the declared trade in agricultural goods, suggesting the potential extent of smuggling in the latter sixteenth century (see Figure 14). In 1628/9, for example, £1,000 worth of beans, £2,000 of beer, £1,400 of butter, and £3,900 worth of calf-skins made up a third of Bristol's recorded exports. Again, there is the possibility that ongoing smuggling may have made the real totals significantly higher.

An expansion of 'industrial' goods was as important as agricultural produce amongst Bristol's exports. Lead from the Mendip mines had always played some part in Bristol's outward trade. In early sixteenth-century customs accounts, lead made up a very small percentage of exports, amounting to little more than £100. By the middle of the sixteenth century, exports of lead to Europe had grown much more significant. In 1545/6, £3,400 worth made up almost a third of Bristol's continental exports. Lead remained a steady presence amongst the goods Bristol shipped to the continent throughout the late sixteenth and early seventeenth centuries. Despite the introduction of additional New Imposition duties, both 1618/19 and 1620/1 saw around £3,000 worth of lead exported from Bristol, about 16 per cent of continental exports. In large part this is likely to be a result of the significant developments in the extractive industries of England and Wales in the Tudor and Stuart era. New mining technologies, especially in drainage and ventilation, allowed miners to delve much deeper, resulting in a significant increase in output. Output of coal increased by as much as eight times between 1540 and 1640, and extraction of lead and iron also increased.[59] Also worthy of note is that Bristol's lead and iron exports were in the form of metal, rather than ore. The simultaneous adoption of new technologies in milling, casting, and smelting may thus also have played a

56   Jones, *Inside the Illicit Economy*, pp. 103, 107.
57   *Ibid.*, p. 106.
58   *Ibid.*, p. 214.
59   J. U. Nef, 'The Progress of Technology and the Growth of Large-Scale Industry in Great Britain, 1540–1640', *Economic History Review*, 5(1) (1934), pp. 9–11.

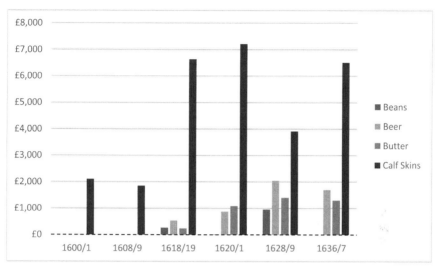

Figure 14. Bristol's agricultural exports as recorded in the Port Books (in pounds sterling).

Sources: 1600/1 Port Book; 1608/9 Port Book; 1618/19 Port Book; 1620/1 Port Book; 1628/9 Port Book; 1636/7 Port Book.

part in increasing output, making Bristol's metallic exports competitive in the continental markets.[60]

Although only occurring right before the Civil War, the most significant sign of things to come was an increase in manufactured goods being exported from Bristol. In the long run, exports of manufactures to foreign markets played an important part in driving the Industrial Revolution.[61] Generally, however, it is thought that the development of a significant export trade in manufactured goods other than cloth did not occur until the eighteenth century.[62] However, manufactured goods were already a significant feature of Bristol's exports to the continent in 1636/7. As discussed in the next chapter, manufactured goods were an even more prominent feature in the Irish trade. Frustratingly the customs officers were not particularly diligent in recording such goods; many entries simply lump together a parcel of 'wares'. It is generally agreed, however, that this generic label represented small manufactured goods such as pins, knives,

60   *Ibid.*, pp. 11–15.
61   K. Morgan, *Slavery, Atlantic Trade and the British Economy, 1660–1800* (Cambridge, 2000), pp. 61–73.
62   R. Davis, *A Commercial Revolution* (London, 1967), p. 9.

glass, tools, wooden tableware, and any number of other everyday items.[63] As much as £3,400 worth of 'wares' are recorded amongst Bristol's exports to the continent in 1636/7. Some sense of what these might have been is given by the small number of entries where the customs officers have noted particular types of manufactured goods. The 1636/7 account, for example, records an assortment of stockings, hose, nails, knives, wire, cordage and shot being sent to Europe.

The New World Influence

How Bristol was able to achieve such a profitable and diverse export trade is best explained by looking at the markets to which these goods were being sent. In particular, developments in the south of the Iberian Peninsula were crucial to Bristol's fortunes, as the influx of New World silver created high demand and high prices for all manner of English goods. As Figure 15 shows, by the early seventeenth century Bristol's Iberian trade was principally focused on the south of the Peninsula. In particular, the outports of Sevilla were the key centre for Bristol's southern commerce. In 1600/1, for example, of £6,600 worth of Spanish goods, £3,600 came from Cadiz, £500 from Puerto de Santa Maria, and £800 from Sanlúcar de Barrameda. The data from 1618/19 shows a similar pattern, when of £7,500 worth of goods imported from mainland Spain, £2,300 came from Sanlúcar and £2,200 from Cadiz. Malaga, the other major port in Andalusia, also featured regularly, with £1,700 worth of goods in 1600/1, £6,000 in 1620/1, and £13,100 in 1637/8, surpassing the Sevilla outports in that year.

Sacks has suggested that there was a shift towards the Mediterranean in Bristol's Iberian trade during this period, with the city's merchants seeking lower prices by heading straight to the source of supply of exotic goods. The evidence presented here, however, does not support this conclusion. The Port Books show Bristol's merchants to have rarely ventured far beyond the Straits of Gibraltar, with very little trade occurring up Spain's eastern coast. While other ports, such as Malaga, were opened up as more regular destinations, the commodities they shipped to Bristol were very familiar south Iberian fare. However, Sacks was correct in suggesting a shift in the locus of Bristol's Iberian trade, with the decline of connections with northern Castile. Summer voyages to pick up cargoes of Biscayan iron had been a regular feature of Bristol's annual commercial cycle in the late fifteenth and early sixteenth centuries.[64] By the beginning of the seventeenth century, however, trade in Spanish iron had ceased to be economically significant. There are a number of potential explanations for this decline. It may simply be the case that Bristol's merchants

63   D. M. Woodward, *The Trade of Elizabethan Chester* (Hull, 1970), pp. 12–22; D. M. Woodward, 'The Overseas Trade of Chester, 1600–1650', *Transactions of the Historic Society of Lancashire and Cheshire*, CXXII (1970), p. 33.
64   Stone, 'Bristol's Overseas Trade', p. 192.

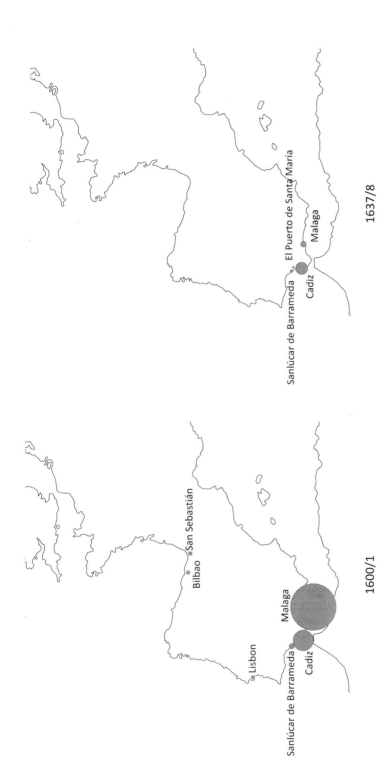

Figure 15. Distribution of Bristol's imports from the Iberian Peninsula 1600/1 and 1637/8, as recorded in the Port Books (in pounds sterling).

Sources: 1600/1 Port Book; 1637/8 Port Book.

were finding greater profits elsewhere, in particular in the light of the growth of the southern trades. Equally, however, it may have been a result of changes in demand. As discussed above, England's extractive industries underwent significant developments in the late sixteenth century, and the resultant increase in output may have driven the price of domestically-produced iron down to the point where Spanish imports could not compete.

It is difficult to look past Sevilla when seeking an explanation for the expansion of Bristol's Andalusian trade. Sevilla held a monopoly on all Spanish trade with the New World. In this period, it thus established itself as one of the most important commercial centres in the world.[65] The result was a dynamic economy in the region, and high prices driven up by the influx of New World bullion. It was this that allowed John Smyth to achieve such high profits on his exports of leather and grain.[66] Sevilla itself rarely features as a destination in Bristol's customs records, but its outports such as Cádiz, Sanlúcar de Barremeda, and El Puerto de Santa María formed the backbone of the city's Iberian trade. A similar phenomenon can also be noted with Lisbon, one of the most important centres for Portugal's trade with its Brazilian colonies. Bristol had strong ties with Lisbon from at least the mid-fifteenth century, when it accounted for as much as 80 per cent of Bristol's Iberian trade.[67] Coinciding with the growth of transatlantic trade, commercial connections with Lisbon gained a new lease of life in the mid-sixteenth century. In 1575/6 Lisbon accounted for half of Bristol's Iberian trade, and a third of trade as a whole, with nearly £2,000 worth of goods sent to the Portuguese city, and £6,000 received in return. This strong focus of Bristol's Iberian trade on the major centres of New World commerce suggests that we should look as much to England's exports as its imports to account for the growth of trade at this time.

At this juncture, it is worth pausing to reflect on the links between Bristol and the transatlantic slave economy. Much has been said, both in print and in impassioned discussions within the city, about the extent to which Bristol benefited from both slavery and the slave trade during their eighteenth-century heyday. Even Bristol's harshest critics, however, have not thought to push this influence back to the days of the Tudors. A very strong case can be made, however, that Bristol was benefiting from the labour of enslaved people in the New World as early as the mid-sixteenth century. If Bristol's late sixteenth- and early seventeenth-century commercial success was linked to the rise of New World trade and its impact on the Iberian economy, then it rested to a large degree on the backs of the enslaved people who laboured in the silver mines of

65   Davis, *The Rise of the Atlantic Economies*, p. 63.
66   *Ibid.*, p. 69; Jones, *Inside the Illicit Economy*, pp. 103, 107.
67   Stone, 'Bristol's Overseas Trade', pp. 194–5.

Mexico and Peru.[68] In Sevilla itself, enslaved people also made up a crucial part of the labour force, working in all manner of professions. Although numbers are uncertain, a 1565 census showed 6,327 slaves out of 85,538 people, meaning that roughly one in fourteen people in the city were enslaved. Again, proportions are uncertain, but in the second half of the century the majority of these enslaved people would have come from Africa.[69] While Portugal did not benefit in the same way as Spain from silver produced by enslaved people, the taint of slavery is also present in the growth of Bristol's trade with Lisbon. By 1550, 9,500 enslaved people made up 10 per cent of the population of Lisbon, and there were as many as 32,370 enslaved people in Portugal.[70] Beyond this, much of Lisbon's renewed success also rested on imports of sugar from the slave-worked plantations in Brazil. As discussed above, following the difficult years for the Netherlands broadcloth trade, the Iberian trades also became increasingly important to London, accounting for much of the growth of the capital's commerce in the early seventeenth century.[71] Even beyond Bristol, therefore, we need to push back the date where the exploitation of enslaved people in the New World had a significant impact on English economic development.

Overall, then, the story of Bristol's export trade in the sixteenth and early seventeenth centuries is not, as Sacks supposed, one of decline and desperation, but instead of innovation and opportunity. With prices driven up by the influx of New World bullion, Spain and Portugal offered a buoyant market for English exports. With output growing from increasingly commercialised agriculture, extractive goods and metalware from the adoption of new techniques in mining and industry, and new varieties of cloth better suited to warmer southern climes, Bristol was well positioned to take advantage of this opportunity. Given that his profits on fabrics were lower than those on other types of exports, it is in fact dubious whether sixteenth-century Bristol merchant John Smyth would have been especially bothered by London merchants buying up broadcloth. Thinking beyond Bristol, this potentially suggests that the diversification of exports (which, for Davis, was one of the key aspects of the Commercial Revolution) was happening earlier than previously thought. Furthermore, it seems that it may have been driven by the emergence of a profitable new market for exports, rather than, as previously thought, the need to replace lost broadcloth exports. Fisher witnessed a similar refocusing on trade with Spain and the Mediterranean in the available trade statistics from London, with non-broadcloth exports expanding fivefold, and southern markets coming to equal those in the Low

68   R. Blackburn, *The Making of New World Slavery: From the Baroque to the Modern, 1492–1800* (London, 2010), pp. 129–56.
69   R. Pike, 'Sevillian Society in the Sixteenth Century; Slaves and Freedmen', *The Hispanic American Historical Review*, 47(3) (1967), pp. 344–59.
70   Blackburn, *Making of New World Slavery*, pp. 112–13.
71   Fisher, 'London's Export Trade', pp. 154–5.

Countries by the eve of the Civil War.[72] This expansion in London, however, has tended to be misinterpreted as a result of the concurrent decline in the Netherlands broadcloth trade that had been the city's main focus. London figures may also conceal some of the diversity of England's export trade at this time. Fisher's figures showed the London expansion to have been driven primarily by new types of cloth, with only comparatively small quantities of minerals and other manufactured goods. He also, unsurprisingly, saw little of the illicitly exported agricultural goods. As Fisher himself suggested, it may well be that bulkier goods were shipped from provincial ports rather than first being carried to London.[73] The figures from Bristol thus show England's economic development to have been more diverse and more developed than the London-based picture would suggest.

Conclusions

Reflecting on the broader context, it is easy to understand why the Bristol merchants who loaded Spanish goods on the *Red Lyon* of Haarlem in 1595 were prepared to run the risks of trading with an enemy nation, and saw their commercial connections as superseding the state of war and religious differences. It was not, as their own petitions and broader historiographical thinking would suggest, because the decline of trade had left them in a state of poverty and decay (quite the opposite).[74] The past century had seen Bristol develop an increasingly flourishing trade with Spain, and as soon as peace returned in 1604 this growth accelerated. The city's merchants were thus prepared to run against the tide of public opinion, and risk their goods and ships being seized, simply because trade with Spain was such a profitable opportunity at this time. This was driven in part by the growing market for semi-luxury Iberian goods such as wine, dried fruit and sugar in England, but also by the high prices in Spain and Portugal for all manner of English agricultural and mineral produce, cloth and other manufactured goods. This in turn was caused by the influx of New World bullion into the south of the Peninsula driving up prices, showing the extent to which the Atlantic economy was already integrated at this early stage. The activities of the Spanish and Portuguese in Central and South America had profound consequences for the English economy, creating a significant opportunity for merchants to exploit the price differential, and incentive to innovate and become more market-oriented to meet this new demand. Previous studies of English trade in this period have tended to play down the significance of the

72   *Ibid.*, pp. 152–5.
73   *Ibid.*, p. 159.
74   Davis, *Commercial Revolution*, pp. 5–6.

Atlantic economy, suggesting instead that moves to open up new markets were driven by desperation as the Netherlands broadcloth trade declined.[75] As Bristol had never traded with the Low Countries to any great extent, however, we need to put much greater emphasis on the strength of the Iberian markets, and ask whether merchants from London and elsewhere were drawn to them by opportunity rather than desperation. This also means that the accepted chronology for the development of early modern English trade may need to be rethought. Rather than three phases following the boom and bust of the broadcloth trade and then emergence of new markets, with periods of decline and stagnation in between, instead we should see a more continuous expansion of the Atlantic economy, which first compensated for the decline of the broadcloth trade and then superseded it. The importance of a diverse range of exports to these Iberian trades is also significant to the ongoing debate regarding the role of slavery in driving English economic development.[76] Given the importance of slavery to the Spanish and Portuguese New World empires, and the subsequent impact on prices for English goods in the Iberian Peninsula, slavery can clearly be seen to have been driving economic development and even industrialisation in England as early as the sixteenth century.

75 Davis, *The Rise of the Atlantic Economies*, pp. xiii, 207.
76 Joseph Inikori has also discussed the role of the Spanish and Portuguese American colonies in shaping European economic development: J. Inikori, 'Atlantic Slavery and the Rise of the Capitalist Global Economy', *Current Archaeology*, 61 (2020), p. 163.

2

Ireland: Beyond 'the First "Colonial" Trade'

The *Mary Fortune* of Wexford is typical of ships involved in Bristol's Irish trade in the sixteenth and early seventeenth centuries. Of just seven or eight tons burthen, in April 1576 her master William Butler loaded her with a cargo of metal, hops and millstones to be taken back to Wexford.[1] By June she was already back in Bristol, ready to load another cargo (beans) to be taken to Wexford.[2] Such little ships making regular short voyages between Bristol and the ports of south-east Ireland were the backbone of this bustling commerce. Another ship, though, reflects how Bristol's trade with Ireland diversified in the seventeenth century. Between 6 and 16 August 1672, the *Joseph* of Bristol loaded a diverse range of goods for her voyage to Ireland. She was carrying a wide range of cloth: serges, sempiterams, tickins, fustians and more. In her hold was also bacon, cheese, butter, and a range of other foodstuffs and drinks, as well as shoes, hats, stockings, nails, curtains, saddles, and some more exotic goods such as sugar and logwood.[3] What makes her most interesting, however, is her list of declared destinations. In Ireland she was due to call at Londonderry, Belfast, and Carrickfergus, all ports in the north of the country that would have been very unusual for a ship such as the *Mary Fortune* in the previous century. She was then due to sail on to Virginia. This is new, and characteristic of the changes to Ireland's place in the Atlantic economy that occurred in the sixteenth and seventeenth centuries. It was no longer an economic backwater, trading with the nearby English ports in fish and hides. Instead, Ireland was a fully-fledged node in Atlantic commerce, with sophisticated tastes of its own, growing provisions bound for North America. Quick shuttle voyages between Bristol and the ports of south-east Ireland did not stop; indeed they remained the backbone of England's trade with Ireland. Increasingly, however, they were just part of a much more complex picture.

Ireland has tended to be overlooked in discussions of the development of the Atlantic economy. It has certainly not been without its historians, but their studies have tended to either view the Irish economy as an entity in itself, or

1   1575/6 Port Book, f. 7v.
2   *Ibid.*, f. 13r.
3   1670/1 Port Book, ff. 115r–119v.

focus on Ireland's economic relationship with England alone. In particular, much attention has been given to assessing how 'colonial' England's commercial relationship with Ireland was.[4] Often Ireland is considered a *Terra Florida*, a testing ground for the colonial schemes eventually to be used when England established its New World colonies.[5] Ultimately, the Irish economy in the sixteenth and early seventeenth centuries has been seen as backward and under-developed, exporting unprocessed raw materials, and relying on imports of manufactured goods.[6] As an 'appendage of England', Ireland has not been given any great significance in the development of the Atlantic economy, other than perhaps being seen as a stepping-stone for English dreams of conquering the New World. In recent decades, however, a range of studies have begun to question these negative perceptions of Ireland's trade and economy. Manufacturing within Ireland has been increasingly recognised, in particular significant centres of cloth production, and a significant 'consumer culture' in the south-east. Rather than seeing developments as a result of interactions with England, recently historians have given greater attention to both factors internal to Ireland, and direct connections between Ireland and the continent.[7]

The English Port Books have come to be one of the key sources for studying developments in the Irish economy.[8] Following the destruction of many of Ireland's own records with the burning of the Irish Public Record Office in 1922, these sources shed a valuable light on an economic world that might otherwise be obscured. As a trade that consisted predominantly of goods low in value

4 For a recent summary of scholarship on Ireland's economy in this period, see R. Gillespie, 'Economic Life, 1550–1730', in J. Ohylmer (ed.), *The Cambridge History of Ireland, Volume II: 1550–1730* (Cambridge, 2018).

5 K. S. Bottigheimer, 'Kingdom and Colony: Ireland in the Westward Enterprise, 1536–1660', in K. R. Andrews, N. P. Canny and P. E. H. Hair (eds), *The Westward Enterprise: English Activities in Ireland, the Atlantic and America 1480–1650* (Liverpool, 1978), pp. 45–65; N. Canny, 'The Ideology of English Colonization: From Ireland to America', *The William and Mary Quarterly*, 30(4) (October 1973), pp. 575–98; N. Canny, *Kingdom and Colony: Ireland in the Atlantic World, 1560–1800* (London, 1988), pp. 1–29.

6 L. M. Cullen, *Anglo-Irish Trade, 1660–1800* (Manchester, 1968), pp. 4–6; S. Flavin, *Consumption and Material Culture in Sixteenth-Century Ireland: Saffron, Stockings and Silk* (Woodbridge, 2014), p. 6; A. K. Longfield, *Anglo-Irish Trade in the Sixteenth Century* (London, 1929), p. 191; D. H. Sacks, *The Widening Gate: Bristol and the Atlantic Economy 1450–1700* (Berkeley, 1991), p. 39.

7 Flavin, *Consumption and Culture*, pp. 244–5; Gillespie, 'Economic Life', p. 536.

8 This approach was taken by the ESRC-funded project 'Ireland-Bristol Trade in the Sixteenth Century' (RES-000-23-1461) between 2006 and 2008. See also: Flavin, *Consumption and Culture*; S. Flavin, 'Consumption and Material Culture in Sixteenth-Century Ireland', *Economic History Review*, 64(4) (November 2011), pp. 1144–74; Gillespie, 'Economic Life', p. 536; D. M. Woodward, *The Trade of Elizabethan Chester* (Hull, 1970), pp. 5–36; D. M. Woodward, 'The Overseas Trade of Chester, 1600–1650', *Transactions of the Historic Society of Lancashire and Cheshire*, CXXII (1970), pp. 32–7.

in relation to their bulk, the nearby ports of Bristol and Chester offered cost-efficient short voyages that dominated England's Irish trade in this period. The Port Books of Chester and those from sixteenth-century Bristol have already been studied in depth from an Irish perspective.[9] Bristol's seventeenth-century customs records, however, have not received such scrutiny. The data presented in this chapter, therefore, attempts to deepen our understanding of the development of Ireland in this key period.

This chapter builds on recent work, arguing that while there are some similarities with Bristol's trade with the North American colonies, commercial connections with Ireland were much more complex than simply being 'Bristol's first colonial trade'. The chapter opens by tracking the overall prosperity of Irish trade in the sixteenth and seventeenth centuries, witnessing significant expansion as the buoyancy of the Irish economy in the early seventeenth century led it to become one of Bristol's most important markets. It also shows how seriously Ireland could be impacted by both warfare and restrictive economic legislation. Next, the chapter focuses on the commodities involved in Irish trade. The range of goods brought from Ireland to Bristol shows both the rapid development of Irish agriculture in the seventeenth century, as well as continued and significant cloth manufacture. Bristol's exports to Ireland, meanwhile, show that the 'consumer revolution' recently revealed in sixteenth-century Ireland continued over the next hundred years.[10] Finally, attention turns to the expansion of Irish economic activity into new areas, taking in both growing trade with the ports serving the settler communities in the north of the island, and also Ireland's role in providing agricultural provisions to the North American colonies. From a Bristol perspective, trade with Ireland could all too easily be omitted from the narrative of development in the sixteenth and seventeenth centuries. Indeed, it has at times been virtually omitted from analysis by previous scholars.[11] As this chapter shows, however, while overshadowed by the later growth of the New World colonies, having such a dynamic economy on its doorstep was fundamental to Bristol's commercial growth in this period.

Expansion of Irish Trade

Overall, the story of Bristol's Irish trade in the sixteenth and seventeenth centuries is one of considerable growth, even at times outstripping the expansion of the continental trades discussed in the last chapter (see Figure 16).

---

9   Flavin, 'Consumption and Material Culture'; Woodward, *Trade of Elizabethan Chester*; Woodward, 'Overseas Trade of Chester'.
10 Flavin, *Consumption and Culture*, p. 243.
11 Sacks, *Widening Gate*, pp. 39–41.

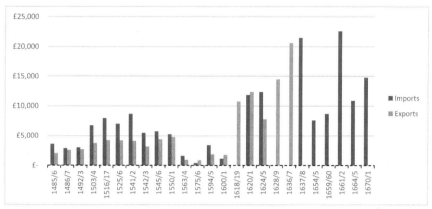

Figure 16. Value of Bristol's Irish trade as recorded in the Port Books, Wharfage Books, and Particular Accounts (in pounds sterling).

Sources: 1485/6, 1486/7, 1492/3, 1503/4, 1516/17, 1525/6, 1541/2, 1542/3, 1545/6 and 1550/1 Particular Accounts; 1563/4, 1575/6, 1594/5, 1600/1, 1620/1, 1624/5, 1637/8, 1670/1 and 1671/2 Port Books; 1654/5, 1659/60 and 1664/5 Wharfage Books. In all graphs throughout this chapter, figures prior to 1558 have been doubled to account for changes in the Book of Rates valuations. Unlike other branches of trade, however, the valuations on goods imported from Ireland did not undergo significant revisions in the 1640s. Figures from after 1642, therefore, have not been adjusted. See the Technical Appendix for a fuller discussion.

In other respects, however, it is something of a paradox. While in absolute terms Bristol's Irish trade had expanded by as much as four times in the century before 1670, in relative terms its significance had declined considerably. Where once Ireland was one of Bristol's key trading partners, accounting for perhaps a quarter of the city's trade, by the end of the seventeenth century it had been completely overshadowed by developments elsewhere, making up less than 3 per cent of the city's imports (Figure 17). This trade was also extremely prone to disruption. While trade with Ireland was clearly benefiting from the general buoyancy of the economy along Europe's Atlantic littoral, this prosperity could be brought crashing down by the political conflicts that so often rent the third Stuart kingdom, and the misguided regulation of English administrators.

Like the continental trades discussed in the last chapter, Bristol's trade with Ireland experienced a significant decline in the middle decades of the sixteenth century. Imports dropped to a low point of just £400 in 1575/6, and exports similarly had fallen to just over £800. Unlike trade with France and Spain, however, Irish commerce remained in the doldrums for the rest of the sixteenth century. Although 1594/5 shows a brief revival, with £3,400 worth of goods coming into Bristol from Ireland, much of this was Spanish goods such as sweet

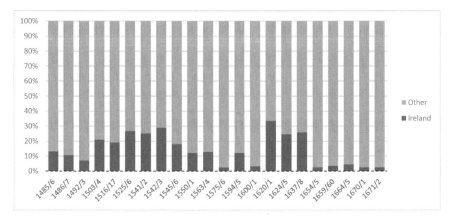

Figure 17. Irish trade as a percentage of Bristol's total recorded imports, as recorded in the Port Books, Wharfage Books, and Particular Accounts (in pounds sterling).

Sources: As for Figure 16.

seck wine, olive oil, and merino wool.[12] By the turn of the century, however, trade with Ireland had declined again. Less than £800 worth of goods were recorded from Ireland in 1601/2, accounting for little more than 2 per cent of Bristol's import trade.

Susan Flavin has concluded that this decline in Irish trade was not a result of weakness of the Irish economy, which was in fact prospering at this time to such an extent that there was a significant increase in the range of consumer goods shipped to Ireland.[13] Neither was it a result of disruption caused by the Munster rebellions, as the decline in trade pre-dated the outbreak of war. Overall, Flavin concludes that the most likely cause was increased trade between Ireland and the continent, directing activity away from Bristol.[14] There are a few hints in the Bristol customs records of Ireland's trade with France and Spain, in the form of commodities being shipped to Bristol that must have originated on the continent. As noted, Spanish goods were particularly prominent during the years of the Anglo-Spanish War, when Ireland would have made a useful alternative source of supply for commodities that Bristol would normally have sourced from the Iberian Peninsula. Such re-exports made up around 30 per

12   Imports recorded from Ireland in that year included £608 worth of seck, £100 of olive oil, £125 of Spanish hat wool, and also £170 worth of French wine. In all, these re-exported goods made up 30 per cent of imports from Ireland in that year. 1594/5 Port Book.

13   Flavin, *Consumption and Culture*, pp. 28–42.

14   *Ibid.*, pp. 35–42.

cent of Bristol's imports from Ireland in both 1594/5 and 1600/1.[15] Even in peacetime, there is some indication of Ireland's own trade with the continent, such as the ton of wine shipped from Ireland to Bristol in 1563/4.[16]

While the Bristol Port Books only permit occasional glimpses of Ireland's continental trade, other sources can help to fill the gaps. Particularly useful is a report on Ireland's trade conducted in 1611, which Raymond Gillespie has suggested is equally applicable to the latter sixteenth century.[17] This suggests that some of the more southerly Irish ports, such as Galway and Cork, were principally trading with Spain at this time. Waterford, the most important port for Bristol's sixteenth-century Irish trade, developed a triangular trade including both Spain and England. Irish goods were sent to Spain to be exchanged for wine, iron and salt, which were then sold in Bristol, where a cargo of English goods was picked up and shipped back to Waterford. This helps to explain the imbalance between Bristol's exports to and imports from Ireland, which is apparent in many of the late sixteenth- and early seventeenth-century accounts (Figure 16). By the late sixteenth century, Ireland was clearly more than an appendage of England, fully integrated into the Atlantic economy, with its own substantial direct trading links to prosperous Spanish markets. Far from being reliant on England, Ireland's economy flourished even when trade with England declined.

Bristol's Irish trade underwent a significant expansion in the first four decades of the seventeenth century. From less than £800 in 1601/2, imports from Ireland were up to £11,800 in 1620/1. By 1637/8, Irish imports of £21,500 worth of goods made up 26 per cent of Bristol's total import trade that year. Exports to Ireland underwent similarly dramatic growth. From £1,400 in 1601/2, they rose to £10,700 by 1618/19, and £20,600 in 1636/7. Booming of Irish trade made a very significant contribution to Bristol's prosperity in these years, making up 53 per cent of recorded exports in 1628/9. This more than twenty-fold growth has been completely overlooked in the previous literature on Bristol's trade in the early seventeenth century. D. H. Sacks, for example, when discussing the 1620s remarked that 'the picture for the Irish trade is virtually the same as in 1575–76'.[18] This is a complete mischaracterisation. At £12,300, Irish imports in the 1624/5 Port Book that Sacks was examining were exponentially higher than the £400 recorded in 1575/6, and exports had experienced similar (if slightly less spectacular) growth. This oversight can only be explained by the fact that Sacks paid relatively little attention to Irish trade, claiming that 'virtually all of this traffic was in the hands of the Irish themselves', and that

15   1594/5 and 1600/1 Port Books.
16   1563/4 Port Book, f. 6r.
17   R. Gillespie, *The Transformation of the Irish Economy 1550–1700* (Dublin, 1998), p. 5.
18   Sacks, *Widening Gate*, p. 41.

'Irish trade only complemented Bristol's traffic with European markets'.[19] This again completely misrepresents the situation. By the 1620s, Irish trade was integral to Bristol's commercial world. In the 1620s and 1630s Ireland accounted for a quarter of Bristol's import trade, and between a third and half of her exports. It was also not true that this trade was exclusively, even predominantly, in Irish hands. Unfortunately, the omission of domicile data from the seventeenth-century Port Books means that the origins of the merchants handling the trade cannot be analysed as they can for the sixteenth century. However, the home ports of the ships involved in the trade give some indication. In the mid-sixteenth century these were predominantly from south-east Ireland, with Irish vessels carrying around 80 per cent of the goods shipped from Ireland to Bristol in both 1563/4 and 1575/6.[20] By 1637/8, however, the dominance of Irish shipping had declined, with English and Welsh ships carrying 57 per cent of Bristol's recorded Irish trade.[21]

The outbreak of the 'War of the Three Kingdoms' (Civil War) in the 1640s was disastrous for Ireland. Ireland was one of the bloodiest theatres of the war, and English military efforts to suppress Irish independence continued until 1653, as did a plague that began in 1649.[22] The combination of war and disease had a dramatic effect on the Irish population, which fell from 2.1 million in 1641 to 1.7 million in 1672.[23] The 1640s and early 1650s were thus a tough time for the Irish economy.[24] As a result, Bristol's trade with Ireland collapsed. Imports from Ireland fell from a pre-war height of £21,500 to just £7,600 in 1654/5. Five years later, still only £8,700 worth of goods were coming from Ireland. Ireland returned to the margins of Bristol's commercial world, accounting for less than 4 per cent of the total value of imports. Frustratingly, due to adjustments in the valuations of the manufactured goods that accounted for much of Irish trade, export figures from the second half of the seventeenth century cannot reliably be compared with earlier figures.

As the Irish economy recovered, the 1660s saw something of a return to the pre-war prosperity of Irish trade. Indeed, Bristol imported £22,600 worth of goods from Ireland in 1664/5, surpassing the heights of the 1630s. This period of renewed success, however, was short. In 1670/1 imports from Ireland had fallen

19   *Ibid.*, pp. 39–40.
20   1563/4 and 1575/6 Port Books. In 1563/4 Irish ships carried £1,333.42 worth of goods imported into Bristol (82.59 per cent), and in 1575/6, £316 (78.27 per cent). The remainder was carried by English and Welsh ships.
21   1637/8 Port Book. The breakdown was: England, £7,744.58; Ireland, £8,624.33; Wales £4,300.50; Unknown/Other, £766.84.
22   Gillespie, *Transformation*, pp. 39–40.
23   L. M. Cullen, 'Population Trends in Seventeenth Century Ireland', *Economic and Social Review*, 6(2) (1975), p. 163.
24   Gillespie, *Transformation*, pp. 38–40.

to £10,900. The following year, they were just a little better at £14,800. This renewed decline was not the result of further outbreaks of disease or conflict, and most likely reflects the effect of restrictive economic legislation enacted in the 1660s, such as the ban on Irish cattle exports, which created much uncertainty in the Irish economy.[25] Nevertheless, taking a longer view, the prospects for Bristol's Irish trade looked much more positive. The slight drop-off in the early 1670s may have meant that Irish trade was not as prosperous as in the 1630s. It had, nonetheless, still come a long way since the difficult times in the late sixteenth century, and Irish imports and exports in 1671/2 were still in excess of the values recorded in 1624/5.

While Bristol's trade with Ireland was still vulnerable to disruption, there can be no doubt that the story of the sixteenth and seventeenth centuries overall was one of stunning expansion. Again, this development has all too often been overlooked by previous scholarship, either due to the growth of Irish trade being overshadowed by the much more dramatic expansion of transatlantic trade, or through simply assuming that Ireland was marginal to Bristol's merchants. The roots of this trade expansion lay in the development and increasing prosperity of the Irish economy across these two centuries, and thus we consider the types of goods Bristol was both importing from and sending to Ireland.

Imports from Ireland – A Colonial Economy?

At the outset of the period covered by this book, Bristol's imports from Ireland were based on a very limited range of commodities. In the latter fifteenth century, Irish trade was dominated by fish, which accounted for three-quarters of the total (see Figure 18).[26] There were some sheepskins and cow-hides, and also some cloth in the form of linens and Irish mantles. On the whole, however, this was a simple trade, based largely on fisheries, and a limited amount of agricultural surplus. As discussed elsewhere, however, over the next two centuries the Irish economy underwent a transformation.[27] From an economy dominated by local lords and focused on redistributive consumption (such as feasting

---

25   *Ibid.*, p. 41.
26   T. Bowly, '"Herring of Sligo and Salmon of Bann": Bristol's Maritime Trade with Ireland in the Fifteenth Century', in R. Gorski (ed.), *Roles of the Sea in Medieval England* (Woodbridge, 2012), pp. 147–66; E. M. Carus-Wilson, 'The Overseas Trade of Bristol', in E. Power and M. M. Postan (eds), *Studies in English Trade in the Fifteenth* Century (London, 1933), pp. 191–201; R. Stone, 'The Overseas Trade of Bristol in the Later Fifteenth Century: The Evidence of the Particular Customs Accounts', in E. T. Jones and R. Stone (eds), *The World of the Newport Medieval Ship: Trade, Politics and Shipping in the Mid-Fifteenth Century* (Cardiff, 2018), pp. 197–8.
27   Gillespie, 'Economic Life'.

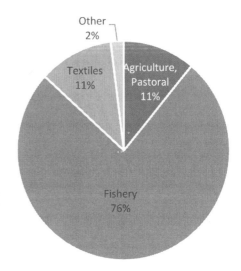

Figure 18. Bristol's imports from
Ireland in the late fifteenth century
(in pounds sterling).

Sources: 1485/6, 1486/7 and 1492/3
Particular Accounts.

in great halls to secure the loyalty of those under their authority), Ireland
became increasingly commercialised from the late sixteenth century onwards.[28]
Combined with the significant increase in Ireland's population from 1 million
in 1500 to 2.2 million in 1687, this led to significant increases in agricultural
output, all clearly reflected in the Bristol Port Books.[29]

The mid-sixteenth century customs accounts paint a very different picture
of Bristol's imports from Ireland than those of the latter fifteenth century
(Figure 19). Particularly notable is growth in the amount of cloth sent from
Ireland to Bristol. Cloth imports of almost £1,300 in 1550/1 made up half of
Bristol's Irish trade in that year. While cloth exports dropped in 1563/4, they
again accounted for more than 50 per cent of imports from Ireland in 1575/6. As
Susan Flavin and Evan Jones have highlighted, this suggests that the economy
of southern Ireland was already experiencing considerable development as early
as the mid-sixteenth century (prior to significant English intervention, usually
seen as the key trigger of development), including establishing a noteworthy
manufacturing industry.[30] The most striking change, however, is the decline in
exports of fish. Having made up three-quarters of imports from Ireland in the
previous century, by 1550/1 the £631 worth of fish represented just 24 per cent
of Bristol's imports from Ireland in that year. Rather than a genuine drop-off

28   *Ibid.*, p. 554.
29   Cullen, 'Population Trends in Seventeenth-Century Ireland'; Gillespie, *Transformation*,
pp. 19–29.
30   S. Flavin and E. T. Jones, 'Introduction', in S. Flavin and E. T. Jones (eds), *Bristol's
Trade with Ireland and the Continent, 1503–1601: The Evidence of the Exchequer Customs
Accounts*, Bristol Record Society Vol. 61 (Dublin, 2009), p. xvii.

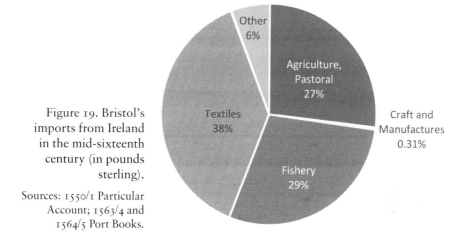

Figure 19. Bristol's imports from Ireland in the mid-sixteenth century (in pounds sterling).

Sources: 1550/1 Particular Account; 1563/4 and 1564/5 Port Books.

in trade, however, this may simply reflect a change in recording policy by the customs officers, as by this time caught fish (as opposed to purchased) did not pay import duties. Therefore, this change may simply reflect much of the produce of the Irish fisheries no longer appearing in the customs accounts.[31]

The accounts across the close of the century show a different picture again (Figure 20). From their dominance a century earlier, imports of fish from Ireland had almost completely dwindled away, making up just 2 per cent of trade. In their place was a considerable amount of wine and olive oil re-exported from Spain, as discussed above, evidence of Ireland's growing trade connections with the continent. In addition to the oft-cited religious sympathies between Catholic Ireland and Spain, it is also worth mentioning that the nature of the Irish economy also made it well suited to trade with the Iberian Peninsula. As discussed in the previous chapter, it was Bristol's ability to provide agricultural goods and increasingly cheap manufactured wares that allowed it to capitalise on the economic opportunities provided by the south of the Peninsula in the sixteenth century. While Ireland had less to offer in terms of manufactured goods, it had access to the foodstuffs and animal-skins that Bristol's merchants sought to smuggle to Spain in abundance. With religious fast days still a significant part of the Spanish calendar, Ireland was also able to capitalise on the same demand for fish that made Bristol keen to develop its presence in the Newfoundland fishery (see Chapter 3).[32] While still largely focused on agricul-

31   E. T. Jones, 'Bristol and Newfoundland, 1490–1570', in I. Bulgin (ed.), *Cabot and His World Symposium* (Newfoundland Historical Society, St. Johns, 1999), p. 76.
32   J. Williams, *Food and Religious Identities in Spain, 1400–1600* (London, 2017), p. 3.

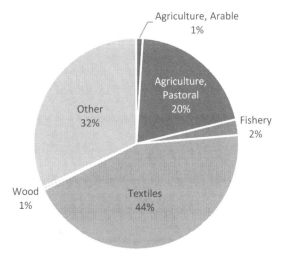

Figure 20. Bristol's imports from Ireland in the late sixteenth century (in pounds sterling).

Sources: 1594/5 and 1600/1 Port Books.

tural produce, the late sixteenth-century customs accounts point to the fact that Ireland still had a noteworthy manufacturing sector. Exports of Irish cloth remained healthy, accounting for over 40 per cent of Bristol's imports from Ireland.

It was, though, the first four decades of the seventeenth century that saw the real transformation of imports from Ireland. By the end of the 1630s, the amount of goods shipped from Ireland to Bristol had not only grown exponentially in value, but also become more diverse in character (Figure 21). The trade in Irish cloth had continued to expand, with almost £5,000 worth of cloth (in particular Irish rugs) arriving in 1637/8. There were also £400 worth of stockings, and £170 worth of yarn. Most notable, though, is the growth in output of Irish agriculture. In 1637/8, Bristol received almost £6,500 worth of skins and hides from Ireland, £4,600 worth of wool, and £1,600 of tallow. There were also some exports of beef from Ireland, but no sign of the significant trade in live cattle that was so important to Chester, the other major port for trade with Ireland.[33] There are a few potential explanations for this. One is that cattle, for one reason or another, were simply not being declared at Bristol, and thus, like the fisheries, the trade does not appear in the Port Books. Omitting cattle from the Port Books has certainly been widely noted in both the sixteenth and seventeenth centuries.[34] Another possibility is that this reflects Bristol's greater distance from the grazing grounds, with the more southern city instead receiving preserved beef and other more portable agricultural outputs. Notably Chester's

33   Woodward, 'Overseas Trade of Chester', pp. 34–9.
34   Gillespie, *Transformation*, p. 5; D. M. Woodward, 'The Anglo-Irish Livestock Trade of the Seventeenth Century', *Irish Historical Studies*, 18(72) (1973), p. 495.

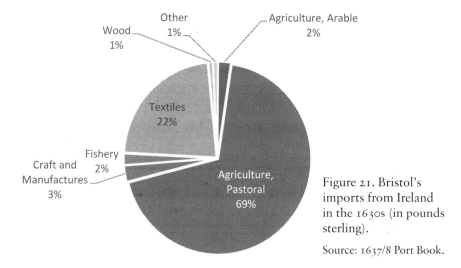

Figure 21. Bristol's imports from Ireland in the 1630s (in pounds sterling).

Source: 1637/8 Port Book.

cattle imports principally came from Dublin, and more northern ports such as Strangford and Drogheda.[35] Finally, for similar reasons of distance, it may be that cattle were taken straight to some of the smaller ports of the Bristol Channel, such as Ilfracombe and Minehead, which, as Donald Woodward has shown, certainly received large numbers of both Irish cattle and sheep in the 1660s.[36] Even without a live cattle trade, however, it is clear that the revolution in Irish farming had a significant impact on trade with Bristol. In all, the produce of pastoral agriculture made up approaching 70 per cent of Bristol's imports from Ireland in 1637/8.

The Wharfage Books from the 1650s and Port Books from the 1670s suggest that, after the changes of the previous century, Bristol's imports from Ireland had now settled into a new pattern dominated by agricultural produce. There were still some fluctuations (for example the complete absence of any Irish cloth in the disrupted years of the 1650s), but broadly the pattern over all four accounts examined here was similar to that of 1637/8. To an extent, this exchange of agricultural produce for the consumer goods discussed in the next section suggests that English trade with Ireland had developed into a colonial-type relationship. Other aspects of the trade, however, point to something more complex, with the Irish economy clearly more developed than a simple colony. The resumption of the cloth trade by the 1670s shows that Ireland still had manufacturing of its own, and indeed was producing goods for export as well as home consumption. While down on pre-war levels, 1670/1 and 1671/2 saw

35   Woodward, 'Overseas Trade of Chester', p. 35.
36   Woodward, 'Anglo-Irish Livestock Trade', p. 498.

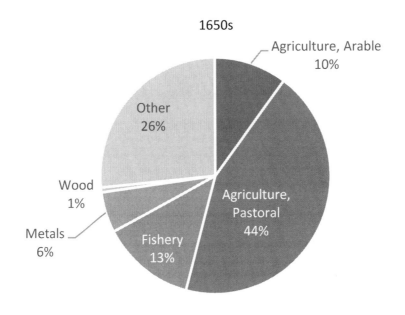

1650s

Agriculture, Arable
10%

Other
26%

Agriculture,
Pastoral
44%

Wood
1%

Metals
6%

Fishery
13%

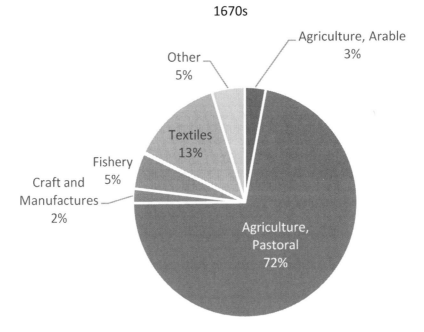

1670s

Agriculture, Arable
3%

Other
5%

Textiles
13%

Fishery
5%

Craft and
Manufactures
2%

Agriculture,
Pastoral
72%

Figure 22. Bristol's imports from Ireland in the mid-late seventeenth century (in pounds sterling).

Sources: 1654/5 and 1659/60 Wharfage Books; 1670 Port Book.

Irish ports send £1,400 and £1,900 worth of cloth to Bristol respectively, around 13 per cent of trade. Perhaps most interesting, though, is the continued presence of continental re-exports among the goods Bristol received from Ireland. At almost £2,900, these made up a significant proportion of the trade in 1654/5. While not quite as significant by the 1670s, the continued presence of a few hundred pounds' worth of goods from the Iberian Peninsula shows that Ireland still had connections to the continent independent of England. As had been the case since the previous century, Irish agricultural produce was in sufficient demand to justify a much longer sea voyage than a quick hop across the Irish Sea. Ireland was thus no simple colony, but an independent economy with both levels of development beyond agriculture, and trading connections of its own.

Exports to Ireland – A Consumer Revolution

The range of goods that Ireland could send to Bristol, and indeed to its continental connections, was key to the success of its overseas trade in the sixteenth and seventeenth centuries. However, Irish demand for a whole range of commodities also had an important part to play. Recent research by Susan Flavin has shown that the sixteenth-century Irish were sophisticated consumers, keeping up with the latest fashions of Europe and demanding a wide range of consumer goods. Based on the same Bristol Port Books that form the core of this study's analysis of sixteenth-century trade, Flavin has identified an ongoing 'consumer revolution' in sixteenth-century Ireland. Her analysis revealed a 'progressively complex range of goods imported into Ireland', showing that the Irish were 'gaining access to the increasingly sophisticated and diversified range of consumer goods being produced and traded in England and mainland Europe at this time'.[37] This included substantial cultural changes in both dress and dining, and was driven not by English immigration but from within Irish society. This change is perhaps best illustrated by the range of individual commodities shipped from Bristol to Ireland. In the early sixteenth century only around sixty distinct types of goods were sent to Ireland, but by the 1590s the Bristol Port Books record almost four hundred.[38]

   In an ideal world, this chapter would continue Flavin's analysis of Ireland's 'consumer revolution' into the seventeenth century. Unfortunately, however, historical records were not created with the needs of the historian in mind, and their authors simply kept records in the way that made most sense to them at the time. So, while the sixteenth-century Port Books record item by item the goods sent from Bristol to Ireland, the same is not true of their seventeenth-century

37   Flavin, *Consumption and Culture*, p. 243.
38   *Ibid.*, pp. 18–22.

counterparts. For the Customer and Controller whose Port Books form the core of the datasets used in this book, it was the tax payable on goods that mattered, rather than the nature of the goods themselves. As seen in the previous section, this led to the non-customable fish disappearing from the Port Books in the mid-sixteenth century. No tax was payable on them, so there was simply no reason for them to be recorded. In the case of Bristol's exports to Ireland, the sheer variety of commodities sent was highly laborious to record. Instead, customs officers lumped them together under headings such as 'other goods valued at ...' or simply 'wares'. By the mid-seventeenth century, this agglomerating tendency on the part of the customs officers rendered the Bristol Port Books virtually unusable for the type of analysis of Irish consumption carried out by Flavin. In 1636/7, for example, almost 85 per cent of Bristol's exports to Ireland (measured by value) were simply labelled 'wares'.[39] Similar trends have been noted elsewhere, with Donald Woodward estimating that up to 80 per cent of goods in Chester's 1583/4 account were grouped together.[40] Nonetheless, even such compromised data allow a valuable conclusion to be drawn. While we can never be certain what made up the 'wares' shipped from Bristol, it seems highly likely that these included a similar range of cloth, clothing and accessories, pieces for dressmaking, food and drink, and domestic utensils to those found by Flavin in the more detailed sixteenth-century accounts. It is thus reasonable to suppose that the sophisticated consumer culture that Flavin uncovered in sixteenth-century Ireland continued into the early seventeenth century and provided a considerable impetus to both Bristol's overseas trade, and manufacturing in the region. Indeed, while the nature of the data means that little can be said about the range of 'wares' Bristol shipped to Ireland in the early seventeenth century, the quantity clearly increased considerably. In 1600/1, the last dataset used by Flavin, Bristol's total exports to Ireland were worth less than £1,800 (much of which was re-exported Iberian goods).[41] By 1636/7, however, Bristol was sending as much as £17,300 worth of 'wares' across the Irish Sea.[42] The buoyancy of the Irish economy, and consequent demand for consumer goods, was thus one of the key drivers of the success of Bristol's overseas trade in the first four decades of the seventeenth century.

While the tendency to lump goods together as 'wares' was common in the latter seventeenth-century Bristol Port Books, customs officers appear to have been more diligent in recording the range of goods shipped to Ireland. In 1671/2, just £2,100 worth of 'wares' were recorded, making up 21 per cent of the goods Bristol sent to Ireland.[43] Rather than a decline in small manufactured

39   1636/7 Port Book.
40   Woodward, *Trade of Elizabethan Chester*, p. 12.
41   1600/1 Port Book.
42   1636/7 Port Book.
43   1671/2 Port Book.

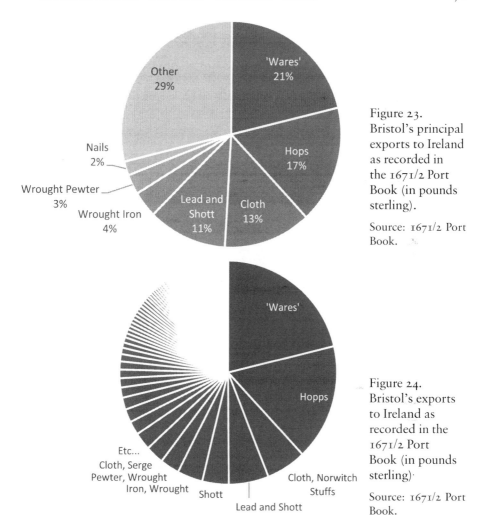

Figure 23.
Bristol's principal
exports to Ireland
as recorded in
the 1671/2 Port
Book (in pounds
sterling).

Source: 1671/2 Port
Book.

Figure 24.
Bristol's exports
to Ireland as
recorded in the
1671/2 Port
Book (in pounds
sterling).

Source: 1671/2 Port
Book.

goods sent to Ireland, however, this was a result of greater diligence on the part
of customs officers in recording small quantities of goods. Manufactured goods
accounted for almost 57 per cent of Bristol's exports to Ireland in 1671/2 (Figure
23). A sizeable percentage of these consisted of a variety of different types of
cloth, which made up 13 per cent of exports, and there was also £196 worth
of nails (2 per cent). The most important single commodity was hops, which
comprised 17 per cent of exports, and there was also more than £1,100 worth
of lead and shot (12 per cent). In all, the 1671/2 customs account records 231
different classes of goods being sent to Ireland, such diversity that Microsoft
Excel cannot present it coherently (see Figure 24)! These included everything

from virginals and cobweb lace to leather chairs and earthenware. While not as diverse as the almost four hundred types of goods identified by Flavin in the 1590s Irish trade, it must be remembered that the 'wares' label almost certainly conceals greater variety.[44] Clearly, Ireland still had diverse consumer tastes, including large quantities of goods sourced from its nearest neighbour.

Broadening Horizons: Regional Distribution of Bristol's Irish Trade

If trends in the goods that Bristol traded with Ireland in the sixteenth and seventeenth centuries are striking, changes in the regional distribution of this trade are even more so. Historically Bristol's trade with Ireland was concentrated in the south-east of the country, the region closest to Bristol both geographically and culturally. The connection between Bristol and this region was very old, with Bristol's links to Waterford dating back to the twelfth century and growing significantly from the fourteenth.[45] This was the core of the English settlement in medieval Ireland, and the country's most economically developed area. Bristol, as the leading English port on the Irish Sea, and little more than a day's sail from south-east Ireland, played an important part in facilitating connections, both political and economic. While Bristol's trade with Ireland was in decline in the latter part of the sixteenth century, it was still focused on key ports in the south-east such as Waterford, Wexford and Youghal. Indeed, in 1594/5 as much as 75 per cent of Bristol's Irish trade was conducted through the old stronghold of Waterford.

By the end of the seventeenth century, although the traditional ports of the south-east remained important, Bristol was increasingly establishing commercial links with ports in central and northern Ireland (see Figure 25). Although Bristol had links with Dublin dating back to the twelfth century, in the latter sixteenth century it did not feature to any significant extent as a destination for Bristol's trade.[46] From the very beginning of these commercial links, though, Bristol had to compete with Chester, which was geographically much closer to Dublin.[47] It is therefore perhaps unsurprising that, by the sixteenth century, Bristol was focused instead on the ports of Waterford and Wexford, which were little more than a day's sail away.[48] By 1637/8, however, Bristol was importing as much as £2,800 worth of goods from Dublin, which made up 16

44   Flavin, *Consumption and Culture*, p. 18.
45   B. Smith, 'Late Medieval Ireland and the English Connection: Waterford and Bristol c.1360–c.1460', *Journal of British Studies*, 50(3) (2011), pp. 546–65.
46   A. Gwynn, 'Medieval Bristol and Dublin', *Irish Historical Studies*, 5(20) (1947), p. 279.
47   *Ibid.*, p. 278.
48   Woodward, 'Anglo-Irish Livestock Trade', p. 512.

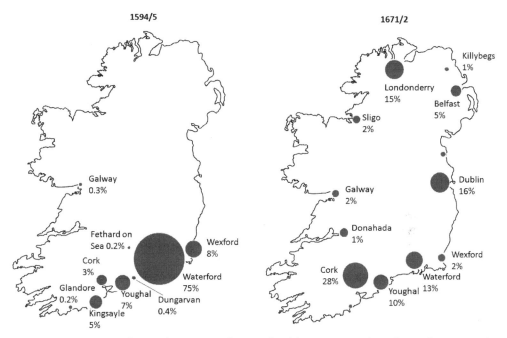

Figure 25. Percentage of Bristol's imports from Ireland by port, 1594/5 and 1671/2 (in pounds sterling).

Sources: 1671/2 Port Book.1594/5 Port Book; 1671/2 Port Book.

per cent of Bristol's Irish trade. The increasing commercialisation of the Irish economy saw Dublin grow exponentially in this period, with its population up from 5,000 in 1600 to 62,000 at the beginning of the eighteenth century.[49] It is thus unsurprising that merchants from Bristol were increasingly drawn there. More striking, though, is the development of trade with the north of Ireland. Imports from Londonderry totalling £2,300 accounted for 15 per cent of Bristol's Irish trade in 1671/2, and £700 worth of goods from Belfast constituted nearly 5 per cent of Irish imports. By this stage, trade with the south-east of Ireland, which had completely dominated in previous centuries, made up barely 50 per cent of Bristol's imports from Ireland. This is perhaps best reflected by the decline in the centrality of Waterford. Having accounted for 75 per cent of Bristol's Irish trade in 1594/5, by 1671/2 just 13 per cent of Bristol's Irish imports came from Waterford. It is important to note that this does not necessarily reflect a decline of Bristol's trade with its old Irish haunts. Imports from the south-eastern ports in 1671/2 were worth as much as £8,200, which, even

49   Gillespie, 'Economic Life', p. 548.

accounting for inflation, is a significant increase on the late sixteenth century. Instead, this represents a growth of opportunities as new areas of Ireland were devoted to intensive cultivation. To an extent, the geographical distribution of Bristol's Irish trade had already begun to diversify by the 1630s. In 1637/8, for example, Bristol imported £477 worth of goods from Coleraine, £292 from Drogheda, £701 from Limerick, and £485 from Londonderry. Development of trade with the north of Ireland, however, probably owes most to the increased spread of colonisation and immigration into the north of Ireland in the years after the Civil War. Increased English and Scottish settlement in these regions made them much more attractive propositions for trade, both through offering a new market for English consumer goods, and through stimulating agricultural production.[50]

The Transatlantic Provisions Trade

As the example of the *Joseph* at the beginning of this chapter shows, by the mid-seventeenth century, Ireland was also integrated into the Atlantic economy through trade with the American colonies. The tobacco colonies of the Chesapeake and the Caribbean sugar colonies focused almost exclusively on producing cash crops. They were therefore reliant on imports from elsewhere to provide them with all manner of necessities, including food.[51] With the rapid expansion of its agricultural production, Ireland was an ideal source of food to be shipped to the colonies. The export of horses and provisions directly from Ireland was also exempt from the Staple Act, which normally required all goods shipped to English colonies to be loaded in England.[52] Many English ships, therefore, stopped off in Ireland en route to the Americas to acquire a cargo of provisions.[53] With a limited amount of detective work, this Irish provision trade can be seen in the Bristol Port Books. As well as being an important market in its own right, Ireland thus also played an important part in facilitating the growth of the transatlantic trades that were to be the defining feature of Bristol's commerce in the second half of the seventeenth century (see Chapter 4).

50   Gillespie, *Transformation*, pp. 16–19.
51   R. Davis, *The Rise of the English Shipping Industry in the 17th and 18th Centuries* (Newton Abbot, 1972), pp. 268–9; N. Zahedieh, *The Capital and the Colonies: London and the Atlantic Economy 1660–1700* (Cambridge, 2010), pp. 252–3.
52   N. Zahedieh, 'Overseas Expansion and Trade in the Seventeenth Century', in N. Canny (ed.), *The Oxford History of the British Empire, Volume I: The Origins of Empire – British Overseas Enterprise to the Close of the Seventeenth Century* (Oxford, 1998), p. 406.
53   Davis, *The Rise of the English Shipping Industry*, p. 269.

A few entries in the Port Books actually declare dual destinations in Ireland and America.[54] The *Ruby*, which cleared Bristol in September 1672, for example, declared a destination of 'Cork and Nevis', although this was relatively rare, and it may be that others just recorded the initial destination in Ireland or indeed left in ballast. Further evidence of stops in Ireland comes from the Bristol Deposition Books, a collection of sworn statements of events made by individuals in front of a magistrate, in the event that they may later be needed in legal proceedings. The *Love's Increase*, for example, leaked very badly during a voyage from Bristol to Ireland and the West Indies, and Edward Yeamans made a loan to some of the crew of the *Mayflower* of Bristol during a voyage from Bristol to Ireland and St. Sebastians.[55]

The most regular evidence for ships from Bristol stopping off in Ireland comes from the numerous occasions on which different consignments on the same ship were declared in the Port Books for different destinations. When goods were loaded onto the *Abraham* of Bristol on 16 July 1672, for example, she was stated as bound for Virginia. Two days later, however, the entries say that she was going to Dublin.[56] Even though the pool of ship names used was relatively small, such instances can be confirmed to be the same vessel as the name of the master responsible remains the same. Why exactly this happened is unclear. In all probability, it was simply lazy entry, as the destination of the vessel was not important to the customs officers for tax purposes. Individual merchants were responsible for entering their goods at the customs house, so it may be that different merchants loading goods on the same ship simply interpreted the question of where it was going differently, some declaring the immediate destination in Ireland, and others the ultimate destination in America.

The number of ships declaring multiple destinations in Ireland and America in the 1671/2 Port Book suggests that this was a substantial part of the transatlantic trade. Of the twenty-eight ships leaving Bristol for North America in that year, six also list destinations in Ireland (21 per cent). Of thirty-one ships bound for the Caribbean, eight appear to have been also stopping off in Ireland (26 per cent). Overall, of the fifty-nine vessels conducting transatlantic voyages from Bristol in that year, at least fourteen (24 per cent) stated that they were visiting ports in Ireland. Irish provisions thus appear to have made up a significant proportion of the goods Bristol sent to the New World. Exactly what goods were being purchased in Ireland is, unfortunately, impossible to determine from the Bristol records. The few surviving Irish customs records, however, show that

---

54 1671/2 Port Book, ff. 27r, 112r, 122r, 126v.
55 P. V. McGrath, 'Merchant Shipping in the Seventeenth Century: The Evidence of the Bristol Deposition Books, Part I', *Mariner's Mirror*, XL (1954), p. 293; P. V. McGrath, 'Merchant Shipping Part II', *Mariner's Mirror*, XLI (1955), p. 29.
56 1671/2 Port Book, ff. 112r–113v.

salted provisions such as beef, pork, butter and fish dominated (beef exports accounted for two-thirds of the total in the latter part of the seventeenth century).[57] In some respects, Ireland's place in the transatlantic trade network was similar to that of northern American colonies such as New England. While Ireland did not produce profitable cash crops itself, it nonetheless played a facilitating role by provisioning plantation colonies unable to feed themselves.[58] It is a chilling thought for the historian of Ireland that the expansion of the pastoral economy in the second half of the seventeenth century was due in no small part to the need to fill the bellies of American enslaved people and their masters.

Bristol's trade in Irish provisions was conducted predominantly through Dublin and the old strongholds in the south-east of the country.[59] Two Virginia-bound voyages do, though, list Londonderry in the far north of Ireland as an outward destination, one of which (the *Joseph*) also declared goods for Carrickfergus and Belfast.[60] Another vessel lists Sligo on the north-west coast as a stopping point en route to Barbados.[61] While the new English colonies in the north of Ireland played some part in this trade, therefore, it was predominantly conducted through the well-established ports of the Pale. R. C. Nash has suggested that the provisions trade was mostly conducted by small partnerships of English merchants.[62] The evidence from the Bristol customs records certainly supports this. Unfortunately, the latter seventeenth-century Port Books do not contain information about the origins of the merchants recorded, so it is not possible to separate Irish and English merchants as can be done with the earlier data. The shipping that they used, however, perhaps gives a better indication. In contrast to the Irish trade more broadly, where shipping from Ireland played a significant part, the American provisions trade was conducted entirely by English vessels. The vast majority of this trade was conducted on Bristolian ships, although single vessels from Liverpool and the Devon port Bideford were also involved.

---

57   R. C. Nash, 'Irish Atlantic Trade in the Seventeenth and Eighteenth Centuries', *The William and Mary Quarterly*, 42(3) (1985), pp. 330–1; R. Dunlop, 'A Note on the Export Trade of Ireland in 1641, 1665, and 1669', *English Historical Review*, 22(8) (1907), pp. 754–6.
58   Zahedieh, *Capital and the Colonies*, pp. 253–4.
59   The following Irish ports were listed by ships also bound for the Americas: Cork (five times), Dublin (three times), Londonderry (twice), Kinsale (twice), and Youghall, Belfast, Carrickfergus, Sligo and Waterford by single vessels.
60   1671/2 Port Book, ff. 112r, 115r–119v.
61   1671/2 Port Book, f. 122r.
62   Nash, 'Irish Atlantic Trade', p. 344.

Conclusions

Over the course of the sixteenth and seventeenth centuries, the story of Bristol's Irish trade is both complex, and crucial. Far from being (as Sacks has dubbed it) a mere complement to Bristol's continental trade, Irish commerce played a key role in shaping Bristol's commercial development in this period.[63] There were clearly fluctuations, with the Irish trade highly susceptible to disruption both from the wars that struck Ireland in this period, but also from the potentially more profitable commercial opportunities available to the Irish through direct trade with the continent. Yet there were also periods of real prosperity, with the first third of the seventeenth century in particular seeing Ireland as arguably Bristol's most important export market, taking 42 per cent of all goods leaving Bristol. By the 1630s, Bristol's Irish exports and imports had both grown tenfold. Although the following decades were to see Bristol's Irish trade overshadowed by growing trade with the New World, it remained significantly higher than in previous centuries. Ireland also continued to play a key role in Bristol's wider Atlantic trading network. In particular, the growing output of Ireland's 'agricultural revolution' allowed it to function, alongside New England, as 'ghost acres' for the American and Caribbean plantation colonies, providing a share of the provisions that fed their workforce.[64]

Examining Irish trade through Bristol's seventeenth-century customs accounts confirms many of the recent trends in Irish economic history. Economically, Ireland was much more than a mere colony of England at this time, acting in its own right as an important node in the nascent Atlantic economy. Flavin's sixteenth-century consumer revolution continued apace into the seventeenth century. Although the lack of detail in the seventeenth-century accounts makes it difficult to comment on the range of goods being sent to Ireland, their value expanded dramatically. The £17,300 worth of manufactured 'wares' that Bristol sent to Ireland in 1636/7 is almost ten times that of the last dataset examined by Flavin.[65] Ireland's manufacturing base also continued to grow, with almost £5,000 worth of cloth sent to Bristol in a single year, and the beginnings of a trade in Irish stockings. Finally, there is also continued evidence of Ireland maintaining its own significant trading connections with the continent. In most years this is only reflected in a steady trickle of Iberian goods into Bristol, but when England was at war with Spain, Ireland could be an important source of goods from the Peninsula, which would otherwise be difficult to acquire. It would be an oversimplification to suggest that there were

63   Sacks, *Widening Gate*, p. 40.
64   For New England's role in supplying provisions to the plantation colonies, see J. J. McCusker and R. R. Menard, *The Economy of British America, 1607–1789* (London, 1985), pp. 91–116.
65   Flavin, *Consumption and Culture*.

no elements akin to 'colonial' trade in Bristol's seventeenth-century relationship with Ireland. Whilst the old strongholds in the south-east and Dublin remained key, a noteworthy proportion of Bristol's expanded Irish trade in the latter seventeenth century was with the plantations of the north. Also, as was the case in Bristol's new American trades (see Chapters 5 and 6), the goods sent to Ireland were predominantly manufactured, and those received in return were mostly agricultural produce. However, as shown in Chapter 1, a similar pattern had also long predominated in Bristol's continental trades, with cloth and other manufactures being exchanged for wine, wool, olive oil, fruit and other agricultural goods. Ireland, then, was never Bristol's 'first colonial trade', but an important actor in its own right, both shaping and sharing in the expansion of the Atlantic economy. While not a stepping-stone in terms of trialling colonial methods, the prosperity Ireland's dynamic commercialising economy brought to Bristol perhaps gave Bristol's merchants the capital and the confidence to take up the opportunities in the New World which, as the next chapters show, transformed the city.

3

A 'Quest' for New Markets?

On 12 August 1504, under the careful eyes of her master William Claron, the 50-ton *Matthew* of Bristol was unloading a cargo of woad, salt and vinegar from Bordeaux. She had been to Ireland in the spring, bringing back hides, skins and fish, and was shortly to set sail once again for Spain with her hold full of broadcloth, lead and tin.[1] This was not remarkable: these were the three core trade routes for early sixteenth-century Bristol, and a versatile mid-sized ship like the *Matthew* could be used on any of them.[2] More than five hundred years later, the *Matthew* of Bristol lies moored outside the city's M Shed museum, resplendent in her Tudor green-and-white livery, and with the water of the Floating Harbour lapping gently at her carvel-built hull. She is, of course, not the original *Matthew*, but a replica constructed to resemble her as closely as possible. Built more than a quarter of a century ago, she has almost certainly existed for longer than the original *Matthew* ever did. It is not because of her regular voyages along Europe's Atlantic coast that the city of Bristol has chosen to remember the original *Matthew*, but rather because she was chartered by Venetian navigator John Cabot when he set sail from Bristol on the famous voyage on which he accidentally 'discovered' North America. Nonetheless, thinking about her humdrum voyages in 1504 tells us something important about more famous voyages. The *Matthew* was not a special ship purpose-built for voyages of 'discovery', but a normal merchantman hired for the purpose. Nor was she celebrated and placed on a pedestal for the part she played in events which we, centuries later, consider momentous. Instead, she went back to the day-to-day business of European trade.[3] Without the benefits of hindsight, the 1497 voyage was, to Cabot's Bristol backers, just another business venture. It was not the first time they had sent out a vessel to try to

---

1   1503/4 Particular Account, ff. 12v, 51r, 55v, 67r, 72r.
2   E. T. Jones, 'The Shipping Industry of the Severn Sea', in E. T. Jones and R. Stone (eds), *The World of the Newport Medieval Ship: Trade, Politics and Shipping in the Mid-Fifteenth Century* (Cardiff, 2018), pp. 149–50.
3   E. T. Jones, 'The *Matthew* of Bristol and the Financiers of John Cabot's 1497 Voyage to North America', *English Historical Review*, 121(492) (2006), pp. 778–95.

open up a new branch of trade, and it would not be the last. It was not even, in their eyes, the most successful.

Reading some of the mid-twentieth-century works on Bristol's overseas trade, you could be forgiven for thinking that the period 1500–1700 was one dominated by the 'quest' to open up new markets. Indeed, they give the impression that the city's merchants were primarily engaged in an inevitable progression, from John Cabot's discovery of 'new' lands across the Atlantic in 1497, to the establishment of an empire founded on transatlantic trade. The early chapter headings of Charles MacInnes's canonical *Gateway of Empire* neatly encapsulate this: 'I – The Period of Preparation', 'II – Marking Time', 'III – Pioneers of Empire', 'IV – From Massachusetts to Cathay', 'V – Newfoundland and Virginia', 'VI – The Northwest Passage'.[4] Writing in the 1930s, MacInnes represents the last flowering of the Whig tradition of historical writing, which presented a teleological version of history, tracing the development of the 'great institutions' of late nineteenth- and early twentieth-century Britain and its Empire.[5] The tradition of including early English Atlantic voyages in a continuous narrative leading to the first colonisation ventures dates back to the late sixteenth century. Propagandists of England's imperial aspirations, such as the two Richard Hakluyts, sought to prove a sustained English connection with the New World to support claims of legitimacy, and also to hold up the 'great deeds' of earlier pioneers to inspire future venturers.[6] The tendency to cast all American ventures, from Cabot to colonisation, into a single teleological narrative is thus both a product of the prevailing approach to historical writing in the nineteenth and twentieth centuries, and shaped by the concerns of the early promoters of English colonisation. Even for the most recent generations of historians, new ventures and new trades receive a significant amount of attention. The latest publications on Bristol's early modern commerce, for example, include a volume on Robert Sturmy's pioneering attempts to break into Mediterranean trade in the 1450s, and numerous works by the Cabot Project looking at Bristol's role in the late fifteenth- and early sixteenth-century 'discovery' voyages.[7] Although the days of idolising those who built the British

4   C. M. MacInnes, *A Gateway of Empire* (Newton Abbot, 1968).
5   R. Hutton, *Debates in Stuart History* (Basingstoke, 2004), pp. 6–31.
6   N. Canny, 'England's New World and the Old', in N. Canny (ed.), *The Oxford History of the British Empire, Volume I: The Origins of Empire – British Overseas Enterprise to the Close of the Seventeenth Century* (Oxford, 1998), pp. 150–1.
7   See, for example: S. Jenks (ed.), *Robert Sturmy's Commercial Expedition to the Mediterranean, 1457/8*, Bristol Record Society Vol. 58 (Bristol, 2006); Jones, 'The *Matthew* of Bristol'; E. T. Jones, 'Alwyn Ruddock: "John Cabot and the Discovery of America"', *Historical Research*, 81(212) (2007); E. T. Jones, 'Henry VII and the Bristol Expeditions to North America: The Condon Documents', *Historical Research*, 83(221) (2010); E. T. Jones and M. Condon, *Cabot and Bristol's Age of Discovery: The Bristol Discovery Voyages 1480–1508* (Bristol, 2016).

Empire are gone, historic examples of innovation and entrepreneurship still appeal to modern eyes.

This chapter seeks to reassess the place of 'new' trades within our understanding of the mindset of early modern English merchants. This was not, for them, an inevitable process of progression towards a globe-spanning overseas empire, but a series of short-term experiments designed to test the waters of potential profits. As historians, we must remember that we look back with the benefit of hindsight. We know that colonisation of the Americas transformed the European economy and made countless individual fortunes. To the merchants of Tudor and early Stuart England, however, this was not apparent. Indeed, in 1613 establishing a colony in Newfoundland was akin to establishing a colony on Mars today.[8] Virtually past the reach of communications, and with a hostile climate, such ventures could be a complete financial failure. On the other hand, bringing into circulation vast amounts of previously untappable resources, such ventures could be truly epoch-making, and fundamentally transform the nature of the global economy.

As previous chapters have made clear, attempts to establish new trade routes were not, as sometimes thought, desperate gambits on the part of merchants who needed to replace lost markets. While it fluctuated, Bristol's overseas trade underwent a sustained period of expansion in the sixteenth and early seventeenth centuries. Rather than seeking to replace lost trade, therefore, such ventures were experiments from a point of strength. Again, like those investing in prospective Martian ventures or other speculative schemes in the early twenty-first century, this is a case of already successful businessmen risking some of their spare capital on schemes that may or may not yield great returns. Instead of a teleological 'grand narrative', the story of Bristol's attempts to break into new trades is thus one of fits and starts. Experimental voyages to new markets were actually a fairly regular feature of the fifteenth, sixteenth and seventeenth centuries. Many of these amounted to little and have thus been neither remembered nor remarked on, surviving only as details in the customs records. Beginning with the most well-known activities in the Americas, this chapter uses the customs and other records to track Bristol's non-core trades. From the 'discovery' and colonisation of North America, it moves on to attempts to break into the Mediterranean trades, arguably a greater prize for Bristol's sixteenth- and early seventeenth-century merchants. Finally, it considers early commercial contact with Africa, peripheral markets such as those in the Baltic and the Netherlands, and opportunities that Bristol's merchants did not pursue, such as the East India trade.

---

8   Plans are under discussion. See, for example, R. Coppinger, 'Elon Musk Outlines Mars Colony Vision', September 2016, http://www.bbc.co.uk/news/science-environment-37486372 (accessed 02/03/18).

America

Perhaps no branch of the city's commerce shows the short-term experimental nature of Bristol's forays into new trades better than the Americas. Through their involvement in John Cabot's discovery voyages in the 1490s, Bristol merchants were involved right from the start of England's engagement with the New World. While, as is well known today, ultimately Bristol's fortunes were made by trade with English colonies in the Americas, the path from Cabot's discovery to the Atlantic economy of Bristol's 'Golden Age' was not steady. It took more than a century and a half, and a significant number of failed ventures and blind alleys before Cabot's 'discovery' was seen as anything other than a disappointment to Bristol. Indeed, for much of this time Bristol's merchant community were indifferent to the New World. By the time England's first successful colonies were eventually established in the early seventeenth century, Bristol was confined to waiting in the wings. Far from taking the lead, as in Cabot's day, Bristol only seriously began to trade with America once the colonies were firmly established. This section examines the reasons for this initial reluctance to enter transatlantic commerce, considering what influenced Bristol's merchants and how significant the obstacles they faced were.

The history of Cabot's 'discovery' voyages is a significant subject in itself and I provide only a brief summary here.[9] Cabot was a Venetian navigator who, like Columbus, hoped to cut out the middle-men in the overland trade with Asia by sailing west from Europe, thus gaining direct access to these markets. If successful, this would have provided access to a wealth of Eastern goods at significantly reduced prices, fundamentally altering the nature of global commerce, and making the fortunes of all involved. Having secured backing from Henry VII, and investment from both London's Italian merchants and the Bristol mercantile community, Cabot set out on a series of exploratory voyages from Bristol in the 1490s. The first voyage in 1496 was abortive, but during the second in 1497 Cabot encountered new land across the Atlantic. A further expedition was launched in 1498, but it quickly became apparent that the continent which Cabot had discovered was not Asia. Over the next decade, a series of voyages to the New World were launched from Bristol, and a 'Company of Adventurers to the New Found Land' was established in the city. While several voyages brought back sizeable cargoes of fish (along with exotic hawks, mountain cats, and other curiosities to please the King), these imported goods took up considerably less space than the cargo capacity of the ships, suggesting that these were still primarily voyages of exploration.[10] From

---

9   The best account of the Cabot voyages to date is E. T. Jones and M. M. Condon, *Cabot and Bristol's Age of Discovery* (Bristol, 2016). A much-anticipated monograph by Condon and Jones on the subject is also currently in preparation.

10   Jones and Condon, *Cabot and Bristol's Age of Discovery*, pp. 60–70.

the voyage of William Weston in 1499, the principal aim appears to have been to find a way around the new landmass to the Asian markets which had always been their ultimate goal.[11] By 1510, it was becoming increasingly clear that no such route was to be found, and Bristol's interest in 'New Found Land' waned.

For much of the sixteenth century, there is virtually no evidence of direct Bristolian involvement with the Americas. Bearing in mind the nature of the lands that Cabot 'found', this is not a surprise. Whereas the Spanish discoveries contained sizeable deposits of gold and silver, civilised peoples, and a climate suited to exotic crops, England found a barren and inhospitable land. Newfoundland's Beothuk people were nomadic hunter-gatherers, so offered little prospect of trade or easy exploitation.[12] Similarly, the climate was too cold to grow crops, so the only resource Newfoundland offered was the rich Grand Bank cod fishery. Fishing voyages are unfortunately very hard to detect in the customs records. With no established colonies in Canada, ships usually left England in ballast, as there was no market for exported goods. Similarly, fish that had been caught rather than purchased did not pay customs duties and thus it was possible for a fishing voyage to sail into and out of Bristol without appearing in the customs records at all.[13] While French and Portuguese vessels flocked to Newfoundland in the first half of the sixteenth century, there is little evidence that the English made any sustained attempt to establish a fishery there.[14] For England more broadly, this lack of interest is likely to have been a result of easy access to supplies of stockfish in Iceland. Bristol, on the other hand, had already more or less abandoned its Icelandic trade by the late fifteenth century.[15] Evan Jones has argued that Bristol's lack of interest in the fisheries was a result of greater commercial opportunities offered by Iberian trade.[16] Equally, however, access to large supplies of fish from Ireland meant that Bristol had little need of either Iceland or Newfoundland. In the last two decades of the fifteenth century, Bristol was consistently importing more than

---

11   M. M. Condon and E. T. Jones, 'William Weston: Early Voyager to the New World', *Historical Research*, 91 (2018), pp. 628–46.

12   G. T. Cell, *Newfoundland Discovered: English Attempts at Colonisation 1610–1630* (London, 1982), p. 10; I. Marshall, *A History and Ethnography of the Beothuk* (Montreal, 1996), pp. 13–41.

13   E. T. Jones, 'Bristol and Newfoundland, 1490–1570', in I. Bulgin, *Cabot and His World Symposium* (St. Johns, 1999), p. 76.

14   *Ibid.*, pp. 76–9. Joshua Ivinson has recently identified two previously unknown English fishing voyages to Newfoundland in 1535, suggesting that some interest may have continued. See J. Ivinson, '"To cleere the course scarse knowne": A Re-Evaluation of Richard Hakluyt's "Voyage of Master Hore" and the Development of English Atlantic Enterprise in the Early Sixteenth Century', *Historical Research*, 94(263) (2021), pp. 1–27.

15   R. Stone, 'Bristol's Overseas Trade in the Later Fifteenth Century: The Evidence of the "Particular" Customs Accounts', in Jones and Stone (eds), *The World of the Newport Medieval Ship*, p. 199.

16   Jones, 'Bristol and Newfoundland', p. 80.

£1,000 worth of fish a year from Ireland (constituting as much as 80 per cent of Bristol's Irish imports).[17] Even as late as 1563/4, £700 worth of fish made up 45 per cent of Bristol's imports from Ireland.[18] This reinforces the point that merchants did not exploit new opportunities for their own sake: there had to be a financial incentive. Just because a Bristol venture had discovered a new continent did not mean that the city's merchants would try to trade with it. They had been looking for a route to Asia, not new fishing grounds, which Bristolians simply did not need.

The early seventeenth century saw a gradual escalation of English involvement with both North America and the Caribbean. The first successful English colony was founded at Jamestown in Virginia in 1607, and by the eve of the Civil War in 1642 colonies in both North America and the Caribbean were well established. With this growth in population came significant growth in English transatlantic trade, making vast fortunes for merchants who capitalised on this new opportunity.[19] While Bristol merchants were involved in a number of ventures in these years, American trade has left little trace in pre-Civil War Port Books, suggesting that colonial commerce remained of minor economic importance to the city. Other than the now regular, but still small-scale, Newfoundland fishing voyages, the only significant evidence of these activities in the Port Book records is £1,168 worth of imports from New England and Somers Island in 1624/5. This made up less than 2.5 per cent of Bristol's imports in that year, and indeed even this figure is likely to be an exaggeration, as tobacco was subject to a disproportionately high rate of poundage in relation to other commodities. Indeed, closer inspection shows this new trade to have been made up of just two consignments on one ship, totalling little more than 5,000 lb of tobacco. Even this exceptional interest seems to have been short-lived, as the 1637/8 Port Book shows just £60 worth of goods imported from the American colonies.

With its ideal position on England's west coast, it is perhaps surprising that Bristol was not more prominently involved in North America. A number of factors appear to have contributed to the continued indifference of Bristol's merchants to transatlantic ventures. The first of these is simple: the first ventures in which they invested did not succeed. In the first decade of the seventeenth century, merchants from Bristol were involved in a number of American projects. The first of these appears to have been predominantly a Bristol-based venture, encouraged by Richard Hakluyt.[20] Two small ships under the command of

17   Stone, 'Bristol's Overseas Trade', p. 198.
18   1563/4 Particular Account.
19   R. Brenner, *Merchants and Revolution: Commercial Change, Political Conflict, and London's Overseas Traders, 1550–1653* (London, 2003), pp. 114–95.
20   P. V. McGrath, 'Bristol and America, 1481–1631', in K. R. Andrews, N. P. Canny and P. E. H. Hair (eds), *The Westward Enterprise: English Activities in Ireland, the Atlantic and America 1480–1650* (Liverpool, 1978), p. 97.

Martin Pring set out from Bristol in 1603, bound for 'Northern Virginia' (which at this stage could have meant anywhere on the eastern seaboard of North America), to undertake a mixture of exploration, cultivation, and fur-trading. Exact details of the financing of this voyage are not known, although the two principal investors were leading Bristol merchants Robert Aldworth and John Whitson, and it is likely that much of the £1,000 capital was raised in the city.[21] Unfortunately, no detailed customs records survive from that year, so it is impossible to gauge the financial returns of the voyage (although both ships returned safely to Bristol). There is no evidence, however, that the experiment was repeated, and when they were next asked to participate in a colonising venture, Bristolians' response was lukewarm.

In 1606, Bristol's merchants were again involved in an unsuccessful American venture, although this time their contribution was more modest. Thirteen members of Bristol's Common Council were persuaded to invest in the Plymouth Company, rival of the London Company that established the famous colony at Jamestown the following year.[22] Compared to the £1,000 invested in 1603, Bristol's contribution to the Plymouth Company was small. Five men agreed to contribute between £12 and £14 each annually for five years, and the others between £2 and £5 each. In all, Bristol's contribution came to only £90 a year.[23] For a port that imported £30,000–40,000 worth of goods a year at this time, this was a drop in the ocean.[24] Two ships were sent out from Bristol in 1606, and the following year, just months after Jamestown was established, the Company founded its own Popham Colony in what is now Maine.[25] Faced with a freezing winter and no sign of any mineral wealth that would yield an easy profit, the colonists returned home in 1608, and there is no evidence that the Company remained active after that.[26] The exact motivations of the Bristol merchants who invested in the Plymouth Company are hard to gauge. Several of the largest contributors had ongoing connections with American ventures, in particular Robert Aldworth, John Guy, and Thomas James. Patrick McGrath also suggested that there may have been a political element to their motivation, with the Common Council initially stating that Bristol would not participate 'unless yt shall please the Kinges Majestie to undertake the same'.[27] Clearly, however, this is a long way from notions of the inevitable progress of Bristol's imperial designs. Ultimately, the small amount of money committed

21   McGrath, 'Bristol and America', p. 97.
22   J. Latimer, *The Annals of Bristol in the Seventeenth Century* (Bristol, 1900), p. 27.
23   McGrath, 'Bristol and America', p. 98.
24   1601/2 Port Book and 1612/13 Port Book.
25   C. M. MacInnes, *Ferdinando Gorges and New England* (Bristol, 1965), p. 6; Latimer, *Annals*, pp. 27–8.
26   MacInnes, *Ferdinando Gorges*, p. 6.
27   McGrath, 'Bristol and America', pp. 97–8.

is probably the crucial factor. These were wealthy men (Robert Aldworth had imported more than £3,000 worth of goods in 1600/1, and Thomas James £1,600), so a speculation of £10 or so did not require a great deal of thought or commitment.[28]

A more ambitious endeavour, and one that appears to have shown both greater commitment and greater agency on the part of Bristol's merchants, was the establishment in 1610 of a colony at Cupid's Cove in Newfoundland. After Jamestown in 1607, this was only the second permanent English colony in the New World, and the first in Canada. The enterprise began around 1608, when Bristol merchant John Guy wrote a (now lost) treatise arguing for the merits of a colony in Newfoundland. Having failed to garner sufficient financial support in Bristol, Guy approached potential investors in London, and in 1610, 'certaine merchantes of London and Bristoll' petitioned the king with a proposal to found a new colony. With Letters Patent granted on 2 May, a joint stock company was formed, with each of the forty-four subscribers paying £25 each. Of these, six were courtiers, eleven Bristol merchants and twenty-seven London merchants.[29] While the initial impetus came from Bristol, this was thus at best a joint venture, and to a large extent a London one. With John Guy as its governor, the colony of around forty people was established at the secluded harbour of Cupid's Cove on Newfoundland's Avalon peninsula in August 1610. Its purpose was to focus on fishing, with the intention of securing the best sites for the (largely onshore) fishery before the migratory fishermen arrived in the spring. There was also some attempt to make contact with the indigenous Beothuk people, most notably a voyage in the *Indeavour*, which Guy led in autumn 1612 in the hope of opening up trading relations. However, the Beothuk, apart from one brief meeting, were elusive, and the colony's fishing activities also faltered. The difficulties of surviving and maintaining a settlement in such a harsh environment took labour away from the work of fishing, and disputes with migratory fishermen resulted in compromise agreements that gave little advantage to the permanent colonists. With the colony struggling, Guy returned to England in 1613. While the Company continued, it appears that the departure of Guy also marked the end of Bristolian involvement.[30]

Bristol's interest in Newfoundland did not end with the breakup of the Newfoundland Company, with a grant of land being made to the Bristol Society of Merchant Venturers in 1617.[31] They established a colony (Bristol's Hope) at what is now Harbour Grace. Unfortunately, Bristol's Hope has left little trace

28   1600/1 Port Book.
29   A. F. Williams (edited by G. Hancock and C. W. Sanger), *John Guy of Bristol and Newfoundland* (St. Johns, 2010), pp. 48–53.
30   Williams, *John Guy*, p. 148.
31   P. V. McGrath, *Records Relating to the Society of Merchant Venturers of the City of Bristol in the Seventeenth Century*, Bristol Record Society Vol. 17 (Bristol, 1952), p. 200.

in the records, although Gillian Cell suggested that it was among the more successful early Newfoundland plantations. In spite of the incompetence of its first governor (Oxford graduate Robert Hayman, who appears to have been more interested in writing poetry than running the colony), Bristol's Hope was still in existence in 1631, when it was mentioned in a letter by Nicholas Guy.[32] Nevertheless, settlement in Newfoundland was still on a very small scale in the first half of the seventeenth century.[33] The Bristol colony left little trace in the city's customs records, showing that it was of minimal economic significance. Occasionally ships sailed to the Newfoundland colonies, with £700 worth of exports recorded in 1620/1, £900 in 1624/5, and £1,300 in 1636/7.[34] These, however, only ever accounted for 2–3 per cent of Bristol's export trade. Bristol simply was not as heavily involved with Newfoundland as some smaller west coast ports such as Plymouth and Dartmouth, which could be virtually taken over by the fishing fleet during September and October.[35] In 1638, for example, only three ships returned directly from Newfoundland to Bristol, compared to twenty-two to Dartmouth and twenty-five to Plymouth.[36]

Beyond the foundation of Bristol's Hope in 1618, the city showed little interest in establishing a permanent presence on American soil. In the early 1620s, Bristol, along with several other West Country towns, was approached by the Company of New England regarding the formation of subsidiary companies for further colonisation, but there was little enthusiasm. Numerous letters were sent to the mayor of Bristol urging him to encourage the city's merchants to invest, including one sent at the instigation of the King, but Bristol could not be persuaded. Instead, the Society of Merchant Venturers instructed the two Bristol MPs to investigate the best terms that they could secure for fishing rights in New England waters.[37] A final pre-Civil War venture that always features in the catalogue of Bristol's American endeavours is the voyage of Thomas James in 1631. This was a Bristolian venture, funded by several individual merchants from the city to the tune of at least £800, and underwritten by the Society of Merchant Venturers.[38] This was, however, a voyage of exploration. Its goal was to find a North-West Passage: a route around the north of Newfoundland,

---

32 Cell, *Newfoundland Discovered*, pp. 17–19.

33 As late as 1677 there were just 6,464 English colonists in Newfoundland. P. E. Pope, *Fish into Wine: The Newfoundland Plantation in the Seventeenth Century* (Chapel Hill, NC, 2004), p. 208.

34 1620/21 Port Book; 1624/5 Port Book; 1636/7 Port Book.

35 G. T. Cell, *English Enterprise in Newfoundland, 1577–1660* (Toronto, 1969), p. 5; Pope, *Fish into Wine*, p. 93; G. D. Ramsay, *English Overseas Trade during the Centuries of Emergence: Studies in Some Modern Origins of the English-Speaking World* (London, 1957), p. 141.

36 Cell, *English Enterprise*, p. 140.

37 McGrath, 'Bristol and America', pp. 100–1.

38 *Ibid.*, p. 101.

renewing the dreams of Cabot and Columbus of establishing a westward route to Asia.

Following the failure of the colonisation ventures in which they did invest, Bristol merchants were barred from engaging with the fledgling American trades by several pieces of legislation. The first of these was a monopoly on all tobacco imports, which was held by the Virginia Company from its inception in 1619 until 1625 when it was disbanded.[39] Although this did not completely bar Bristol merchants from trade with the American colonies, excluding them from its staple commodity would have been a major, and indeed probably insurmountable, disincentive. From 1616 when commercial cultivation began, the economy of the Chesapeake colonies was dominated by tobacco production, to the extent that if you could not trade in tobacco, you could not trade with Virginia or Maryland.[40] In the Caribbean colonies, tobacco and cotton were the dominant cash crops in the early years (sugar cultivation did not take off on a significant scale until the 1640s).[41] New England lacked a staple commodity, instead surviving partly through subsistence agriculture and limited manufacture of goods that would otherwise have to be imported, and partly through supplying the cash crop colonies.[42] There were, thus, few opportunities to allow Bristol's merchants to develop trade links. The tobacco imports appearing in the 1624/5 Port Book may, thus, represent a first experiment into American trade by Bristol merchants after the ending of the tobacco monopoly, but this window of opportunity was short. Just six years later, a Royal Proclamation, issued in January 1631, forbade the import of tobacco into any port other than London.[43] This proclamation was re-issued twice, in May 1634 and January 1638, and, like the monopoly before it, was a major obstacle to any Bristolian desire to develop connections with the Americas. It was withdrawn in January 1639, after a petition from the farmers of the Customs who felt that they were losing out greatly on customs duties as a result of tobacco being smuggled into western ports (including Bristol).[44]

The nature of trade with the early American colonies also served to discourage Bristol's involvement. As Robert Brenner has highlighted, it was simply not possible to purchase American tobacco on a large scale without being directly involved in its production.[45] Even by the 1620s, the colonies

---

39   A. M. Millard, 'The Import Trade of London' (unpublished PhD thesis, University of London, 1956), pp. 303, 305.

40   J. J. McCusker and R. R. Menard, *The Economy of British America, 1607–1789* (London, 1985), pp. 118–19.

41   *Ibid.*, pp. 148–9.

42   *Ibid.*, p. 92.

43   Latimer, *Annals*, p. 116.

44   *Ibid.*, p. 144.

45   Brenner, *Merchants and Revolution*, p. 103.

were still very much in a nascent state, reliant on regular injections of capital and manpower to survive. Therefore, a system of merchant-planter partnerships developed, where the merchant would supply set-up capital and ongoing loans to the planter in return for tobacco.[46] Little tobacco was thus available on the open market, so in order to trade, merchants had to be willing to tie up their capital in long-term investments in colonising ventures. In the case of London's merchants, Brenner has suggested that those who were already successful were unwilling to invest in colonial trade after the initial Company phase. With profitable opportunities available in their existing trades, they were not attracted to colonial investments. Instead, in his view, it was a new group of merchants from less established socio-economic backgrounds who were prepared to take the risks, and ultimately profit from the early American trades.[47] This interpretation has recently been challenged by Edmond Smith through investigation of the investors in the East India Company. Smith's work has shown social networks were key to fostering investment in the big trading companies, with connections to merchants with previous experience in either the Levant Company or even Merchant Adventurers being crucial to drawing in new capital from people previously unconnected to overseas ventures.[48] The attitude of Bristol's merchants seems to reflect a little of both Brenner's and Smith's arguments. As their involvement in the Cupid's colony shows, Bristol merchants could and did have access to the London networks which fostered investment in the big companies. However, hundreds of miles away from the capital, and more often than not, not involved in London schemes, they were also very much on the fringes of such networks. Equally importantly, the early seventeenth century, as Chapters 1 and 2 show, was a profitable time for Bristol's existing trades along Europe's Atlantic coast. While, therefore, they were prepared to speculate on new ventures that either tied in well with existing interests or had potential to yield significant profits, they were not prepared to make long-term investments in American projects that did not guarantee a significant return. There were simply easier ways for them to make money.

There is some evidence that by the 1630s Bristolians were beginning to develop a new interest in the potential of the American colonies. While tobacco imports were still officially restricted to London, significant quantities of leaf were smuggled into Bristol. One case, involving two merchants described as 'patentees of London', occurred on 14 December 1638, little more than a month before the prohibition was lifted. Most unusually for a smuggled consignment, these imports appear in the Port Book. The details are not specific, with no duty paid and two of the three entries recorded as unknown quantities. The

---

46 *Ibid.*, pp. 103–4.
47 *Ibid.*, pp. 111–12.
48 E. Smith, 'The Social Networks of Investment in Early Modern England', *The Historical Journal*, 64(4) (2021), pp. 937–9.

customs officer noted that they were 'resting in ye warehouse' and added that 'these former parcels of Tobacco landed without lawfull order and much more is ommited in thy account; in regard whereof I stand not chargable in thi[s] account'.[49] Further evidence, this time concerning Bristolian merchants, comes from a 1641 court case relating to the allegations of a Bristol Customs Waiter.[50] Depositions were given stating that a licence had been granted to land a cargo of tobacco from St. Kitts in November 1637, and again in January 1638 for 90 cwt from Barbados. The Waiter also suggested that further large quantities of tobacco had been brought into the Avon and landed from there, but that he had been thwarted in his attempts to seize the contraband. This new wave of interest may have been triggered by the increasing financial stability of the Chesapeake colonies. As the planters became more established, they became less reliant on their financiers, and so were able to offer their goods on the open market, and it was thus possible for a casual trader to purchase American tobacco on the spot, rather than having to invest in colonising ventures to secure a pre-arranged deal.[51] With much of the risk, and the need for long-term financial commitment removed, American trade once again appeared profitable to Bristol's merchants.

Overall, then, Bristol's involvement with the American continent remained consistent in character from the time of the Cabot voyages in the late fifteenth century through to the outbreak of the English Civil War almost a hundred and fifty years later. To Bristol merchants, investment in New World schemes was not ideological, as it was for the Raleighs and Hakluyts of the Elizabethan world, but purely commercial. Rather than a noble endeavour to establish England on the world stage, these were experimental ventures, seeking to open up trades that may or may not greatly increase their fortunes. Such experiments were not desperate attempts to find new markets to see the merchants through difficult times, but speculations from a point of strength, funded with capital that they could afford to lose. When these ventures did not pay off, Bristol's merchants simply cut their losses and focused on their profitable existing markets, leaving the risk-taking to others. There can be no doubt that they faced some obstacles to participation in the early American trades, but ultimately these were subsidiary factors. Restrictive legislation may have played a part in preventing the development of a Bristol tobacco trade at this time, although (as was so often the case), once the profits outweighed the risks, the city's merchants were happy to smuggle American goods into England. The nature of the colonies, and the need to invest in colonisation to gain access to tobacco supplies, is more significant. Equally, however, Bristol's merchants could make such investments when they wanted to; they simply did not see

49   TNA PRO E190/1136/10, f. 29v.
50   Latimer, *Annals*, pp. 152–3.
51   R. Davis, *The Rise of the English Shipping Industry in the Seventeenth and Eighteenth Centuries* (London, 1962), p. 270.

this as an opportunity worth pursuing. They did not know how successful transatlantic commerce was to become, so in the early seventeenth century it made more sense to focus on the established European trades. It was only in the second half of the century, once the American colonies had become a significant economic entity, that they began to draw serious attention from the Bristol merchant community.

The Mediterranean

There is a tendency when studying innovation in Bristol's early modern trade to focus on America and the Atlantic (including in the title of this book). Again, however, this focus is principally a result of hindsight, and the knowledge that these later became the most significant markets for Bristol in succeeding centuries. From a sixteenth- or early seventeenth-century perspective, it would have seemed equally likely that breaking into the Mediterranean trades would transform Bristol's commercial fortunes.

Bristol's interest in establishing trade with the Mediterranean dates back as far as the 1440s. The middle decades of the fifteenth century saw leading Bristol merchant Robert Sturmy make two attempts to break into Mediterranean trade, at the time dominated by Italian merchants trading through Southampton.[52] In 1446 Sturmy sent the *Cog Anne*, carrying a cargo of wool and 160 pilgrims, on a voyage in search of Eastern goods. The pilgrims were safely delivered to Jaffa (part of Tel Aviv) in Israel, but the *Cog Anne* was then wrecked off the island of Modon on the Greek coast.[53] In 1457 Sturmy sent three ships to the Levant. This voyage was bound ultimately for Chios off the coast of Turkey, but also stopped in Pisa and Naples.[54] This was clearly a significant undertaking, with Sturmy acquiring a licence to export goods worth £37,000, and compensation of £6,000 being paid after the ill-fated voyage.[55] While there were some outside investors, the bulk of the finance for this voyage came from Bristol's merchant elite, with the twenty-five Bristolian backers representing almost all of the city's leading overseas traders.[56] Again Sturmy's plans ended in failure, with two of his ships falling prey to an attack from pirates backed by the Genoese, who

---

52   A. A. Ruddock, *Italian Merchants and Shipping in Southampton, 1270–1600* (Southampton, 1951).

53   E. M. Carus-Wilson, 'The Overseas Trade of Bristol', in E. Power and M. M. Postan (eds), *Studies in English Trade in the Fifteenth Century* (London, 1933), pp. 224–6.

54   S. Jenks, *Robert Sturmy's Commercial Expedition to the Mediterranean (1457/8)*, Bristol Record Society Vol. 58 (Bristol, 2006), pp. 7–8.

55   *Ibid.*, pp. 3–4.

56   *Ibid.*, pp. 25–8.

were extremely hostile to this intrusion into their commercial territory.[57] Carus-Wilson and Jenks had different interpretations of whether Sturmy's voyages should be viewed as a precursor of the early modern 'discovery voyages'. Carus-Wilson argued that Sturmy's voyage marked the beginning of 'an intrepid spirit of daring' for Bristol's merchants that would culminate in Cabot voyaging off into the unknown, whereas Jenks has highlighted that Mediterranean trade was already well-known, and Bristol's merchants simply wanted a share.[58] Clearly, however, this was a major endeavour, and an attempt by Bristol's merchants to open up a profitable new market. In some respects, this falls within the ongoing tradition of 'experimentation' already discussed with regard to America. With more than forty backers to share the cost, the financial risks taken by all but the leading proponents are unlikely to have been substantial.[59] The rewards, however, had the venture come off, had the potential to be great. At a time when Bristol faced commercial difficulties in its core French trade, this was a speculation from a point of strength by already wealthy merchants.[60]

Recent work shows that Bristol's interest in developing commercial links with the Mediterranean did not die with Sturmy. Thirty years later in 1485/6 the Particular Accounts show £530 worth of goods being imported into Bristol from the 'Leauvant' (eastern Mediterranean). This voyage appears to have been a joint Anglo-Castilian venture, but most of the cargo was owned by Bristol merchants. Accounts from 1486/7 and 1492/3 do not show any similar ventures, suggesting that Mediterranean trade was not a regular feature for Bristol at this stage.[61] Equally, however, the patchy survival of detailed customs records means that there may well be other examples of which we are not aware. Clearly Bristol was still experimenting with new trades in the latter part of the fifteenth century, and new routes to the East (which was after all the main goal of Cabot's voyages) were foremost.

Unfortunately, the data provided by the surviving Particular Accounts and Port Books for much of the sixteenth century is sub-optimal and does not record the last port of call of ships coming into the country from 1516/17 to 1564/5. It is therefore difficult to establish whether Bristol's experiments with Mediterranean trade continued into the reign of Henry VIII and beyond. Legal records do give occasional glimpses of Bristolian merchants continuing to trade to the Mediterranean. In 1546, for example, an Italian merchant, Francis Galiardet, brought a case to the High Court of Admiralty regarding a voyage that imported over 200 tons of wine from Crete to Bristol. The case (regarding non-payment of freight fees and the profits from Galiardet's share of goods)

57   *Ibid.*, p. 7.
58   *Ibid.*, pp. 28–48; Carus-Wilson, 'Overseas Trade of Bristol', pp. 225–30.
59   Jenks, *Robert Sturmy's Commercial Expedition*, pp. 16–28.
60   Stone, 'Bristol's Overseas Trade', pp. 192–7.
61   *Ibid.*, pp. 199–200.

was brought against the late Bristolian merchant Nicholas Thorne. Galiardet claimed that Thorne had formed a company with other Bristolian merchants to trade with Sicilian and Levantine ports, but there is no further evidence of this company, so it seems unlikely that Mediterranean trade ever became a staple of the city's commerce.[62] Trade with France, Ireland and Iberia continued to dominate, but it is certainly possible that there were other odd voyages not recorded in the available sources.

From the 1570s onwards, trading conditions in the Mediterranean became more favourable for English merchants. The diversification of the English cloth industry, greater defensibility of English ships against piracy, and Italian economic decline all combined to allow merchants from England and the Low Countries to seize control of trades previously dominated by the Italian states.[63] For Bristol this could have meant a profitable new opportunity, but other factors combined to prevent the city's merchants from establishing themselves in the Mediterranean trades. As part of its attempts to increase revenues, in the latter part of Elizabeth I's reign the Crown devised a new policy of selling monopolies on trade with particular areas to groups of merchants. The Mediterranean was one such region, with exclusive trading rights granted to the Turkey Company (founded in 1581) and the Venice Company (founded in 1583). In 1592, these two companies were merged to form the Levant Company.[64] In theory, membership of these companies was open to merchants from Bristol and other provincial ports, but in reality high joining fees meant that the monopoly companies were almost exclusively composed of London merchants.[65] In effect, therefore, Bristol merchants were not legally allowed to trade to the Mediterranean.

Despite legal restrictions, from the 1590s Bristol's merchants remained keen to break into the Mediterranean trade. In 1597, the mayor of Bristol and five other senior merchants petitioned Lord Burghley, asking that they 'maie obteyne libertie to traffique and sende their shippes to any place within the Straightes [of Gibraltar]', specifically to 'Venice or to any place within the terretories theirof or to Turkey or Barberye'.[66] The following year a similar petition was sent to Burghley by the then mayor and a different group of Bristol merchants (only the name of Thomas Aldworth is repeated). Rather than unrestricted trade, they asked that Burghley might license 'the citizens of Bristoll to trade yerely to the Seigniories of Venice and Turkie with such shippes or shippe and for such

---

62   J. M. Vanes, *Documents Illustrating the Overseas Trade of Bristol in the Sixteenth Century*, Bristol Record Society Vol. 31 (Bristol, 1979), p. 161.

63   R. Davis, 'England and the Mediterranean, 1570–1670', in F. J. Fisher (ed.), *Essays in the Economic and Social History of Tudor and Stuart England* (Cambridge, 1961), pp. 117–37.

64   P. Croft, 'Fresh Light on Bate's Case', *The Historical Journal*, 30(3) (1987), p. 524.

65   P. V. McGrath, *The Merchant Venturers of Bristol* (Bristol, 1975), p. 52.

66   Vanes, *Documents*, p. 37.

consideration towards the patentees as to your wisdom shalbee thought fytt'.[67] The Port Books show that, even though a favourable answer from the Lord High Treasurer was not forthcoming, Bristol's leading merchants continued with their plans to trade to the Mediterranean. In 1600/1, 23 per cent of Bristol's declared exports were sent to the Mediterranean, although notably the declared destinations (Toulon and Livorno) both lay outside the Levant Company's monopoly-protected area.[68] The following year, five ships came into Bristol from Italy, the *Charles*, *Moyses* and *Hopewell* from Civitavecchia, the *Dolphin* from Livorno, and the *Gabriell* from Venice. Between them they carried cargoes, principally of alum, worth £5,700, 15 per cent of Bristol's total imports in that year.[69] While not necessarily an annual venture as there are no imports from Italy recorded in 1600/1, this trade was clearly both a substantial and a fairly regular part of Bristol's commercial activities in the latter years of the Anglo-Spanish War. April 1599 had also seen ships from Venice, Civitavecchia, and the Greek island of Zante come into Bristol, and in 1601/2 ships bound for Italy once again made up almost a quarter of Bristol's declared exports.[70]

For the first four decades of the seventeenth century, the Port Books provide scant evidence of Bristol's involvement in Mediterranean trade. In 1624/5 a London ship declared 200 butts of muscadell wine from Candia in Crete, and occasionally vessels left Bristol for Livorno.[71] On this evidence, therefore, it seems Bristolian merchants' Mediterranean ambitions had been stilled. However, other sources show that they continued to devote considerable attention to challenging the Levant Company monopoly, and may even have conducted an illicit trade in Levantine currants. As early as January 1601, Bristol's Common Council appointed representatives 'to consider of the objections and demaundes made unto the merchauntes of Bristoll by the Governors of the Turkye Companye touchinge the trade into the Levante Seas'.[72] Four years later this was still an issue, with the Common Council minutes for 1605 stating that 'Master John Aldworthe and John Gwye [Guy], marchauntes shalbe sente to London to aunswere the lettres touchinge the trade into the Levante Sea, viz. to Venice and Turkey'.[73] It is worth noting that those championing Bristol's attempts to break into the Mediterranean trade had also backed the city's American ventures. John Guy, as discussed, was the moving force behind the London-Bristol Newfoundland Company, and the

67   *Ibid.*, p. 38.
68   1600/1 Port Book.
69   1601/2 Port Book.
70   Vanes, *Documents*, pp. 162–3.
71   1624/5 Port Book.
72   Vanes, *Documents*, p. 163.
73   *Ibid.*, p. 163.

signatories of the various surviving letters and petitions concerning the Levant trade contain many of the names of investors in Bristol's American voyages.[74]

The leading members of Bristol's merchant community pursued their Mediterranean project into the 1620s and beyond. In March 1625, for example, according to Adams's Chronicle, the Chief Basha of Constantinople was 'royally entertained' by the mayor and many of Bristol's merchants who would 'not suffer him, or any of his followers to spend one penny' in the city. The Basha was given a gelding by the merchants to carry him on the remainder of his journey to London, 'fitted with rich furniture beseeming his greatnes and theire credit', and he was treated by them to supper at his lodgings 'with admirable cost, & provision uppon so short a warning'.[75] Although the Basha's principal reason for visiting England was to bring gifts to the newly-crowned King, the enthusiasm with which Bristol's merchants entertained him certainly suggests that they were keen to cultivate influential connections in the East. They also continued their legal battles with the Levant Company, now in the guise of the newly re-founded Bristol Society of Merchant Venturers.[76] The Society continued to petition the Privy Council, and in 1618 Bristol's merchants were granted the right to import 200 tons of currants a year (one of the most sought-after commodities of the Levantine trade) in return for the payment of an imposition of 4d. per cwt to the Levant Company.[77] According to the Book of Rates valuations, 200 tons of currants would have been worth £6,000, so this would have constituted about 12 per cent of Bristol's total imports in 1624/5.[78] Two ships were sent to the Levant in 1618 and 1619 to exercise this right, in the later year carrying goods worth £5,406.[79] Although frustratingly the Port Books provide no record, it appears that Bristol maintained this trade for at least the next sixteen years. In 1632, the Levant Company wrote to the aldermen of Bristol complaining that the 4d. per cwt duty due on imported currants had not been paid.[80] The Society's response that, while paying arrears would sadly be impossible, they would ensure that the duty was paid in future, seems to tacitly acknowledge that they had been carrying out an illicit trade.[81]

In 1643 Charles I granted a new charter to Bristol's Society of Merchant Venturers, in part as a reward for the city's loyalty to the Royalist cause.

---

74 McGrath, *Records*, pp. 213–17.
75 BRO 13748/4.
76 The ongoing battle between the Society of Merchant Venturers and the Levant Company is discussed in greater depth by McGrath, *Merchant Venturers*, pp. 55–7.
77 See BRO SMV/2/1/1/34, pp. 51–4.
78 1604 Book of Rates
79 M. Epstein, *The English Levant Company: Its Foundation and Its History to 1640* (London, 1908), p. 113.
80 BRO SMV/2/1/1/34, pp. 205–6.
81 McGrath, *Merchant Venturers*, pp. 55–6.

This charter permitted members of the Bristol Society to trade without restriction with several previously monopoly-protected areas, including the Mediterranean.[82] In the years after the Restoration, the Society fought hard to confirm the terms of the 1643 charter, eventually succeeding in 1665.[83] While far from being as spectacular as the growth of the city's American trades, some of Bristol's leading merchants developed significant trade with the Greek islands in the years after the Civil War. There was no sign of this trade in 1654/5, but in 1659/60 imports from Zante amounted to £19,000. This was 8 per cent of total imports in that year and even surpassed recorded imports from France, the historic bastion of Bristol's commercial world. Thereafter, this trade became a regular feature for Bristol, with imports of between £18,500 and £20,200 worth of olive oil and currants from Zante and Cephalonia recorded in each of the post-Restoration accounts. This was certainly significant, and if it were not for the more spectacular growth of the American trades it would have received far more attention. Even accounting for the adjustment of the Book of Rates, the value of this Greek trade is greater than Bristol's total imports in 1594/5. By the 1670s, however, it accounted for less than 5 per cent of Bristol's total imports. It also appears to have been restricted to a relatively small group of merchants, with just thirteen individuals importing goods from Greece in 1671/2, three of whom controlled 66 per cent of the trade. The growth of Bristol's Greek interest, therefore, while certainly still significant, only represents a sideline to its main commercial interests in the latter seventeenth century. The merchants' hopes of a profitable Mediterranean trade had finally been fulfilled, but, in the meantime, they had become overshadowed by developments elsewhere.

If, then, there is a long-term narrative running from Bristol's fifteenth-century pioneers to the eventual establishment of a regular trade in the latter seventeenth century, it begins with Sturmy and the Mediterranean. Unlike the more speculative and uncertain early American ventures, trade with the Mediterranean was a known entity. There were well-established commodities with a ready market in Britain, and the obstacles to participation were not uncertainties about the viability and profitability of this trade but the jealous guarding of a monopoly by whichever group of merchants controlled the trade at that time. It is therefore completely logical that, when seeking potential new trade opportunities, the Mediterranean was high on the priority list of Bristolian merchants, even when participation carried the risks associated with illegal ventures. It is thus unsurprising that those same Bristol merchants who ventured small amounts of capital on various American projects were even more keen to break into this new branch of trade much nearer to home. Ultimately activity in the Mediterranean was overshadowed by the dramatic and unanticipated growth

82   J. Latimer, *The History of the Society of Merchant Venturers of the City of Bristol, with Some Account of the Anterior Merchants' Guilds* (New York, 1970), pp. 106–7.
83   McGrath, *Records*, p. xx.

of trade with the New World colonies, but until the mid-seventeenth century, the Mediterranean simply looked a better horse to back.

Africa

Bristol is infamous for its trade with Africa, as Britain's leading slave-trading port in the 1730s and 1740s.[84] Bristol's first commercial connections with Africa, however, were more than a century and a half earlier. Arguments that Bristol was illegally interloping into the slave trade in the post-Restoration years are examined in Chapter 6. The city's earliest contacts with Africa were very different in character from the traffic in enslaved people that later dominated. These either focused on the north of the continent, extending Bristol's Iberian trade, or focused on goods such as ivory and hides rather than human beings.

Trade with Africa does not appear in the surviving Bristol customs records before the early seventeenth century. The first African entry was for £213 worth of goods brought in from Guinea in West Africa on the 70-ton *Gabriel* in April 1601. This included large quantities of hides and salt, as well as 170 elephant's tusks.[85] Given the patchy survival of Port Books from this period, it is certainly possible that there were earlier Bristolian voyages to Africa. Indeed, evidence from other sources suggests that Bristol may have had trading contacts with Africa as much as half a century before this. In 1552, for example, two vessels (including one appropriately named the *Lyon*) left Bristol for Barbary on the North African coast. While this was principally a London venture, several Bristolian merchants were amongst those who loaded goods on the *Lyon*.[86] By 1576, prominent Bristol merchants Dominic Chester and Thomas Aldworth claimed to have a regular trade with Barbary, although no ships either to or from Africa are recorded in the Bristol Port Books of that year.[87] Voyages to Africa were clearly already part of the commercial repertoire of Bristol's merchants by the end of the sixteenth century. They were not, however, as Jean Vanes also concluded, a regular or significant feature of the city's commerce.[88] Across all the four Port Books examined for the period 1575/6–1601/2, just one African voyage is recorded, which represented less than 1 per cent of Bristol's trade that year.

After the 1601 voyage from Guinea, West African trade does not feature again in the Bristol customs records until after the Restoration. Such voyages as

---

84   K. Morgan, *Bristol and the Atlantic Trade in the Eighteenth Century* (Cambridge, 1993), p. 132.
85   TNA PRO E190/1132/11, f. 7r.
86   Vanes, *Documents*, p. 158.
87   *Ibid.*, p. 24; 1575/6 Port Book.
88   Vanes, *Documents*, p. 24.

do appear in the second half of the century also seem to have been tied up with Bristol's illegal involvement in the early slave trade (see Chapter 6). There are several potential explanations for Bristol's apparent lack of interest in pursuing trade with sub-Saharan Africa beyond this single exploratory voyage. It must, of course, also be added that the patchy survival of the Port Books may mean that there were other attempts of which no record survives. The most obvious explanation is the existence of monopoly companies granted exclusive legal rights to African trade. Initially this came in the form of the Guinea Company, founded in 1618 and which survived until the Restoration. It was succeeded by the Company of Royal Adventurers into Africa in 1660, and eventually the Royal African Company in 1672.[89] Unlike the Mediterranean trade, however, there is little evidence that Bristolian merchants challenged the monopoly of the various African companies until 1690 when the Society of Merchant Venturers mounted a sustained attack on the Royal African Company's exclusive right to African trade.[90] It should be noted here that Edward Colston, who became Deputy Governor of the Royal African Company, was only Bristolian by birth. He was apprenticed in London, and spent the majority of his career operating from there, and thus should be thought of primarily as a London merchant.[91] Colston's Bristol-based father William and brother Thomas both supplied goods such as cloth and beads to the Company, and the elderly William did purchase £400 worth of shares in 1674, but this was atypical of Bristol merchants and probably owes more to the connections of his son.[92]

It seems, therefore, that Bristol's merchants were genuinely uninterested in exploring African trade, rather than prevented by legal barriers. The reasons for this were very similar to those that prevented sustained interest in the early American trades: the need for long-term investment of capital to be able to trade, and the fact that the trade had not been shown to be profitable. In the seventeenth century (unlike in the eighteenth, when African traders tended to remain offshore and rely on local contacts to bring enslaved people to them), trade with West Africa was conducted by establishing coastal forts. These were hugely expensive to build, staff and maintain, with the Royal African Company paying around £20,000 per annum in salaries and upkeep.[93] This model was adopted from the early days of English trade in Africa, with the Guinea Company establishing six factories along the coast between 1632 and 1650.[94] Added to

---

89   K. G. Davies, *The Royal African Company* (London, 1957), pp. 39–44.

90   McGrath, *Merchant Venturers*, p. 59.

91   K. Morgan, *Edward Colston and Bristol* (Bristol, 1999), pp. 1–3.

92   M. Steeds and R. Ball, *From Wulfstan to Colston: Severing the Sinews of Slavery in Bristol* (Bristol, 2020), pp. 50–1.

93   Davies, *Royal African Company*, p. 259.

94   P. E. Hair and R. Law, 'The English in Western Africa to 1700', in Canny (ed.), *The Oxford History*, p. 253.

the expense of a permanent presence was the relatively uncertain nature of African trade, which did not firmly settle down into focusing on trading in enslaved people until the last third of the seventeenth century. In the sixteenth and early seventeenth centuries, English trade with Africa lacked a clear staple commodity. Other than the three Hawkins voyages of the Elizabethan era, there is little evidence of English merchants trading in enslaved people prior to the 1640s (it is certainly not mentioned in the charter of the Guinea Company in 1618). Instead, the African voyages experimented with a variety of commodities such as wax, hides, pepper and redwood, alongside financially disastrous attempts to break into the gold trade.[95] As with the Americas, it was not until a staple was established (in the New World, tobacco and sugar; in Africa, enslaved people) that trade became predictable and profitable. Ultimately, as K. G. Davies noted, such were the uncertainties and costs of nascent African trade that all the companies established to conduct it ended in financial failure.[96] Those who invested in the Royal African Company did so cautiously, with no individuals holding a particularly large stock.[97] It is thus unsurprising that the relatively risk-averse Bristol merchants did not see African trade as worth pursuing.

More common than West Africa ventures (although still irregular) were voyages to the north coast of Africa, which in the seventeenth century was dominated by the four 'Barbary States': Morocco, Algiers, Tunis, and Tripoli. As in the latter sixteenth century, African trade does not feature in every Port Book examined from the sixteenth century. Exports worth £1,400 were, however, sent to Barbary in 1620/1, and £2,500 worth of goods bound for Barbary in 1637 made up 5 per cent of Bristol's export trade.[98] Clearly this represents an expansion in the range of ports Bristol's merchants visited. However, it is questionable whether this truly represents a 'new' branch of trade. Instead, these Barbary voyages should be viewed as an additional part of Bristol's existing Iberian commerce. The Barbary coast was, after all, virtually adjacent to the southern Iberian ports that formed the mainstay of Bristol's continental trade.

Following the Restoration, England acquired its own port on the Barbary coast, with Tangier being granted as part of the deal for Charles II's marriage to the Portuguese Catherine of Braganza in 1661. The English had high hopes for Tangier, spending £340,000 constructing a new harbour, and declaring it a free port to attract merchants from all around the Mediterranean.[99] However, facing ongoing pressure of a Moorish invasion, in 1683 the port was abandoned

95 Ibid., pp. 246–55.
96 Davies, Royal African Company, p. 17.
97 Ibid., pp. 68–9.
98 1620/21 Port Book and 1636/7 Port Book.
99 A. Tinniswood, Pirates of Barbary (London, 2011), pp. 204–8.

and the harbour demolished.[100] Bristol merchants were quick to trade with Tangier. As early as 1662, four Bristol ships (the *Angel Gabriel, Dolphin, Dove* and *William & James*) declared cargoes for Tangier. The goods (worth almost £600, and almost 1 per cent of total exports that year) were fairly typical of Iberian trade, consisting of an assortment of cloth, small manufactured goods, provisions, and a large quantity of 'decayed tobacco'.[101] The next surviving export Port Book from 1672 shows an even more substantial trade, with £2,600 worth of goods declared as destined for Tangier.[102] Closer examination of the four ships involved (the *Bristol Armes, Dolphin, Zant Friggott* and *Nevis Adventure*), however, shows the complex nature of this trade. Other consignments on the same vessels list different destinations, predominantly Cadiz and Malaga in the south of Spain, and Lisbon in Portugal. One set of consignments on the *Nevis Adventure* lists its destination as both 'Tangeer and Mallaga'. Rather than a 'new' trade, therefore, these links with the Barbary coast should be seen more as an extension of Bristol's existing Iberian commerce. Since the sixteenth century, it had been common for vessels sailing to southern markets to stop at multiple ports (including on the Barbary coast).[103] When these vessels returned to Bristol the following year, the cargoes they carried were of typically Iberian goods such as dried fruits and olive oil.[104]

In many respects, then, the attitude of Bristol's merchants to African trade in the pre-slave trade era was very much like their approach to early American ventures. While they did send at least one experimental voyage to the Guinea coast, on the whole the risks, expense and long-term commitment needed meant that this was simply not an attractive enough proposition. The exception was trade with the ports on the Barbary coast, but with their position in North Africa and integration into the European economy this should be seen much more as an extension of Bristol's existing Iberian trades. It is certainly true that monopolies held by chartered companies made it illegal for Bristol to trade to West Africa for most of the seventeenth century. However, as the example of the Mediterranean trades has shown, illegality did not deter Bristolian merchants if they thought it was profitable. Bristol had sources of the key African goods such as hides and wax available closer to home in Ireland, and the quest for gold was risky. It was not, therefore, until enslaved labour began to be used on a large scale on the English New World plantations, integrating Africa firmly into the Atlantic economy, that Bristol merchants saw the continent as a source of a 'commodity' that they both needed and could make a profit from.

100   *Ibid.*, pp. 245–53.
101   TNA PRO E190/1240/6, ff. 85r–92r.
102   1671/2 Port Book.
103   Vanes, *Documents*, p. 21.
104   BRO SMV/7/1/1/5.

Other Markets

While, as discussed, the battle to trade with the Levant Company's Mediterranean markets was important to Bristol's merchants, they showed little interest in other opportunities afforded by the new charter Charles I awarded to the Society of Merchant Venturers in 1643. This included the right to trade with previously monopoly-protected areas in Scandinavia and the Baltic, Russia and the Netherlands.[105] Bristol's merchants did not seek to expand into new markets simply because the opportunity was there, or out of desperation, but rather made a carefully calculated decision based both on the economic potential and perceived risk.

Almost every year, the Port Books show a smattering of ships coming into Bristol from outside its core markets. They were, however, rarely of any great economic significance, and even combined never make up more than 3 per cent of the value of Bristol's trade in any given year. The only noteworthy interest in markets in northern Europe was a small upsurge in trade with the Netherlands. From the 1620s, Bristol received a few ships from the Netherlands, with as much as £1,100 worth of imports recorded in 1637/8. In the years after the Civil War this grew considerably, with Dutch imports as high as £7,800 in 1654/5 and £6,000 in 1670/1.[106] This trade, however, still never accounted for more than 2.5 per cent of Bristol's imports, and was also highly vulnerable to disruption from the recurrent Anglo-Dutch Wars. Imports from the Netherlands were down to £900 in 1664/5, and also dropped significantly in 1671/2. This relative lack of interest in the Low Countries after the Civil War shows a marked contrast to Bristol's near neighbour Exeter. As Stephens showed, Exeter took advantage of the collapse of the Company of Merchant Adventurers monopoly to develop a significant trade with the Netherlands in the second half of the seventeenth century.[107] The principal reason for Bristol's lack of enthusiasm for these markets was a simple matter of geography. The close proximity of London and Exeter to the Netherlands meant that they had a natural advantage over Bristol, which historically had not been involved in these trades even before the advent of legal monopolies. With increased shipping costs from the longer voyage times, Bristol simply could not compete.

As with the Netherlands, Bristol occasionally traded with Baltic ports, but this never became either a regular or a significant feature of the city's commerce.

---

105   McGrath, *Records*, p. xx.

106   As many of the goods imported from the Netherlands were manufactured, the actual increase in value of this trade is less than the figures suggest. Hoping to protect home industries, the customs rates on imported manufactures increased considerably in the 1640s and 1650s (see Technical Appendix).

107   W. B. Stephens, *Seventeenth-Century Exeter: A Study of Industrial and Commercial Development, 1625–1688* (Exeter, 1958), pp. 85–95.

Whilst not present in every year (although perhaps becoming more consistent after the Civil War), Bristol received occasional ships from the Baltic throughout the seventeenth century, with £193 worth of goods coming in from Poland and Norway as early as 1600/1.[108] This never, however, accounted for more than 0.6 per cent of the value of Bristol's trade, with the highest recorded figure being £1,072 in 1670/1.[109] As with the Low Countries, Bristol's geographical position meant that it simply could not compete with the east coast ports in developing a Baltic trade. However, while it was not economically viable to trade with the Baltic on a large scale, the nature of the goods involved meant that there was still a market for occasional voyages direct to Bristol. Imports from the Baltic consisted predominantly of bulky timber goods, such as deal boards and masts. Clearly, with a significant shipping industry, such goods would have been in demand in Bristol, but their size and weight made them difficult and expensive to carry by land. Although not ideally placed for Baltic trade, sending the odd ship direct to Bristol to meet local needs was thus still viable.

One opportunity that Bristol's merchants may have come to rue not taking was investment in the East India Company. After its foundation in 1600, the East India Company underwent some difficult times in its first century. It operated on a joint stock basis, whereby rather than individual members carrying out private trade with the monopoly-protected regions, all capital was pooled, and trade carried out by the Company itself. In 1650, Bristol, along with thirteen other provincial ports, was invited to invest in an East India Company venture. Bristol's merchants, however, showed no interest, stating that 'the said proffer may prove noe way beneficiall'.[110] Again, this reminds us of the benefits of hindsight: we know that the East India Company was to become a global power and generate huge amounts of wealth. At the time, however, Bristol's merchants simply saw this as a risk not worth taking. After all, that the Company had solicited investment from the outports suggested that it was not in rude financial health. In addition, the nature of trade with Asia may have deterred Bristolian investment. The great distances involved meant that voyages could take several years, requiring both significant capital investment, and a potentially long wait before profits were realised. At a time when significant new commercial opportunities were emerging in the Americas (see Chapter 4), it must have seemed to those in Bristol that there were faster and easier ways to increase their fortunes.

By the end of the seventeenth century Bristol's merchants had completely reversed their attitude to the East India trade. In 1681 the Society of Merchant Venturers voted in favour of joining forces with the Levant Company and others, hoping to extract a share of the monopoly from the East India Company.[111] In

108   1600/1 Port Book.
109   1671/2 Port Book.
110   McGrath, *Records*, p. 228.
111   McGrath, *Merchant Venturers*, p. 58.

1691, Bristol's merchants again put together a petition for 'gaining a part of the East India trade to this Citty'. This was clearly quite a serious undertaking, with a committee of seventeen, including some of the city's most senior and successful merchants, meeting twice a week to discuss the proposals. They also offered to send two representatives to London to explain their reasons for having the petition granted to Parliament.[112] By the 1690s, Bristol merchants were clearly seeking new opportunities, with a similar campaign of petitions also prepared to break into the monopoly of the ailing Royal African Company.[113] By this time, the city was experiencing new levels of prosperity created by the rapid growth of new trades with the American colonies. In part, this was expressed in building grandiose new houses, such as those on Queen Square (built between 1699 and 1729).[114] It also meant, however, that the city's merchants had both the confidence and the capital to seek out new commercial opportunities.

Conclusions

Studying the attempts of Bristol's merchants to break into new trades is a valuable counterpoint to one of the core arguments of this book. While the significant influence of the Atlantic economy on the city and its overseas trade is clear throughout the sixteenth and seventeenth centuries, this was not apparent to people at the time. Indeed, for much of the reign of Elizabeth and throughout the early Stuart years, the principal expansionary goal of Bristol's merchants was not to establish a trade with America, but to break into the Mediterranean monopoly of the London-based Levant Company. This was a well-known trade, with established commodities and clear potential profits. The Port Books and other records show a regular smattering of experimental voyages to the Americas, Africa, and elsewhere, but these were sporadic and rarely continued for long. This was certainly not an inevitable progress from Cabot to colonisation. Why Bristol's merchants did not show more interest in the potential of new trades is also frequently misunderstood. As shown, this was clearly not a desperate search for new markets, as Bristol's established trades flourished in the late sixteenth and early seventeenth centuries. Neither was it due to legal obstacles. While Bristol was, for much of this period, excluded from the African trade and parts of the American trade by the monopoly rights of London companies, Levant trade clearly shows that the city's merchants were willing to challenge and even ignore such rules if it suited them. We must, then,

---

112 McGrath, *Records*, pp. 228–30.
113 McGrath, *Merchant Venturers*, p. 59.
114 M. Dresser, *Slavery Obscured: The Social History of the Slave Trade in Bristol* (Bristol, 2007), p. 105.

conclude that their lack of involvement in these new markets was due to either lack of interest; other, more accessible sources of the goods to be acquired in America or Africa (usually in Ireland); or an unwillingness to invest in ventures that were either risky or involved tying up their capital for long periods. This essential conservatism is consistent, and Bristol's merchants were reluctant to invest in new ventures even when the pressure came from the King himself. When Bristol's merchants did experiment with new trades, it tended to be from a point of strength, in the safest way possible, and as a group to spread the risk. Consistently these ventures involved a group of Bristol's leading merchants, sometimes in conjunction with London counterparts. They did not take opportunities simply because they were there. The potential rewards if ventures paid off could be huge, with the scope to change the nature of overseas trade (as indeed did happen with the rise of American trade in the latter seventeenth century). There may also have been an element of fear of missing out, with Bristol merchants putting in a small stake to have a foot in the door if a project did prove to be the next big thing. Finally, there may also have been an element of seeking prestige and recognition, not unlike the involvement of wealthy businessmen such as Richard Branson and Elon Musk in the space race today. These were wealthy businessmen, perhaps feeding their egos and looking for excitement, but without risking their fortunes. Overall, even combined, all these experimental trades were not of particularly great economic significance, rarely amounting to more than 5–10 per cent of Bristol's total trade. Nonetheless, as a mirror of both the ambitions of the merchants, and their own reading of where potential future profits lay, they are certainly worthy of study.

4

Bristol's 'American Revolution': Tobacco and Sugar

There is perhaps no ship that captures the changes to Bristol's commercial world in the middle decades of the seventeenth century better than the *Lisbon Merchant*. She was an English-built and -owned vessel of 80 tons burthen, operated by master John Smith and his English crew. Despite her name, however, when she arrived in Bristol in late February 1672 she had not in fact come from Portugal, but from Virginia. The assortment of bags and hogsheads in her hold contained over £8,000 worth of tobacco grown in the plantations of Chesapeake Bay.[1] That a ship named after one of Bristol's European trades was being used to carry goods from the Americas captures the speed and unprecedented nature of change. As discussed in the opening chapters of this book, as late as the 1630s a voyage to Virginia such as that conducted by the *Lisbon Merchant* in 1671/2 would have been highly exceptional. By the 1670s, the American tobacco trade was a core pillar of Bristol's commercial world. The city's merchants, and its ships, rapidly realigned themselves from the trading patterns they had adopted for centuries in order to take advantage of the significant opportunities that the new colonies presented.

This chapter explores how and why the Atlantic economy developed in the second half of the seventeenth century, as well as examining the impact this had on both the city of Bristol and England more broadly. The middle decades of the seventeenth century are widely recognised as the beginning of a significant transformation of English overseas trade. In particular, the period after the Restoration of the monarchy in 1660 began what is now thought of as a 'Commercial Revolution'.[2] For the first time, England's trade was becoming truly global, with markets in North America and Asia as important as the old European heartlands. This redirection of trade also had significant impacts on the types of commodities involved, with England beginning to import a

---

1   1671/2 Port Book, ff. 10r–16v. The *Lisbon Merchant* was still being used for the purpose that her name suggests at other times, having returned to Bristol the previous year with a cargo of white sugar from Lisbon in Portugal (1670/1 Port Book, ff. 34r–41r).

2   R. Davis, *A Commercial Revolution: English Overseas Trade in the Seventeenth and Eighteenth Centuries* (London, 1967); N. Zahedieh, *The Capital and the Colonies: London and the Atlantic Economy, 1660–1700* (Cambridge, 2010), pp. 3–5.

range of new exotic goods, and exports diversifying away from cloth, which had been the defining feature of medieval and Tudor trade. In its place, ships leaving England now carried a broad range of manufactured goods, as well as re-exporting colonial crops and Asian wares. These were crucial developments, laying the foundations of Britain's economic success as it became one of the wealthiest and most advanced nations in the world in the eighteenth and nineteenth centuries. To understand significant historical events such as the globalisation of English trade, the rise of the British Empire, and the Industrial Revolution, it is thus essential to look in depth at the commercial changes of the latter seventeenth century that set them in motion.

While the development of the Atlantic economy was crucial to England's early modern economic growth, its analysis, in the words of Nuala Zahedieh, has relied 'on scrappy information'.[3] In his canonical study, Ralph Davis used just two sets of data, from 1663 and 1669 and 1699–1701, to trace developments in the post-Restoration years.[4] These have recently been supplemented by Zahedieh's detailed study of London's colonial trade between 1660 and 1700, but even this is based principally around the London Port Books from a single year (1686).[5] Existing datasets are also problematic as they focus almost exclusively on London. This period saw the first signs of a loosening in London's stranglehold on English overseas trade. While the capital continued to be by far the most important player, the shift of the focus of commerce from mainland Europe to the Atlantic led to the beginnings of what G. D. Ramsay described as 'The Rise of the Western Ports'.[6] Bristol pioneered this development. Customs accounts from the capital, therefore, cannot stand as proxy for the development of English overseas trade as a whole in this period.

This chapter uncovers the remarkable growth of Bristol's trades with North America and the Caribbean after the English Civil War (1642–49). Previous estimates by Patrick McGrath, based on the number of ships entering and leaving the port, suggested that New World trade accounted for less than a sixth of Bristol's trade in the 1650s and 1660s, rising to between a quarter and a third in the 1680s.[7] New evidence from the customs records shows that the expansion of the American trade was much faster; the American colonies accounted for around 70 per cent of Bristol's imports by 1654.

3   Zahedieh, *Capital and the Colonies*, p. 9.
4   R. Davis, 'English Foreign Trade, 1660–1700', in W. E. Minchinton (ed.), *The Growth of English Overseas Trade in the 17th and 18th Centuries* (London, 1969), pp. 84–5.
5   Zahedieh, *Capital and the Colonies*, p. 11.
6   G. D. Ramsay, *English Overseas Trade during the Centuries of Emergence* (London, 1957), pp. 132–65; W. E. Minchinton, 'Introduction', in Minchinton (ed.), *Growth of English Overseas Trade*, pp. 32–4.
7   P. V. McGrath, *Merchants and Merchandise in Seventeenth-Century Bristol*, Bristol Record Society Vol. 19 (Bristol, 1968), p. xxi.

This is astonishing, given that Bristol had barely engaged in any trade with the Americas before the Civil War, as the earlier discussion of the Bristol customs accounts made clear (see Chapter 1). At some point between 1638 and 1654, a commercial pattern that had remained essentially unaltered since the Middle Ages changed radically. Bristol's American and Caribbean trades continued to grow: the value of these routes doubled by the 1670s and peaked in the 1680s.

After discussing the new evidence for the remarkable growth of Bristol's American trades in the decades after the Civil War, the chapter examines the prosperity in the city which accompanied it. Rather than replacing Bristol's existing trades, the dawn of New World commerce saw the continuing expansion of Bristol's imports that had characterised the decades before the Civil War. The next section delves deeper into the customs data, revealing the types of commodities involved in the American trades, and the regions with which Bristol was (and was not) trading. The impact of this revolution in trade is then considered in greater depth, including the development of significant tobacco- and sugar-processing industries, and the growth of a sizeable new re-export trade with Ireland and the continent. The causes of these dramatic changes are then considered. The role of both legislative and market-driven factors is assessed. This includes the role of the Navigation and Staple Acts that protected English involvement in colonial trade, and the move away from restrictive legislation and monopoly companies that opened the door for new players with lesser capital reserves than the London oligarchs. Some consideration is given to the role of the Anglo-Dutch Wars in diverting shipping to Bristol, before turning to the growth in the market for tobacco and sugar occasioned by the crash in prices as colonial production escalated. Finally, existing figures for the trade of England as a whole with the Americas are reconsidered. It is suggested that the valuations for key commodities adopted by previous studies are too low, and thus, as has been shown to be the case with Bristol, English New World trade may have developed significantly faster and earlier than previously supposed.

Americanisation of Trade

The political turmoil and administrative breakdown of the middle years of the seventeenth century seem to have been mirrored in the customs house. The survival of Port Books from Bristol is patchy at best, and for the years of the Civil War and Interregnum (1642–60) they are virtually non-existent. Indeed, apart from one coastal book from 1649, and a couple of fragmentary wine accounts from the same year, no usable Bristol customs records survive from

1638 until after the Restoration in 1660.[8] Fortunately this gap in the Exchequer sources can be filled by another type of record: the Wharfage Books of the Bristol Society of Merchant Venturers, which in many respects replicate the Port Books.[9] These have been sampled at five-year intervals for the Interregnum and immediate post-Restoration period, giving accounts for the years 1654/5, 1659/60, and 1664/5.[10]

It is unclear exactly when Bristol first became involved in trade with the American colonies on a significant scale. It seems likely, however, that it emerged over the course of the 1640s and early 1650s. As shown in the last chapter, in the years before the Civil War Bristol's involvement in New World commerce was minimal, with just a few fishing voyages to Newfoundland, and small, irregular shipments of tobacco. American trade had never amounted to much more than 3 per cent of Bristol's total trade. Statistical records for the 1640s and early 1650s are lacking, but qualitative sources permit us to glimpse the emergence of Bristol's American trades through the fog of Civil War. One particularly valuable source in this regard is the first volume of the Bristol Deposition Books, covering the period 1643–47.[11] These contain several snippets of information on Bristol's American trade during the war. The earliest refers to a voyage in 1638, initially heading to Newfoundland and then on to Virginia.[12] Another example, this time from 1645, refers to a ship that came into Chepstow from Barbados, where the governor took four rolls of tobacco from the ship.[13] The 1646 depositions yield two further cases. One refers to various hogsheads of tobacco brought home by the merchant Thomas Weston, on which £60 of customs were due.[14] The other refers to rows between the master and crew on a Dutch ship, the *Bordeaux* of Flushing, which sailed from the West Indies to Ireland.[15] A final example comes from 1649, where a widow refers to her husband's share in an 80-ton ship, the *Richard and Francis*, which had sailed

---

8   TNA PRO E190/1136/11 is an outwards coastal book from Lady Day until Christmas 1649. Interestingly, it is on paper (rather than the usual parchment), perhaps representative of the disruption of these years. E122/221/75 is a Quarter Book for wine, with accounts covering December 1648 to March 1649, and June–July 1649. The Quarter Books were the original records, later used by the customs officers to write up the fair copy Port Books. This is the only surviving example from Bristol in this period.
9   For a full discussion of the Wharfage Books and how they have been processed, see the Technical Appendix.
10   BRO SMV/7/1/1/1; SMV/7/1/1/2.
11   H. E. Nott (ed.), *The Deposition Books of Bristol, Volume I: 1643–1647*, Bristol Record Society Vol. 6 (Bristol, 1935). Depositions were sworn statements of events made by individuals in front of a magistrate in case they were later needed in legal proceedings.
12   P. V. McGrath, 'Merchant Shipping Part II', *Mariner's Mirror*, XL (1954), p. 28.
13   *Ibid.*, p. 292.
14   *Ibid.*
15   *Ibid.*, p. 23.

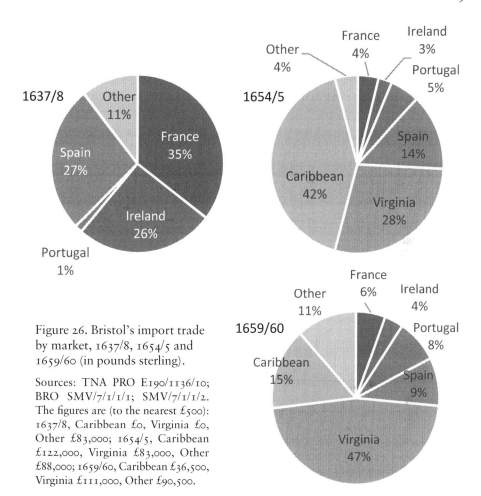

Figure 26. Bristol's import trade by market, 1637/8, 1654/5 and 1659/60 (in pounds sterling).

Sources: TNA PRO E190/1136/10; BRO SMV/7/1/1/1; SMV/7/1/1/2. The figures are (to the nearest £500): 1637/8, Caribbean £0, Virginia £0, Other £83,000; 1654/5, Caribbean £122,000, Virginia £83,000, Other £88,000; 1659/60, Caribbean £36,500, Virginia £111,000, Other £90,500.

to Barbados.[16] Unfortunately these depositions can never be more than a fragmentary record, and we can glean little from them about the extent to which Bristol's involvement with the Americas had grown. They do, however, suggest that, despite the difficulties of the Civil War, transatlantic voyages from Bristol were becoming common in the late 1640s.

Although the exact origins of Bristol's American trades remain shrouded in mystery, by the time records are once more available in 1654/5 these trades had become extremely significant. In 1654/5 trade with North America and the Caribbean accounted for about 70 per cent of Bristol's import trade (see Figure 26). More than £83,000 worth of goods from Virginia made up 28 per

16 *Ibid.*, p. 286.

cent of Bristol's imports, and almost £122,000 worth from the Caribbean 42 per cent. The next sampled set of Wharfage accounts confirms that this was not an exceptional year. In 1659/60, American imports made up almost two-thirds of Bristol's total. Over the course of little more than a decade, New World trade had become firmly established at Bristol.

The declining amount of detail recorded in the Wharfage Books means that data from the third year sampled, 1664/5, is slightly less reliable than that of earlier accounts. Nonetheless, it shows clearly that the dramatic growth of Bristol's New World trades seen in the 1650s was far from the end of the city's 'American Revolution'. As much as £335,000 worth of goods was imported on ships likely to have come from the Chesapeake in 1664/5 (almost 68 per cent of total imports). A further £55,000 worth of goods, the makeup of which suggests they came from the Caribbean, brings the colonial share of Bristol's import trade to almost 80 per cent. From the 1670s, Port Book records are once more available in decent quantities, with a reasonably good sample surviving for the remainder of the century. Two Port Books from the early 1670s have been fully transcribed, and confirm ongoing growth (see Figure 27 and Table 1). In 1670/1 American trade made up 60 per cent of Bristol's total trade. This comprised £205,000 worth of imports from the mainland colonies, and £47,000 from the Caribbean (49 per cent and 11 per cent of Bristol's imports respectively). Recorded trade the following year was considerably higher, showing the potential extent of annual fluctuation. A staggering £461,000 worth of goods from the colonies made up 81 per cent of Bristol's import trade in 1671/2. The vast majority of this came in the form of tobacco from the Chesapeake, worth £394,000.

Table 1. Regional distribution of Bristol's imports, 1637/8, 1654/5, 1659/60, 1670/1 and 1671/2 (to the nearest £500).

Country	1637/8	1654/5	1659/60	1670/1	1671/2
Caribbean	£0	£122,000	£36,500	£47,500	£66,500
France	£29,000	£11,500	£13,500	£41,000	£23,000
Ireland	£21,500	£7,500	£8,500	£11,000	£15,000
Mediterranean	£0	£0	£19,000	£20,000	£18,500
Portugal	£1,000	£16,000	£19,000	£47,000	£15,500
Spain	£22,000	£40,500	£21,500	£39,500	£36,500
Virginia	£0	£83,400	£111,000	£203,000	£394,500

Sources: TNA PRO E190/1136/10, 1137/3, 1138/1; BRO SMV/7/1/1/1; SMV/7/1/1/2.

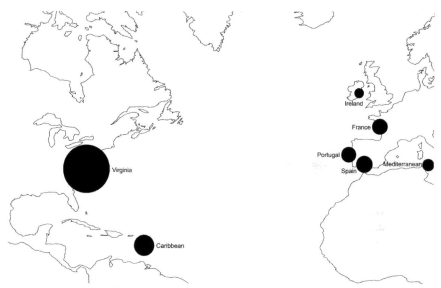

Figure 27. Regional distribution of Bristol's import trade, 1670/1 and 1671/2 (in pounds sterling).

Sources: TNA PRO E190/1137/3, 1138/1.

In all five years of accounts examined here, American trade consistently accounted for more than 60 per cent of Bristol's imports, and at times as much as 80 per cent. This reveals a significantly faster 'Americanisation' of Bristol's trade than has been assumed, with the prevailing tendency being to see Bristol's 'Golden Age' as ushered in by the city's entry into the slave trade in the early eighteenth century.[17] The only previous attempt to chart the rise of Bristol's American and West Indian trades in the second half of the seventeenth century was made by Patrick McGrath, who estimated the importance of these trades to Bristol through a simple count of the number of ships entering and leaving the port.[18] This survey suggested that colonial commerce grew steadily over the second half of the century. McGrath's figures show that shipping bound either to or from the Caribbean and the mainland colonies made up around a seventh of all Bristol's traffic over the period 1658 to 1660, rising to a sixth in 1667–68, and between a quarter and a third in the years 1685–87. These figures greatly underestimate the significance of Bristol's New World commerce. With

17   See, for example: K. Morgan, *Bristol and the Atlantic Trade in the Eighteenth Century* (Cambridge, 1993), p. 1; McGrath, *Merchants and Merchandise*; Ramsay, *English Overseas Trade*, pp. 144–6; D. H. Sacks, *The Widening Gate: Bristol and the Atlantic Economy 1450–1700* (Berkeley, 1991).
18   McGrath, *Merchants and Merchandise*, p. xxi.

much of the regular shipping coming into and out of Bristol consisting of small vessels making regular trips carrying low-value goods to and from Ireland, the much larger transatlantic vessels, which undertook only one voyage a year and carried high-value tobacco and sugar, are naturally elided by a simple count of arrivals and departures. The new customs value-based figures reveal how great this distortion is. Rather than 14 per cent of trade, as suggested by McGrath's shipping figures, New World imports already made up 70 per cent of the total by 1654/5, and thus Bristol's trade was already fully 'Americanised' by the 1650s.

Expansion of Trade

Bristol's newfound transatlantic trades were not a replacement for declining trade with the city's traditional markets. With the first surviving year's accounts to record this trade, from 1654/5, just five years after the end of the English Civil War (1642–49) we might expect to see disruption and decline in Bristol's trade. The opposite, however, was the case. Whatever the disruption of the war years (and given the lack of surviving evidence it may never be possible to calculate this), it is clear that Bristol's trade bounced back with vigour. As previous chapters have shown, Bristol's Irish trade slowed in the 1650s and 1660s, and growth in continental trade slowed after significant expansion in the late sixteenth and early seventeenth centuries. Nonetheless, both imports and exports in all of these branches of trade remained high. Overall, the rise of the new American trades saw the value of Bristol's import trades reach unprecedented levels, as the city's economy thrived in the decades after the Civil War.

As a result of changes in the customs valuations that occurred several times during the Civil War and Interregnum, it is not possible to directly compare trade values from the latter half of the century with those from the first (a full explanation of how valuations have been adjusted appears in the Technical Appendix). For the sake of brevity, however, it is enough to state here that a rough doubling of pre-1642 import valuations allows them to be compared accurately with those used here for customs accounts from the second half of the seventeenth century. With exported goods, a direct comparison of total values is not possible. This is a result of considerable modifications of the customs valuations, beyond mere adjustment for inflation, which were implemented in order to encourage the export of manufactured goods and discourage the export of raw materials.

Bristol's recorded imports totalled £293,000 in 1654/5, and £238,000 in 1659/60 (see Figure 28). After adjusting for inflation, this shows that Bristol's import trade had increased by around one-and-a-half times between the late 1630s and the mid-/late 1650s. Bearing in mind that the sixteen years between 1638 and 1654 included seven years of hard-fought civil war, this is a remarkable

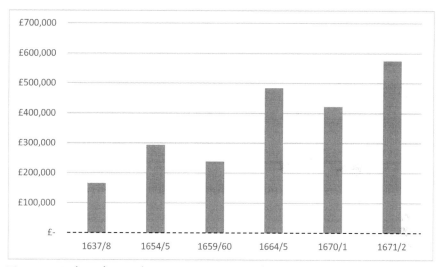

Figure 28. Value of Bristol's overseas import trade as recorded in the Port Books and Wharfage Books, 1637/8–1671/2 (in pounds sterling).

Sources: TNA PRO E190/1136/10, 1137/3, 1138/1; BRO SMV/1/1/1/1; SMV1/1/1/2. The figure for 1637/8 on the graph has been doubled to account for changes in the customs rates that occurred in 1642. To the nearest £500, the values are: 1637/8 £83,000; 1654/5 £293,000; 1659/60 £238,500; 1664/5 £484,000; 1670/1 £422,000; 1671/2 £575,000.

expansion. The development of trade with profitable new markets across the Atlantic allowed Bristol's merchants to continue the growth of their trades at rates that equalled, or even exceeded, that of the pre-war decades. The Port and Wharfage Books from the 1660s and 1670s show the expansion of Bristol's import trades to have continued apace in the decades after the Restoration. By 1664/5 imports had reached £484,000. Although 1670/1 saw a slightly lower figure, imports were even higher again in 1671/2 with almost £575,000 worth of goods brought into Bristol. Between the 1650s and the early 1670s, therefore, Bristol's import trade doubled in value, taking it to almost three-and-a-half times the pre-Civil War level. This is an expansion of overseas trade almost unprecedented in the city's commercial history, only perhaps equalled by Bristol's sudden rise to become England's premier cloth exporting centre in the 1350s and 1360s.[19]

The initial expansion of Bristol's American trades appears to have been over by the late 1670s. Although the sheer volume of work involved in transcribing such detailed records has meant that it has not been possible to undertake

19   E. M. Carus Wilson and O. Coleman, *England's Export Trade 1275–1574* (Oxford, 1963), pp. 76–8, 142.

detailed analysis of the later volumes, simply calculating the total value of trade from the Port Books from the last thirty years of the seventeenth century gives a reasonably good indication of the continued development of trade (see Figure 29). Total imports peaked at just over £600,000 in 1677/8, showing that levels of trade as high as that of 1671/2 could be seen in peacetime. Thereafter, however, recorded import figures drop off slightly. A good run of Bristol Port Books survives from the early 1680s, with three of the first four years of that decade having usable import accounts. Imports were £456,000 in 1679/80, £444,000 the following year, and slightly higher at £492,000 in 1682/3. While down on some of the highest figures recorded, these three accounts suggest that Bristol's trade had stabilised at a level similar to or slightly above that of 1670/1. The phase of rapid growth may, therefore, have been over, but Bristol's imports were still at the highest levels they had ever been.

The most likely explanation of the slowing of the growth of Bristol's trade during the 1680s and 1690s is the continued fall in the price for colonial goods. In the 1680s, English wholesale prices for tobacco dropped below 2s. per lb, falling by as much as 1s. per lb between the early 1670s and 1686. There was, however, no corresponding drop in the farm price in the colonies, meaning that the profitability of the colonial trades was significantly reduced as merchants'

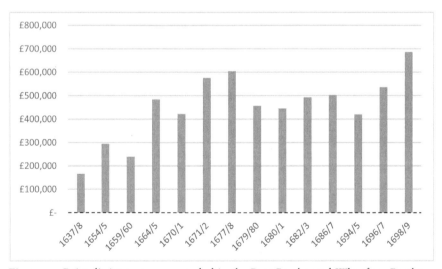

Figure 29. Bristol's imports as recorded in the Port Books and Wharfage Books, 1637/8–1698/9 (in pounds sterling).

Sources: TNA PRO E190/1136/10; BRO SMV/1/1/1/1; SMV/1/1/1/2. Values in addition to those shown in Figure 29 are (to the nearest £500): 1677/8 £604,500; 1678/9 £456,000; 1680/1 £444,500; 1682/3 £492,500; 1686/7 £502,500; 1694/5 £419,500; 1696/7 £536,000; 1698/9 £685,500.

margins were squeezed.[20] This fall in profitability was also aggravated by the introduction of additional Imposition duties on tobacco in 1685, which further cut into merchants' profits. This is perhaps best reflected in the ledger of the Bristol merchant Thomas Speed.[21] Speed's ledger, covering the period 1681–90, is the only private account of a Bristol merchant extant from the seventeenth century.[22] From the Wharfage Books we know that Speed focused on the American trades in the early part of his career. By the 1680s, however, his attentions had shifted primarily to Bristol's traditional wine trade with southern Europe. As there was less money to be made in the colonial trades, Speed simply went elsewhere. Unfortunately, no completed tobacco accounts survive (he did not trade in this product at the time of the ledger), but on the twenty-two consignments of sugar that are recorded, Speed made a 2 per cent overall loss.[23]

The early bonanza of the colonial trades was, it seems, over by the 1680s. The introduction of further customs duties, however, is likely to have increased the level of smuggling in the tobacco trade, potentially resulting in an artificially low level of imports being recorded in the Port Books.[24] Based on a comparison of weights in England and Virginia, R. C. Nash has suggested that tobacco smuggling in the outports was fairly limited in the late seventeenth century. By comparing the amount of tobacco declared for customs with independent records of the ships' lading, he concluded that in 1700 the weight of tobacco declared at Bristol was only 3 per cent less than the true total imported.[25] Other evidence, however, points to a considerably higher level of tobacco smuggling in late seventeenth-century Bristol. For example, in a report on the West Country customs service based on investigations conducted in the early 1680s, William Culliford concluded that Bristol merchants were smuggling tobacco on a significant scale.[26] According to Culliford's evidence, as much as £100 worth of

20   J. E. Thorold Rogers, *A History of Agriculture and Prices in England,* Volume 5 (Oxford, 1887), pp. 467–8; Sacks, *Widening Gate,* pp. 284–5; Russell R. Menard, 'The Tobacco Industry in the Chesapeake Colonies, 1617–1730: An Interpretation', *Research in Economic History,* 5 (1980), pp. 109–77.

21   J. Harlow (ed.), *The Ledger of Thomas Speed, 1681–1690,* Bristol Records Society Vol. 63 (Bristol, 2011).

22   The only other survival of a Bristol merchant's ledger from the period covered by this book is that of John Smythe, covering the period 1538–50. J. M. Vanes (ed.), *The Ledger of John Smythe, 1538–1550,* Bristol Records Society Vol. 28 (Bristol, 1975).

23   Harlow, *Ledger of Thomas* Speed, p. xxxi.

24   Zahedieh, *Capital and the Colonies,* p. 205.

25   R. C. Nash, 'The English and Scottish Tobacco Trades in the Seventeenth and Eighteenth Centuries: Legal and Illegal Trade', *Economic History Review,* 33(2) (1982), pp. 357–9.

26   W. B. Stephens, *The Seventeenth Century Customs Service Surveyed: William Culliford's Investigation of the Western Ports, 1682–84* (Farnham, 2012), p. 47.

tobacco duty was lost on every ship that came in from the colonies.[27] Although these figures are naturally approximate, this suggests that something like 15–20 per cent of tobacco coming into Bristol was smuggled.[28] Particularly in the last two decades of the seventeenth century, therefore (when reduced profit margins on tobacco imports increased the incentive to smuggle), Bristol's trade may have been much greater than the Port Book figures suggest.

Working with tonnage figures from the Wharfage Books, Jonathan Harlow argues that Bristol's trade may have begun to decline by the end of the seventeenth century, reaching little more than its 1650 levels by 1700.[29] The figures presented here do not support this interpretation. Although the pre-1689 Port Books do show a slight drop-off from their 1670s peak, imports remained over £400,000 throughout the 1680s. Indeed, the last two surviving seventeenth-century Port Books from 1696/7 and 1698/9 suggest a return to expansion for Bristol's import trade. Goods worth almost £536,000 were brought into Bristol in 1696/7, and £685,000 the following year. Although beyond the scope of this study, these two accounts are worthy of more detailed attention, particularly as they straddle Bristol's 'official' entry into the slave trade in 1697.

The years between the Civil War and the end of the seventeenth century witnessed a revolution in Bristol's overseas trade. By the 1650s the medieval trading pattern based exclusively on Europe's Atlantic littoral had been swept away, with new transatlantic trades coming rapidly to the fore. While the rapid ongoing expansion driven by the opening up of this new market came to an end after around a quarter of a century, it was spectacular while it lasted. By the 1670s, Bristol's imports were firmly established at around three times the level of just three decades earlier. These new findings re-write previous interpretations of both the Americanisation and expansion of Bristol's trade, locating both firmly in the middle of the seventeenth century. Furthermore, they also improve our understanding of the growth of colonial trade on a national scale. Where previous studies have focused on relatively few data points, the Bristol records provide a more regular data series, giving a clear sense of both the extent and timing of this 'American Revolution'.

27 N. Williams, *Contraband Cargoes: Seven Centuries of Smuggling* (London, 1959), pp. 84–5.

28 The *Barbados Merchant*, for example, paid £495 in duty in 1671/2 when unloading its cargo of tobacco, so if £100 worth of duty had been evaded that would mean 17 per cent of its cargo had been smuggled. PRO E190/1138/1, ff. 95r–105v.

29 J. A. S. Harlow, 'The Life and Times of Thomas Speed' (unpublished PhD thesis, University of the West of England, 2008), pp. 174–5.

Nature of Trade

As has been recognised throughout this book, perhaps the greatest advantage of the Port Books is the level of depth that their data provides, allowing us to look well beyond simple totals for trade. The following sections, therefore, make use of some of this data, examining the types of goods involved in Bristol's nascent New World trades and their regional distribution.

Goods

The goods that Bristol imported from the Americas followed a typical colonial pattern, being dominated by a limited range of cash crops. Indeed, the two staples of the early colonies, tobacco and sugar, accounted for almost the entirety of Bristol's New World imports throughout the post-Civil War decades (see Figure 30 and Table 2). In 1654/5 these two commodities accounted for 92 per cent of Bristol's New World imports, and 98 or 99 per cent in all of the other accounts examined. This is very similar to the pattern observed by Zahedieh in her work on the London customs records of the 1680s, and supports the widely held view that the economy of early colonial America was focused almost exclusively on cash crops for the European market.[30] On the import side at least, this was a much simpler trade than that with Bristol's other commercial partners. As shown in previous chapters, goods from the more mature economies in Ireland, France and the Iberian Peninsula were more diverse, including some manufactured wares as well as agricultural goods and raw materials.

Table 2. Bristol's American imports by commodity, 1670/1 and 1671/2 (to the nearest £10).

Commodity	1670/1	1671/2
Ginger	£570	£930
Indigo	£380	£1,590
Other	£750	£1,500
Sugar, brown	£43,690	£54,750
Sugar, white	£1,930	£1,700
Tobacco	£204,860	£400,560

While their dominance of Bristol's colonial trade remained consistent throughout this period, the absolute volumes of tobacco and sugar imported rose considerably. Bristol's initial forays into the tobacco trade prior to the

30 Zahedieh, *Capital and the Colonies*, p. 189.

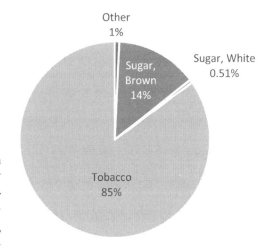

Figure 30. Bristol's American
and Caribbean imports by
commodity, 1670/1 and 1671/2
(in pounds sterling).

Sources: TNA PRO E190/1137/3,
1138/1.

Civil War were relatively modest: just 5,150 lb in 1624/5, and 20,000 lb in 1637/8. By 1654/5 this had risen dramatically to 1,945,250 lb (see Figure 31). This rapid expansion continued into the 1660s and 1670s, with 4.4 million lb of tobacco imported in 1664/5, 2.6 million in 1670/1, and 5 million in 1671/2. Such was the pace of this growth that the amount of tobacco imported into Bristol in the early 1670s was not far short of the volumes attained in Bristol's eighteenth-century 'Golden Age'. For most of the eighteenth century, Bristol's tobacco imports averaged around 4.4 million lb per annum.[31] The 5 million lb imported in 1671/2 surpasses all but the four highest annual imports recorded during the eighteenth century. Indeed, at this stage Bristol was responsible for a sizeable percentage of England's total tobacco imports. Ralph Davis's figures show that 7 million lb of tobacco were imported into London in 1662/3, and 9 million lb in 1668/9.[32] Figures for total English tobacco imports are few and far between for this period, but Menard cites figures of 15 million lb imported from Virginia in 1669, and 17.5 million in 1672.[33] Roughly, therefore, Bristol was responsible for between a fifth and a quarter of English tobacco imports in the 1660s and 1670s, and a significantly higher proportion in war years when trade was diverted from London.

Although Bristol was already importing sizeable quantities of sugar from Spain, none was imported from the American colonies prior to the Civil War. By 1654/5, however, Bristol imported as much as 21,400 cwt from the West Indies and American mainland (see Figure 32). Although prone to some annual

31   Morgan, *Bristol and the Atlantic Trade*, p. 155. This is up until the outbreak of the American Civil War in 1775, when the tobacco trade collapsed.
32   Davis, 'English Foreign Trade', p. 80.
33   Menard, 'Tobacco Industry', p. 159.

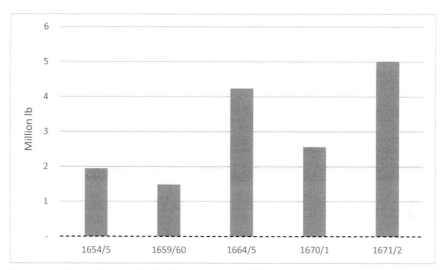

Figure 31. Bristol's recorded tobacco imports (lb).

Sources: BRO SMV/1/1/1/1, SMV/1/1/1/2; TNA PRO E190/1137/3, E190/1138/1. The total recorded volumes of tobacco imports were (to the nearest 1,000 lb: 1654/5 1,946,000 lb; 1659/60 1,485,000 lb; 1664/5 4,233,000 lb; 1670/1 2,562,000 lb; 1671/2 5,007,000 lb.

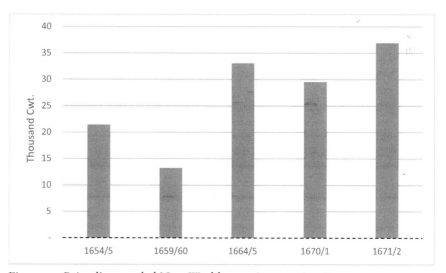

Figure 32. Bristol's recorded New World sugar imports (cwt).

Sources: BRO SMV/1/1/1/1, SMV/1/1/1/2; TNA PRO E190/1137/3, E190/1138/1. To the nearest 100 cwt, total imports were: 1654/5 21,000 cwt; 1659/60 13,200 cwt; 1664/5 33,100 cwt; 1670/1 29,500 cwt; 1671/2 36,900 cwt.

fluctuation, this expansion continued into the 1670s with 37,000 cwt of colonial sugar recorded in 1671/2. This is a significant expansion, but by the 1670s Bristol's sugar imports were still well short of the levels they were to reach in the eighteenth century, when, having become a specialist centre for the import of West Indian sugar, Bristol's sugar imports peaked at 144,000 cwt per annum in the 1730s.[34] Nonetheless, Bristol had already become a significant player in the national sugar trade. London averaged 148,000 cwt of sugar imports in 1662/3 and 1668/9, suggesting that Bristol was responsible for roughly a sixth of English colonial sugar imports at this time.[35]

Regional Distribution

Bristol's trade with the New World was geared almost exclusively towards colonies whose economies were focused on producing crops for export (see Figure 33 and Table 3). While some ships plied the Grand Bank fisheries off Newfoundland, and occasional voyages ventured to New England, the tobacco farms of the Chesapeake and the sugar plantations of the Caribbean accounted for the vast majority of Bristol's transatlantic trade.

Table 3. Regional distribution of Bristol's North American trade (to the nearest £100).

	1654/5	1659/60	1670–71	1671–72
Newfoundland	£800	£60	£300	£300
New England	£–	£400	£2,500	£–
Virginia	£83,400	£111,200	£202,400	£394,300
Caribbean	£121,800	£36,500	£47,300	£66,700

By far the most important destination for Bristol's American trades was Virginia, where tobacco made up between 75 and 85 per cent of Bristol's American imports in 1659/60 and the 1670s accounts. Virginia's exports to Bristol consisted of virtually nothing but tobacco. In 1670/1, for example, of Bristol's £201,600 worth of recorded imports from Virginia, all was tobacco except £100 worth of hides, skins, and wood. This was clearly a cash crop economy, focused almost exclusively on the production of tobacco. This early dominance of the Chesapeake in Bristol's New World trade has interesting implications for how we think about the relationship between the slave economy and the city's growth. Bristol's past is haunted by the words of an anonymous

34   Morgan, *Bristol and the Atlantic Trade*, p. 196.
35   Davis, 'English Foreign Trade', p. 81.

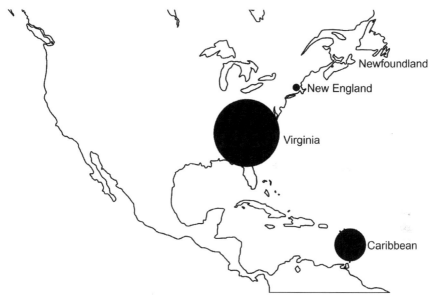

Figure 33. Regional distribution of Bristol's North American trade, 1670/1 (in pounds sterling).

Source: TNA PRO E190/1137/3.

early eighteenth-century annalist, who wrote that 'there is not a brick in the city but what is cemented with the blood of a slave'.[36] Whether this is true of the eighteenth century is a completely different subject, but the findings presented here suggest that the situation in the seventeenth century was more complex. While some enslaved people were certainly present, Virginia did not begin to adopt enslaved labour on a significant scale until after 1680, and it was not until 1720 that it completed the transition to a slave economy.[37] Most of the tobacco which passed through Bristol in the second half of the seventeenth century was, therefore, produced by indentured servants, rather than by enslaved people.

Trade with the Caribbean was generally significantly less valuable than that with Virginia, making up between a quarter and a fifth of Bristol's New World imports. This is a complete contrast to the eighteenth century, when Bristol's specialisation in the sugar trade made the Caribbean its main trading partner.[38] Initially, again tobacco was the most important commodity in Caribbean trade.

36   Cited in M. Dresser, *Slavery Obscured: The Social History of the Slave Trade in Bristol* (Bristol, 2007), p. 96.
37   K. Morgan, *Slavery and Servitude in North America, 1607–1800* (Edinburgh, 2000), pp. 36–9.
38   Morgan, *Bristol and the Atlantic Trade*, p. 13.

Bristol imported £75,000 worth of Caribbean tobacco in 1654/5, making up almost 60 per cent of trade from the region. While in the long run the Caribbean became better known for sugar cultivation, this was still in its early years in the 1650s. It is thus not surprising that other crops still played a significant part in the islands' export economy. Sugar cultivation was first introduced to the Caribbean in the 1630s, but it was not until the 1640s that it began to expand on a significant scale.[39] Producing sugar also needed much greater initial investment than other crops such as tobacco. Harsh working conditions that indentured servants were unwilling to tolerate necessitated an enslaved workforce, and the need to cure sugar within hours of its harvest meant that a semi-industrial boiling house had to be paid for.[40] It was not, therefore, something a settler could launch straight into: time was needed to build up the necessary capital.

In 1659/60 sugar supplanted tobacco as the key import, but tobacco still made up 37 per cent of goods coming from the Caribbean. By the 1670s, however, between 85 and 92 per cent of Bristol's Caribbean imports were sugar. This was mostly in the form of unrefined 'brown' sugar. As with the Chesapeake colonies, the Caribbean was rapidly becoming focused exclusively on the production of a single cash crop. Sugar was, though, still supplemented by moderate quantities of ginger, indigo, and tobacco, with a smattering of other goods. Cotton wool and dyestuffs such as logwood may also be slightly more significant than the Port Book figures suggest, as they were either exempt from duty, or their customs collection was farmed out. At this stage, there was no sign of diversification into the sugar by-products rum and molasses which, for Barbados in particular, became important in the eighteenth century.[41] Also noteworthy are the small quantities of 'elephant's teeth' that appear in the 1671/2 Port Book. Elephants, of course, are not indigenous to either Barbados or Jamaica, so this ivory almost certainly came to the Caribbean in the cargoes of African slave-traders. While slightly more varied in its output than Virginia, throughout the period Bristol's customs records show the Caribbean to have been an economy also geared almost exclusively towards the production of unrefined cash crops for export to Britain.

Bristol's seventeenth-century Caribbean trade was primarily focused on Barbados and the Leeward Islands (see Table 4). Barbados, the most firmly established and economically advanced of the region's colonies, was the key market, accounting for around 60 per cent of Bristol's Caribbean imports. Nevis, and to a lesser extent Antigua, were also significant trading destinations for Bristol. Nevis at times accounted for as much as 40 per cent of the

39   J. J. McCusker and R. R. Menard, *The Economy of British America, 1607–1789* (London, 1985), pp. 148–9; Zahedieh, *Capital and the Colonies*, pp. 211–14.
40   K. Morgan, *Slavery and the British Empire: From Africa to America* (Oxford, 2007), p. 27; McCusker and Menard, *Economy of British America*, p. 152.
41   *Ibid.*, pp. 164–5.

West Indian import trade. Antigua featured less regularly, with no trade at all in some years, and never accounting for more than 8 per cent of trade with the region. The only other Caribbean island that Bristol traded with at this time was Jamaica. Newly acquired by the English as part of Cromwell's Western Design in 1655, it is unsurprising that Bristol did not trade with Jamaica in the 1650s. Nonetheless, as the colony became more firmly established and began to develop a plantation economy, its trade with Bristol grew, reaching as much as £5,300 by 1671/2.[42]

The goods Bristol was importing varied relatively little from island to island, with sugar consistently making up 85–90 per cent by the 1670s, but there was some minor variation in the lesser commodities. For example, around 7 per cent of Barbados's exports were of refined white sugars not produced on the other islands, and tobacco, which was no longer sent from Barbados, still made up 10 per cent of exports from Nevis. Most variation is seen in goods from Jamaica, which was still in the early phases of its transformation from an economy based on piracy to one based on cash crop production.[43] Even there, however, brown sugar still accounted for 70–80 per cent of the trade.

Table 4. Bristol's Caribbean imports by colony (to the nearest £100).

	1654/5	1659/60	1670/1	1671/2
Antigua	£1,300	–	–	£2,900
Barbados	£69,500	£21,300	£28,000	£25,200
Jamaica	–	–	£800	£5,300
Nevis	£41,900	£15,200	£18,500	£33,300

Sources: BRO SMV/1/1/1/1, SMV/1/1/1/2, TNA PRO E190/1137/3, E190/1138/1.

One somewhat perplexing feature of the 1650s Bristol trade records is a significant shift from the Caribbean as the most important source of trans-atlantic imports in 1654/5 to Virginia as the key market in all subsequent seventeenth-century records. The Caribbean accounted for 60 per cent of Bristol's New World imports in 1654/5, and Virginia 40 per cent. In 1659/60, however, the position had switched: 75 per cent of American imports came from the Chesapeake, and just 25 per cent from the Caribbean (see Table 3). While both trades grew in the subsequent decades, their relative proportions remained consistent in the 1670s. It is not entirely clear why this shift occurred, particularly bearing in mind that the Caribbean dominated Bristol's trade in the

---

42 N. Zahedieh, 'Trade, Plunder, and Economic Development in Early English Jamaica, 1655–89', *Economic History Review*, 32(2) (1986), pp. 205–22.
43 *Ibid.*

eighteenth century. It seems most likely that the reason lies in the Caribbean's move from tobacco to sugar production. In 1654/5 Bristol imported £72,000 worth of tobacco from the Caribbean, but by 1659/60 this was down to just £13,000, with Chesapeake tobacco imports growing in its place. This shift from tobacco to sugar may also have had implications for the export side of Bristol's trade. With the Royal African Company monopoly in place, Bristol's supply of exported labour was largely (if not totally) restricted to indentured servants rather than the African enslaved people who had become central to production in the Caribbean. The increasingly high proportion of enslaved people in the Caribbean population may also have impacted the demand for the manufactured goods key to Bristol's American exports. With the enslaved being provided for as cheaply as possible, with a largely locally (and even self-) made material culture, it may be that Bristol at this stage favoured trade with the mainland as this provided a larger market for its export goods.[44]

Although not as significant as trade with the Caribbean and Chesapeake, Bristol also continued the connections with Newfoundland that dominated its earliest interest in New World colonies (see Chapter 3). In addition to being in great demand in England, fish from the Grand Bank (preserved by salting and drying on massive racks or flakes) found a considerable market in southern Europe. Fish was particularly sought after in Catholic communities on the Iberian Peninsula, where it was much in demand for consumption on days when eating meat was not permitted. This led to the evolution of a triangular trade. Ships would leave England either in ballast or carrying a few essential supplies for the colonies, then pick up a cargo of fish from the Newfoundland Banks, either by fishing or from a fishing master in Newfoundland. This cargo would then be sold in Spain, in return for dried fruits and Spanish wines (leading to this route sometimes being described as the Newfoundland sack trade), which would be brought back to England for sale.[45] Unfortunately, trade between Newfoundland and the Iberian Peninsula is virtually impossible to track using the Port Books. Ships going out to Newfoundland tended to leave in ballast and are thus not recorded in the customs records; and on their return only their immediate port of origin in southern Europe is listed. Unlike the produce of the colonies in the West Indies and Virginia, Newfoundland fish was not bound by the Navigation Acts to be exported only to England, so was usually shipped straight to its end markets, rather than first being brought back to

---

44   Archaeological investigations of slave plantations have shown that slaves had access to some imported metalware, particularly the tools used for their work. Domestic objects such as ceramics and musical instruments, however, were often locally made and emulated West African designs. Morgan, *Slavery and the British Empire*, pp. 116–23; J. Walvin, *Slaves and Slavery: The British Colonial Experience* (Manchester, 1992), pp. 65–74.

45   P. E. Pope, *Fish into Wine: The Newfoundland Plantation in the Seventeenth Century* (Chapel Hill, NC, 2004), pp. 79–121.

Bristol. The 1671/2 Port Book shows only one ship bound for Newfoundland, the *Experiment*, which left in mid-June carrying a variety of provisions.[46] Only one ship also appears to have returned from the Banks that year (the *John*, carrying trayne oil and tallow) and just three were recorded in the previous year's Port Book.[47] Evidence from Newfoundland, however, shows that in 1675 as many as nine Bristol ships (averaging 59 tons in size) visited the Banks, all bound directly for southern Europe.[48] It seems, therefore, that this hidden trade may have made a fairly significant contribution to Bristol's overseas commerce in the mid- to late seventeenth century. Interestingly, though, Bristol was not as heavily involved as many smaller west coast ports. Dartmouth, for example, sent forty-one ships to Newfoundland that year, and Bideford twenty-five; in all, 174 ships were recorded, of which Bristol only contributed a little over 9 per cent.[49]

Of the other mainland colonies, there is very little sign in the Bristol customs accounts. Although by 1670 the population of the northern colonies was significantly greater than that of the Chesapeake, only New England traded with Bristol.[50] Even New England only featured in three out of the six years of accounts examined in detail, and it accounted for a very small percentage of recorded trade. In 1660 just one ship, the *Blessing*, came in from New England, carrying 26 bags of wool (worth £195) and 36 tons of trayne (fish) oil (worth £216).[51] In 1662, three ships left Bristol for New England: the *Supply*, the *Mary Fortune*, and the *Huntsman*. In all they carried £300 worth of goods, consisting principally of cloth and clothing.[52] The most significant amount of trade with New England was in 1670/1, when two ships, the *Adventure* and the *Providence*, imported £2,500 worth of goods into Bristol.[53] Both vessels appear to have been New England-owned ships, listing Boston as their home port. The makeup of their cargoes is very interesting, consisting primarily of goods produced in the Caribbean and the Chesapeake. Although there were small quantities of trayne oil and beaver skins, the majority of their cargoes were brown sugar and molasses (46 per cent) and tobacco (45 per cent). While the population of the northern colonies would suggest that they offered a potential market to Bristol, the nature of their economies meant

46   PRO E190/1138/1, ff. 80r–80v.
47   PRO E190/1137/3, ff. 35, 85v–87r, E190/1138/1, ff. 145v–146r.
48   Pope, *Fish into Wine*, p. 111.
49   *Ibid*.
50   In 1670, the population of the Chesapeake colonies is estimated to have been 48,500, and that of the other mainland colonies 59,000. Source: https://www.census.gov/library/publications/1975/compendia/hist_stats_colonial-1970.html, p. 1168.
51   BRO SMV/7/1/1/1/2, p. 56.
52   TNA PRO E190/1240/6, ff. 15–43.
53   TNA PRO E190/1137/3, ff. 8–10 and 94–5.

that they simply were not suited to full integration into the Atlantic economy. The Caribbean and Chesapeake planters were focused on market production from the start, experimenting with different cash crops until they found one that could be marketed in England. In New England, however, the economic vision of the settlers was instead one of 'competency': subsistence farming on a piece of land large enough to sustain themselves and their family.[54] They did not produce significant quantities of goods for export and thus, as the customs accounts show, large numbers of merchants were not attracted there. Instead, the New England settlers' interaction with the Atlantic economy was indirect. As the cargoes of the *Adventure* and *Providence* in 1670/1 reveal, when they needed to buy English manufactured goods, the northern colonists did so via their more market-oriented southern counterparts, either by carrying their goods or providing them with agricultural supplies.[55]

Impacts

Such a significant change in both the character and the extent of Bristol's trade had significant implications beyond the realms of merchants, ships and shipping. Many trades and industries were either created or grew substantially to meet the needs of the bustling port. The relationship between Bristol's New World exports and the expansion of manufacturing in both the city and its hinterland will be dealt with in the next chapter. Here, the focus is the significant employment generated by the need to both process and sell the colonial tobacco and sugar that flooded into the city.

Having received only a rough curing in the Chesapeake before being packed into hogshead casks ready for transport, tobacco needed a good deal of further processing before it was ready for consumption. On being removed from the cask and allowed to dry, the tobacco first needed to be 'cut' to remove the leaves from the stalks, and to shred them to a fine consistency. The leaves were then mixed with sugar, water and other liquors, and spun on a wheel to turn this into a 'roll' of tobacco. This could then be cut up into smaller portions for sale, and ultimately consumed either by smoking or chewing, or grinding up to take as snuff.[56] The limited amounts of tobacco Bristol imported from the Caribbean tended to come ready processed and rolled. Tobacco coming from

---

54   V. Dejohn Anderson, 'New England in the Seventeenth Century', in N. Canny (ed.), *The Oxford History of the British Empire, Volume I: The Origins of Empire, British Overseas Enterprise to the Close of the Seventeenth Century* (Oxford, 1998), p. 210.

55   McCusker and Menard, *Economy of British America*, pp. 100–1.

56   N. C. P. Tyack, 'The Trade Relations of Bristol with Virginia during the 17th Century' (unpublished MA thesis, University of Bristol, 1930), pp. 56–7; Zahedieh, *Capital and the Colonies*, p. 202.

the Chesapeake, however, was unprocessed in hogsheads. The result, therefore, was a fast-growing tobacco-processing industry in Bristol. Indeed, such was the scale of the business by the last quarter of the century that a degree of division of labour appears to have occurred, with specialist 'tobacco cutters' and 'tobacco rollers' enrolled as burgesses of the city, as well as more general 'tobacconists'. From work on the city's apprentice register and burgess books, Nicholas Tyack has estimated that as many as 150 people were employed in tobacco-cutting and rolling in Bristol between 1648 and 1700.[57] To this can be added at least 150 involved in the retail trade in tobacco, and more than a hundred enrolled as burgesses in the related craft of pipe-making.[58] While this represents the total number employed over a fifty-year period, rather than the number working with tobacco at any one time, it was still clearly a significant source of employment in the city. In all, this amounts to at least 400 people employed in tobacco-processing and related trades, in a city whose population was still only 20,000 at the end of the seventeenth century.[59]

While Bristol's early modern tobacco industry has been relatively under-studied, its sugar industry has received a good deal of attention. Here, too, it is clear that the processing of goods imported from the colonies generated a good deal of employment and economic activity in the city. Unlike tobacco, Bristol was already importing some sugar from the Iberian Peninsula and Atlantic islands by the end of the sixteenth century. Indeed, the city's first sugar refinery was opened by the successful merchant Robert Aldworth as early as 1612 at St. Peters in the shadow of the crumbling Bristol Castle.[60] As already shown, Bristol's sugar imports rose significantly in the middle decades of the seventeenth century, from just 178 hogsheads when the first refinery was opened in 1612 to almost 3,400 in 1654.[61] Although an initial boiling was required on the plantations within hours of harvest to prevent spoilage, the vast majority of sugar imported into Bristol was in a 'brown' semi-refined form. A further process of boiling, adding refining agents, and finally setting in moulds and maturing was thus needed before it was ready for sale.[62] Unsurprisingly, therefore, a second, much larger, sugar house was opened in 1653 just off St.

57   Tyack, 'Trade Relations', pp. 56–60.
58   *Ibid.*, p. 64; N. C. P. Tyack, 'Bristol Merchants, Shipwrights, Ship-Carpenters, Sailmakers, Anchorsmiths, Seamen, Tobacco-Cutters, Tobacco-Rollers, Tobacconists, Tobacco Pipe-Makers. A Transcript Chronologically Arranged, from the Bristol Burgess Books: 1607–1700' (unpublished transcript, University of Bristol, 1930), pp. 105–10.
59   W. E. Minchinton (ed.), *The Trade of Bristol in the Eighteenth Century*, Bristol Record Society Vol. 20 (Bristol, 1957), p. ix.
60   D. Jones, *Bristol's Sugar Trade and Refining Industry*, Bristol Historical Association Pamphlets no. 89 (Bristol, 2003), pp. 1–2.
61   *Ibid.*, pp. 2–4.
62   Zahedieh, *Capital and the Colonies*, pp. 218–19.

Augustine's Back.[63] As sugar imports continued to grow (consistently topping 7,000 hogsheads per year by the 1680s), so did the number of sugar refineries built to process them.[64] By the end of the seventeenth century, Bristol had ten sugar refineries, with two opened in the 1660s and five in the 1680s.[65] While setting up a refinery required a good deal of capital, sugar-refining was not labour-intensive.[66] No study has been conducted of the number of people employed in Bristol's seventeenth-century sugar industry, but the thirteen cottages built in the grounds of the St. Augustine's sugar house to accommodate its workers perhaps give some indication.[67]

Not all the tobacco and sugar imported into Bristol in the mid-seventeenth century was bound for domestic consumption. The Navigation Acts prevented produce from the English colonies being sent directly to markets on the continent, thus creating an opportunity for a re-export trade, furnishing European demand for tobacco and sugar. Ralph Davis described the re-export trade as one of the most significant developments in English commerce in the second half of the seventeenth century, with re-exports making up as much as 30 per cent of all English exports by the end of the century.[68] Re-exported goods are unfortunately hard to detect in the customs records. Re-exported tobacco and sugar were exempt from customs duty, so the Customer and Controller did not record them in their versions of the Port Books. Fortunately, however, the Searcher and Waiters were concerned with checking what goods were actually on the ships (rather than what duty they paid), and so tobacco and sugar re-exports are recorded in their accounts. In 1661/2 Bristol's re-export trade was relatively modest. Just £700 worth of sugar and £3,400 worth of tobacco (two-thirds of which was classed as 'decayed') are recorded, amounting to less than 7 per cent of the total value of Bristol's exports.[69] Two decades later, however, this trade had grown considerably. Unfortunately, the account from 1671/2 examined in detail for this study is a Controller's account, and thus does not record re-exported goods. Initial examination of an account from 1678, however, shows a significant volume of re-export trade.[70] A total of 1.5 million lb of tobacco was exported from Bristol. This is roughly typical of

63   Jones, *Bristol's Sugar*, p. 8
64   *Ibid.*, p. 4.
65   *Ibid.*, p. 10; I. V. Hall, 'Whitson Court Sugar House, Bristol, 1665–1824', *Transactions of the Bristol and Gloucestershire Archaeological Society*, 65 (1944); I. V. Hall, 'Bristol's Second Sugar House', *Transactions of the Bristol and Gloucestershire Archaeological Society*, 68 (1949), p. 110.
66   Zahedieh, *Capital and the Colonies*, pp. 218–19.
67   Jones, *Bristol's Sugar*, p. 8.
68   Davis, 'English Foreign Trade', p. 78.
69   TNA PRO E190/1240/6.
70   TNA PRO E190/1139/3. I am extremely grateful to Jonathan Harlow for providing me with these figures.

the wider picture, with approximately a third of England's tobacco imports being re-exported in 1671, and half in 1686.[71] Of Bristol's 1.5 million lb of re-exported tobacco, 60 per cent was bound for Ireland and 15 per cent for Scotland. Surprisingly, continental markets played a relatively modest part, with 75,000 lb sent to France and 147,000 lb to Spain, making up just 15 per cent of Bristol's tobacco re-exports. As discussed in the next chapter and in the Technical Appendix, the customs valuations on the export trade at this time are problematic, and thus it is difficult to determine the exact proportion of Bristol's exports that these colonial products represented. Nonetheless, it is clear that by the 1670s and 1680s a considerable proportion of the tobacco being imported into Bristol was being re-exported, strengthening the integration of both its Irish and continental trades into the Atlantic economy.

Causes

While the expansion of Bristol's American trades and their impact on the city can be traced with relative ease using the customs and other records, the causes of these developments are harder to pinpoint. One factor which can be discounted, however, is a decline in the other branches of Bristol's commerce. As already shown, Bristol's 'American Revolution' witnessed a significant increase in the value of total imports, rather than a straightforward shift from trading with one set of markets to another. As shown in Chapters 1 and 2, while expansion had slowed, trade with Bristol's three traditional markets in France, Ireland and the Iberian Peninsula remained healthy in the second half of the seventeenth century, with some of the city's leading merchants even favouring them over the new transatlantic trades. Instead, therefore, we must look to a multiplicity of other factors to account for the rapid growth of this new branch of trade. Most important was growing consumer demand on both sides of the Atlantic, but the broader political and legislative climate also had a part to play in Bristol capitalising on this.

To an extent, government legislation boosted Bristol's involvement in the American trades. A number of Acts related to colonial trade were introduced in this period, designed to give English shipping an advantage over their Dutch rivals, and establish a total monopoly on trade with the colonies. The two principal pieces of legislation were the Staple Act of 1663, which meant that the colonists were bound to buy almost all English and European goods directly from England; and the Navigation Act, which required virtually all colonial produce (including sugar, tobacco, cotton, and dyestuffs) to be sent directly

---

71   Zahedieh, *Capital and the Colonies*, p. 208.

to England in English or colonial ships.[72] The Navigation Act was passed in 1651, although during the Interregnum it is unlikely that its enforcement was sufficient to exclude the Dutch from trade with the American colonies.[73] In 1660, however, a new Navigation Act was issued including tighter definitions and further measures to ensure its enforcement; indeed, the 1670s Bristol Port Books include occasional notes with regard to the nationality of a ship and its crew.[74] Although it seems unlikely that total enforcement of these Acts was ever possible, in the years after the Restoration the combination of the Staple and Navigation Acts certainly gave English (including Bristolian) merchants an advantage and further stimulated their trade with the rapidly growing American colonies.

Just as important as the introduction of pieces of legislation favourable to Bristol's colonial trade is the move away from legislation that hindered its possibilities. As shown in a previous chapter, several royal Acts and monopolies prevented Bristol from engaging in any significant trade with the Chesapeake prior to the Civil War. In the post-Restoration era, however (with the notable exception of the African trade), there was a general move away from monopolies, which had been one of the many royal policies leading to resentment in the tumultuous early decades of the seventeenth century. In the years after the Civil War, therefore, Bristol's merchants were able to expand into new regions unhindered by restrictive legislation, or the exclusive rights of London-based companies. In many ways, this development was crucial in sparking the 'Rise of the Western Ports'. Atlantic-facing ports such as Bristol and Liverpool had a geographical advantage over London in the Atlantic trade, with shorter voyages meaning lower costs. This, however, would not have outweighed the significant costs of acquiring monopoly rights from the Crown. The unrestricted nature of this trade, therefore, meant that for the first time the opening of a new market was an opportunity for the less capital-rich merchants of the outports, not just wealthy London Company men.

The American trades and access to goods were also becoming much more open from the middle of the seventeenth century. As Robert Brenner has highlighted, in its early days colonial trade was very much bound up with investment in plantations. With the planters in need of set-up capital, many of their crops were often sold to backers long before they were even grown.[75] There was thus little opportunity for a casual speculator to pick up a cargo of tobacco. By the eve of the Civil War, however, this situation had begun to shift,

72   C. Wilson, *England's Apprenticeship, 1603–1763* (London, 1965) pp. 163–4.

73   J. Cooper, 'Social and Economic Policies under the Commonwealth', in G. E. Aylmer (ed.), *The Interregnum: The Quest for Settlement 1646–1660* (London, 1972), p. 135.

74   Wilson, *England's Apprenticeship*, p. 164.

75   R. Brenner, *Merchants and Revolution: Commercial Change, Political Conflict, and London's Overseas Traders, 1550–1653* (London, 2003), p. 103.

with tobacco for sale on the open market. The door was, therefore, open for those who did not want to take the risks of long-term investment to become involved in American trade. The types of goods involved in the trade also meant that it was inherently open to all, not requiring detailed knowledge of what goods to buy and in what proportions in order to secure a safe profit when they were brought home. With just tobacco and sugar on offer, the range of goods available to buy was much more straightforward than in other branches of trade. Crucially, too, no knowledge of foreign languages was needed, and indeed in many cases Bristolians would have had family connections amongst the colonists to facilitate trading links.[76] Again, therefore, the open nature of the American trades from the middle of the seventeenth century onwards created an opportunity for the comparatively less wealthy outport merchants to compete with their London counterparts.

While they may have boosted trade, protective legislation and freedom from restrictions alone were not enough to lead merchants to develop a new branch of trade. As was seen in the last chapter, over the course of the fifteenth, sixteenth and seventeenth centuries Bristol's merchants experimented with new trade routes on a fairly regular basis. On the whole, however, these did not last: for a trade to endure and become established as part of the regular commercial cycle, it had to offer something more in terms of stability, ease of conduct, and, above all, profitability.

In some years at least, Bristol's American trade was boosted by the series of Anglo-Dutch Wars (1652–54, 1665–67, 1672–74), which gave the city a temporary competitive advantage over London. Much of the naval strife, with resulting hazards to merchant shipping, was focused on the English Channel, providing a major obstruction into London.[77] Bristol, on the other hand, had an almost clear run to open water and the Americas. As Figure 34 shows, in each of the three war years from which data has been collected, Bristol's imports were significantly higher. While the wars may well have accelerated Bristol's process of becoming involved in the American trades, this was no more than an accelerant of an independently developing trend. As the two peacetime datasets show, Bristol's American imports were growing significantly, regardless of naval strife.

Ultimately, while many other factors doubtlessly contributed, the simplest cause was the most important in driving the expansion of New World trade between the 1650s and 1670s: the growth in population of the American and Caribbean colonies. In the 1620s, Virginia's population of 2,200 was equivalent to a reasonably-sized English town. By 1650, however, it had reached more than 18,700, growing to 27,000 by 1660 and 35,800 by 1670 (nearly twice the size

---

76   Sacks, *Widening Gate*, pp. 264–7.
77   C. Wilson, *Profit and Power – A Study of England and the Dutch Wars* (London, 1957), p. 62.

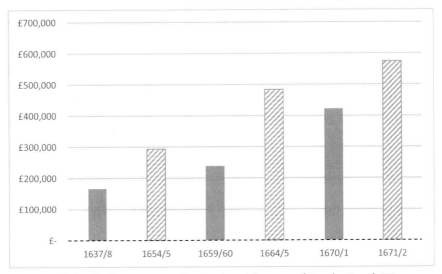

Figure 34. Bristol's imports 1637/8–1671/2, with years of Anglo-Dutch Wars highlighted (in pounds sterling).

Sources: TNA PRO E190/1136/10, 1137/3, 1138/1; BRO SMV/1/1/1/1, SMV1/1/1/2.

of Bristol itself at that time).[78] There were thus simply more opportunities to develop a profitable trade. The need to supply this new colonial population has long been recognised as an important driving force in the growth of English transatlantic trade.[79] Naturally, the newly-founded colonies lacked substantial manufacturing industries, so they relied on English ships for all manner of manufactured wares. Also, even relatively early, the colonies were almost entirely focused on their staple cash crops, devoting little space or effort to the production of food, thus creating a considerable market for the export of provisions from England and Ireland (a trade discussed in Chapter 5).[80]

On the import side, there can be no doubt that growing consumer demand for colonial-produced tobacco and sugar was the principal driver of growth, with these two commodities making up in excess of 99 per cent of Bristol's transatlantic imports. At the start of the century these had been expensive luxuries, available to only the elites.[81] Soaring of colonial production, however, brought prices crashing down. By the 1670s the retail price of both tobacco and sugar had fallen considerably, making them accessible to even the poorest

78   Source: https://www.census.gov/library/publications/1975/compendia/hist_stats_colonial-1970.html, p. 1168.
79   Davis, 'English Foreign Trade', pp. 80, 83.
80   Brenner, *Merchants and Revolution*, p. 95.
81   Davis, 'English Foreign Trade', p. 80.

in society. The retail price for tobacco, for example, fell from 40s. per lb in the 1610s to as little as 1s. per lb in the 1670s.[82] Both became ubiquitous features at all levels in all parts of England: no woodcut of an alehouse or coffeehouse scene from the latter seventeenth century would be complete without several of the revellers sporting tobacco pipes. A French visitor to Bristol in 1670 remarked that smoking was common among both women and schoolboys, and that he had been told over dinner that 'without tobacco one cannot live in England'.[83] In the period after the Restoration, production and consumption of colonial goods entered a virtuous cycle. Increased production led to falling prices, which opened up new markets for these goods, with the increased demand in turn fuelling increases in production and further price falls. Clearly this situation could not endure indefinitely, however, and by the 1680s demand for tobacco had reached saturation point, and the farm price had fallen such that production was much less profitable than it had been.[84] Nonetheless, by this time cultures of consumption in England had been changed forever by these exotic products, and a substantial new trade become firmly established. The taste for tobacco was also not restricted to England. As shown in the previous section, by the 1670s Bristol was playing a redistributive role, with considerable amounts of tobacco being shipped on to Ireland and continental Europe. As the Atlantic economy grew from the latter half of the seventeenth century, port cities such as Bristol benefited as nodal points for the movement of goods between the Old World and the New. This role connecting the 'ghost acres' of North America and the Caribbean with the consumers of the tropical goods that they produced was the principal driver of Bristol's expansion in the second half of the seventeenth century.

England's 'American Revolution'?

This chapter has revealed that Bristol's American trades developed much faster than has previously been accepted. But was this true elsewhere? The standard narrative for other towns and cities is based on similarly 'scrappy evidence'.[85] Work by Ralph Davis and Nuala Zahedieh suggests that trade with the New World colonies accounted for just 12 per cent of London's imports in 1663 and 1669, rising to 20 per cent by the end of the century, implying much slower development than that shown to have occurred at Bristol.[86] The work of Davis and Zahedieh was ground-breaking in terms of quantifying developments and

82   *Ibid.*
83   J. Latimer, *The Annals of Bristol in the Seventeenth Century* (Bristol, 1900), p. 360.
84   Zahedieh, *Capital and the Colonies*, pp. 208–9.
85   *Ibid.*, p. 9.
86   *Ibid.*, pp. 10–11.

identifying the 'Rise of the Atlantic Economy'. Their figures, however, almost certainly underestimate the true significance of American trade.

The main reason the growth rates proposed for Bristol are so different from those for London is that different assumptions have been made about how best to value the chief exports of the American colonies. For 1663 and 1669, Zahedieh and Davis retained the values for tobacco and sugar from their original source, the Book of Tables. The valuations were not added to these until 1678, and are thus based on London prices in the late 1670s rather than prices in either 1663 or 1669.[87] Tobacco, for example, was valued at 6d. per lb. This, as Davis showed, was roughly equivalent to the merchants' price for the lowest grades of tobacco at the end of the 1670s.[88] Yet, as discussed above, soaring production of the colonial cash crops during the 1660s and 1670s meant that retail prices crashed during these decades. The price of tobacco in England, for example, fell from 8s. per lb in 1662 to 2s. 6d. per lb in 1681.[89] Using a price from 1678 will thus considerably undervalue tobacco in 1663 and 1669. As tobacco and sugar were so dominant in the colonial trades throughout the period, using 1678 prices for tobacco and sugar in 1663 and 1669 means that the significance of America in relation to other branches of trade is greatly underestimated.

The valuations used by Davis and Zahedieh for the end of the seventeenth century are equally problematic. These are based on the valuations used in the Inspector General's Ledgers, which begin in 1696, and recorded the price at which goods were *bought* in the Americas. Davis thus valued tobacco recorded in his post-1697 records at 2s. 4d. per lb, and Zahedieh applied the same valuation to tobacco found in her 1686 London Port Books.[90] When examining the significance of a trade to England, however, it is inappropriate to use colonial prices. As Davis pointed out, modern practice does not use the 'first cost' of imported goods: 'imports are today valued at cost up to the point of landing – i.e. including insurance and freight'.[91] The purchase cost of the commodities was, after all, a relatively small proportion of the expense of bringing tobacco and sugar across the Atlantic, given the risks and distances involved.[92] Using figures derived from foreign prices thus grossly underesti-

---

87   Davis, 'English Foreign Trade', pp. 84–5; Zahedieh, *Capital and the Colonies*, p. 189.
88   Davis, 'English Foreign Trade', p. 87.
89   J. E. Thorold Rogers, *A History of Agriculture and Prices in England, Volume V: 1583–1702* (Oxford, 1887), pp. 467–8. Rogers was careful to differentiate between colonial and the more expensive Spanish tobacco.
90   Davis, 'English Foreign Trade', pp. 86–7; Zahedieh, *Capital and the Colonies*, pp. 13, 189.
91   Davis, 'English Foreign Trade', p. 87.
92   For a discussion of the shipping business in the new transatlantic trades, see Zahedieh, *Capital and the Colonies*, pp. 114–95; R. Davis, *The Rise of the English Shipping Industry in the Seventeenth and Eighteenth Centuries* (London, 1962).

mates the value of American goods landed in England. While this may be acceptable when assessing general trends within American trade itself, it causes major problems when assessing the significance of tobacco and sugar relative to other trades.

My study has instead used the valuations from the Book of Rates, which provides figures for all import goods. These are not ideal, since the rates books were only updated occasionally, but they do, however, bear a closer relationship to wholesale prices in England than the prices charged in the colonies. While the Book of Rates had not been significantly altered for almost a century after 1558, it was in fact revised twice during the mid-seventeenth century (in 1642 and 1660).[93] This included significantly reducing the valuations of colonial goods such as tobacco and sugar to account for recent falls in their price.[94] For the 1650s and 1660s, therefore, these valuations can be assumed to be reasonably accurate and up-to-date. The 1660 Book of Rates valued tobacco at 1s. 8d. per lb, and brown sugar at £1 10s. per cwt.[95] As the Technical Appendix shows, comparison with known wholesale prices from the time shows that, despite the collapse of the price for colonial imports, for the 1650s, 1660s and 1670s, these valuations are roughly in line with those of other commodities.[96] These valuations thus give a more realistic indication of the economic significance of the American trades, relative to other branches of English commerce.

Reassessing the valuations to more closely match contemporary market prices in England shows that the American trades grew much faster and much earlier than has been assumed. More detailed work on the customs accounts of London and other ports is clearly needed to verify these conclusions. A rough re-calibration of the figures calculated by Davis and Zahedieh for 1663 and 1669

---

93   *The Rates of Merchandises: That is to say, the Subsidie of Tonnage, the Subsidie of Poundage, and the Subsidie of Woollen, Cloathes, or old Drapery* (London, 1642); *The rates of merchandise, that is to say, the subsidy of tonnage, subsidy of poundage, and the subsidy of woollen clothes or old-drapery, as they are rated and agreed on by the Commons House of Parliament...* (London, 1660).

94   The price of tobacco was reduced from 3s. 4d. a lb. in the 1642 Book of Rates to 1s. 8d. That for brown sugar was cut from £10 a cwt to £1 10s. As price falls were occurring throughout this period, this study uses the 1660 valuation for the 1650s to avoid the risk of overstating the importance of the American trades.

95   *The Act of Tonnage & Poundage, and Book of Rates, with several Statutes at large relating to the Customs* (London, 1675).

96   The relationship between the retail price of commodities and their Book of Rates valuation was not a consistent one, but on the whole the Book of Rates valued goods at between half and a third of their market price. Comparison with known retail prices shows the Book of Rates valuation for brown sugar to have been a quarter of its market value in the 1650s and 1660s, and tobacco a fifth (see Technical Appendix). If anything, therefore, the Book of Rates valuations still underestimate the significance of American trade in the Interregnum and post-Restoration years.

is, however, attempted in Table 5 to give an indication of the likely extent of this growth. This suggests that tobacco has been considerably undervalued, with the Book of Rates valuation being three times that listed by the Book of Tables. As a result, the recalculated total value for American trade is more than double the previous figure, £1.13 million rather than £545,000. This means that the overall importance of American trade to English overseas commerce has been underestimated. Rather than the 12 per cent previously assumed, New World imports in fact made up almost 28 per cent of London's total imports in 1663 and 1669.[97] This is not quite an 'American Revolution' akin to that experienced by Bristol: London participated in a more diverse range of trades and other branches will also have shaped its development. Nonetheless, combined with the significant trade through Bristol shown above, it is clear that American trade in general was expanding much more rapidly than previously supposed, and as a result having a significant impact on English economic development from the middle of the seventeenth century onwards.

Table 5. Revaluation of London's colonial imports, 1663 and 1669.

Commodity	Quantity	Unit	Book of Tables price	Book of Tables value	Book of Rates price	Revised value
Tobacco	8,196,600	lb	6d.	£204,915	1s. 8d.	£683,050
Brown sugar	148,338	cwt	27s.	£200,324	£1. 10s.	£222,507
White sugar	19,860	cwt	56s.	£55,608	£7 6s. 8d.	£145,640
Cotton	6,986	bags	£6	£41,916	n/a	
Cocoa	1,732	cwt	£10	£11,920	n/a	
Beaver skins	14,520	skins	10s.	£7,125	6s. 8d.	£4,840
Otter skins	3,795	skins	5s.	£1,318	5s.	£949
Ginger	2,659	cwt	22s.	£2,924	n/a	
Indigo	15,000	lb	2s.	£1,500	1s.	£750
Other				£17,538		
Total				£545,088		£1,132,034

Sources: Zahedieh, *Capital and the Colonies*, p. 189; *The Act of Tonnage & Poundage, and Book of Rates, with several Statutes at large relating to the Customs* (London, 1675). Direct comparison with the Book of Rates valuations was not possible for cotton, cocoa and ginger, so the original values for these have been included in the revised total.

97   Davis has London's total imports as £3,495,000 in 1663/1669 (Davis, 'English Foreign Trade', p. 92). With the revised value for American trade, however, this becomes £4,082,000.

Conclusions

The middle of the seventeenth century was, then, crucial for the Atlantic economy. As shown above, from at least the mid-sixteenth century, the flow of goods from the Americas to Europe shaped both Bristol's and England's commercial fortunes. The rapid growth of England's American colonies in the decades either side of the Restoration, however, initiated a step change in this transformative process. Even at the height of the Civil War, Bristol's trade grew apace. This was without doubt the most startling commercial transformation the city had ever seen, with the value of its imports tripling in two decades, and previously non-existent transatlantic trades coming to make up as much as three-quarters of the total. With the exception of the New England settlers, this new body of Englishmen in North America and the Caribbean was fully integrated into the Atlantic economy. They developed a symbiotic relationship with the homeland, creating a large new market for the exotic cash crops that they produced at ever-decreasing prices, and relying on provisions, goods and labour from their Old World customers. For ports such as Bristol, the bridging points across the Atlantic, this was transformative. Her docks were busier than ever, but Bristol was not just a transit point. Beyond the world of the merchant and the ship-owner, significant new industries emerged to handle the imported tobacco and sugar and, as we see in the next chapter, countless craftsmen were able to up their output as they found a new market overseas.

These findings again reinforce the importance of firm quantitative evidence. While previous historians were aware that Bristol was beginning to trade with the Americas in the latter half of the seventeenth century, the qualitative evidence and tonnage-based figures that they used do not show the extent of this revolution in trade. We must re-think our narrative of Bristol's development, tracing its 'Americanisation' and expansion back into the mid-seventeenth century, well before the beginning of slave-trading in 1698. This also has significant implications for how we think about developments beyond Bristol. With previous discussions resting on data from just a few years, the evidence presented here gives the clearest picture to date of the development of trade with North America and the Caribbean in the crucial decades after 1650. Furthermore, previous studies have underestimated the speed and extent of the growth of England's American trades. The re-appraisal presented here suggests that the New World already contributed more than a quarter of English imports as early as the 1660s. The Commercial Revolution identified by Davis seems, therefore, to have been progressing much faster than he supposed, and the Atlantic economy to have already been having a significant impact on England as early as the mid-seventeenth century.

5

Exports

On 8 January 1666 the *Speedwell* of Worcester left the port of Gloucester for Bristol. She was carrying a mixed cargo of malt, ironware, salt, wheat, linen cloth, grocery wares, hops, stockings, bellows, haberdashery wares, hats and chairs.[1] The surviving sources do not, of course, allow us to work out where the goods from the *Speedwell* were sent next. Some may well have been destined for consumption in Bristol itself, but others could have made their way onto a ship such as the *Laurell* of Bristol. Bound for Nevis in the Caribbean, on 8 February (alas in a different year, as there are no years from this period where Overseas and Coastal Port Books match up) she loaded a cargo as varied as that of the *Speedwell*. In her hold were beer, shoes, copper manufactures, earthenware, tobacco pipes, cartwheels, leather chairs, four small bedsteads, two tables and two chests of drawers.[2] Every year Bristol would have seen hundreds of little ships such as the *Speedwell*. In 1699, for example, the Coastal Port Books record 491 vessels arriving in Bristol from ports all around the region.[3] They sailed up and down the River Severn and along the coasts of Somerset, Devon and Wales, bringing all manner of goods to and from Welsh Back, the city's main dock for regional trade. This is a valuable reminder that, while entitled *Bristol and the Birth of the Atlantic Economy*, this book is not about one city. Bristol acted as a node that connected a network spanning the west of England and Wales to a broader network spanning the whole Atlantic world. Growth of trade at Bristol thus had knock-on benefits for producers of a wide range of goods across the whole region. It is also an important reminder of the importance of everyday things. While attention naturally focuses on exotic goods such as sugar, spices, and tobacco, the revolution in Bristol's trade was built as much on the need of those who crossed the Atlantic for everyday items such as pots and pans, shoes and saddles, tables and chairs.

As Nuala Zahedieh has remarked, 'historians of early English expansion and the commercial revolution have neglected the colonial export trade', with

1   Gloucester Coastal Port Books.
2   1671/2 Port Book, f. 7v.
3   D. Hussey, *Coastal and River Trade in Pre-Industrial England: Bristol and Its Region, 1680–1730* (Exeter, 2000), p. 40.

attention instead focusing on 'the "revolutionary" changes in the import, and linked, re-export trades'.[4] The research presented in this chapter very much supports this point, and further argues that the export trade more broadly, not just that with the colonies, merits much greater attention. The chapter opens by considering the range of goods Bristol exported in the second half of the seventeenth century, and the radical transformation of the city's export trade from the cloth monoculture of the latter Middle Ages. It then moves on to consider the sources of manufactured and other goods for Bristol's overseas trade, showing that it provided a market for crafts and manufacture, agriculture and extraction in the city, the region, and beyond. The chapter wraps up by considering exports in different branches of Bristol's trade. The nature of Bristol's exports to the colonies is considered alongside the European trades, arguing that elements of a shared Atlantic material culture emerged in this period. Overall, it is argued that demand for exported goods was fundamental to the development of Bristol's overseas commerce in this period, and indeed could prove to be the most profitable part of the trade, and arguably even its driving force.

Of all of the data provided by the sixteenth- and seventeenth-century customs accounts, those for exports are unfortunately the most difficult to analyse. The sheer complexity and range of goods sent from English shores at times simply defies statistical analysis, even with the aid of technology. Combined with this, the survival of export data from Bristol in the seventeenth century is also poor. The Wharfage Books, which for imports bridge the lacuna in the Port Books between the 1630s and the 1670s, do not record Bristol's exports. Surviving Port Books are also, as ever, few and far between, and those that survive contain imperfect datasets. Those of the Customer and Controller omit re-exported goods, and those of the Searcher do not record the nominal value of the goods or the duty paid. Adjustments to the customs valuations, which were much more significant than those on imported goods, also make it impossible to compare the value of Bristol's export trade from the 1660s onwards to that earlier in the century (problems discussed in more depth in the Technical Appendix). Therefore, this chapter focuses on export Port Books from just two years: 1661/2 and 1671/2. Despite these limitations, however, the data presents some important findings crucial to our understanding of the development of both Bristol's and England's overseas trade and the development of craft and industry in England and Wales.

---

4   N. Zahedieh, *The Capital and the Colonies: London and the Atlantic Economy 1660–1700* (Cambridge, 2010), p. 238.

The Range of Exported Goods

Although there was a smattering of other goods, the late fifteenth-century Particular Accounts show that cloth made up 99 per cent of the value of Bristol's exports to the Iberian Peninsula, and 98 per cent of exports to France.[5] This was almost exclusively the heavy high-quality woollen broadcloth that had become the speciality of West Country clothmaking. As shown in Chapters 1 and 2, in the late sixteenth and early seventeenth centuries (unlike London), Bristol was already well on the way to diversifying its exports.[6] It was this shift towards a wider range of raw materials and manufactured goods that allowed Bristol to withstand commercial competition from the capital. In the second half of the seventeenth century, Bristol truly shifted to the pattern of exports dominated by a broad range of manufactured goods and re-exports that was to characterise English overseas trade in the coming centuries.[7]

As Figure 35 shows, the overall pattern of Bristol's exports in the 1660s and 1670s remained broadly similar to that of the 1630s, with manufactures, agricultural goods, and the produce of the region's mines all featuring prominently. Having declined dramatically in importance in the sixteenth and early seventeenth centuries, textiles were seeing something of a renaissance. With the new market provided by the colonies, and the shift to more marketable types of cloth rather than heavy woollen broadcloth, £17,900 worth of textile exports made up 30 per cent of Bristol's total in 1661/2. A new development was the significant amounts of clothing recorded. A broad assortment of felt hats, stockings, bodices, and all kinds of apparel made up 10 per cent of the value of Bristol's exports in 1661/2, and 13 per cent in 1671/2. This is likely to be a significant underestimate of the value of the clothing trade, as many types of garments appear to have been exempt from customs duties. The defining characteristic of Bristol's export trade at this time, however, was the sheer variety of goods involved. In 1661/2, exports to both the Chesapeake and the Caribbean featured more than 270 distinct classes of goods. Much of this variety is a result of the variety of types of manufactured goods sent out from Bristol, including everything from cartwheels to window glass. Combining textiles, clothing, and other craft goods, more than half of all Bristol's recorded exports were manufactures of one sort or another in both 1661/2 and 1671/2.

5   R. Stone, 'Bristol's Overseas Trade in the Later Fifteenth Century: The Evidence of the Particular Customs Accounts', in E. T. Jones and R. Stone (eds), *The World of the Newport Medieval Ship: Trade, Politics and Shipping in the Mid-Fifteenth* Century (Cardiff, 2018), pp. 192–6.
6   See also R. Stone, 'The Overseas Trade of Bristol before the Civil War', *The International Journal of Maritime History*, 23(2) (2011), pp. 211–39.
7   R. Davis, 'English Foreign Trade, 1660–1700', in W. Minchinton (ed.), *The Growth of English Overseas Trade in the Seventeenth and Eighteenth Centuries* (London, 1969), p. 78.

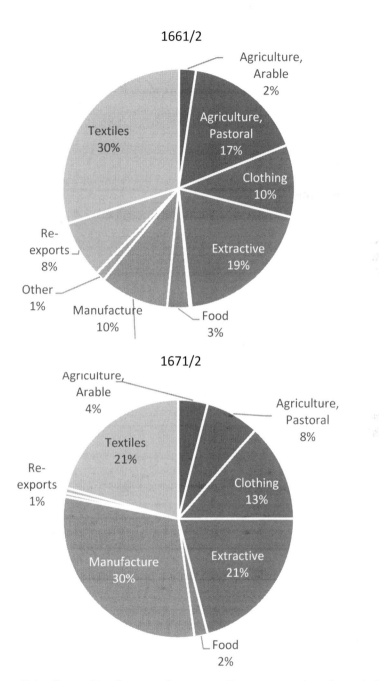

Figure 35. Bristol's combined exports by commodity type, 1661/2 and 1671/2 (in pounds sterling).

Sources: 1661/2 Port Book, 1671/2 Port Book.

Including processed goods takes the total even higher, with most of the iron, lead, and other extracted goods having been refined and processed into bars. Amongst the agricultural goods too, most goods had been processed to aid preservation, including tanned hides, cider and cheese. Interestingly foodstuffs made up a relatively small proportion, highlighting the importance of the Irish provisions trade discussed in Chapter 2.

Re-Exports

One category of Bristol's exports needs separate consideration: re-exports of goods originally produced in the colonies. The terms of the Navigation Acts meant that all tobacco and sugar produced in the English colonies had to be brought back to England. Due to this protectionist legislation, it was not possible to send Virginian tobacco or Barbadian sugar directly to markets in continental Europe.[8] For Ralph Davis, the growth of the re-export trade was one of the most important developments in English commerce in the second half of the seventeenth century. Having barely featured before the Civil War, American and Asian products made up as much as 30 per cent of the English export trade by the end of the century, breaking the centuries-old reliance on woollen cloth.[9] Due to the reliance on customs records to examine overseas trade, Bristol's re-export trade is very difficult to study. Indeed, I have previously erroneously written that there was no evidence of Bristol having a significant trade in re-exported tobacco and sugar in the 1670s.[10] This is because re-exported goods were not liable for customs duties when they were sent out of the country; indeed, they would have received a rebate on any tax paid when they were brought into England, or even held in bonded storage to avoid paying any import duty.[11] As they paid no tax, re-exported tobacco and sugar were of no interest to the Customer and Controller (as their role was

---

8   Zahedieh, *Capital and the Colonies*, pp. 36–8.
9   Davis, 'English Foreign Trade', p. 78.
10   R. Stone, 'The Overseas Trade of Bristol in the Seventeenth Century' (unpublished PhD thesis, University of Bristol, 2012), pp. 202–4. I am extremely grateful to Dr Jonathan Harlow for pointing out to me that the Searchers did record re-exports. This was on the day after I had had the final copies of my PhD thesis bound, and I have wanted to correct this ever since!
11   The existence of a bonded store is hinted at by a couple of small entries of tobacco on the import side of the accounts, recorded as having come from 'the King's Storehouse'. Bonded warehouses for tobacco were not formally introduced until 1733, and it has not been possible to find any reference to either seventeenth-century 'bonded warehouses' or 'the King's Storehouse' in the existing literature on the customs service. There was, however, a 'King's Warehouse' in London dating back to the seventeenth century 'in which goods were stored as security for duties or to await condemnation after seizure'. W. J. Ashworth, *Customs and Excise: Trade, Production, and Consumption in England, 1640–1845* (Oxford, 2003), p. 69; E. E. Hoon, *The Organisation of the English Customs System 1696–1786* (Newton Abbot, 1968), p. 150.

to record the tax collected), and thus they do not appear in the Customer and Controller's Port Books that I used to write my thesis. The Searcher, however, was responsible for checking what goods were actually on the ships, and thus he did record re-exported goods. More recent examination of the 1661/2 Searcher's Port Book has thus revealed that Bristol did re-export colonial goods on a noteworthy scale. This year saw £4,100 worth of re-exports, making up just under 7 per cent of Bristol's total declared export trade. The vast majority was tobacco, with £3,400 worth of the leaf re-exported compared to £700 worth of colonial sugar. Much of this tobacco went to Spain, with £1,300 worth of tobacco and decayed tobacco making up around 8 per cent of Bristol's Iberian exports. Re-exports to France were minimal, consisting of just £237 worth of tobacco. The lion's share, therefore, was sent to Ireland. Tobacco worth £2,100 and £700 worth of sugar made up more than 17 per cent of Bristol's exports to Ireland in 1661/2.

By the 1660s, Bristol's re-export trade was still much less significant than the 30 per cent of English exports that Davis suggested re-exported goods represented by 1700. There are a number of potential explanations. One is Davis's suggestion that 'the outports had little share in this [re-export] trade'.[12] This observation, however, may simply be a result of the London-centric nature of the evidence he had available to him. Secondly, it may be a result of the types of goods Bristol had access to. The most important of England's re-exports at the end of the seventeenth century were Indian linens and calicoes.[13] As the source of these goods was controlled by the London-based East India Company, they did not feature significantly at Bristol. Perhaps most important is simply that 1661/2 was very early in the development of the re-export trade. Indeed, Davis suggested that 'much of that growth certainly took place after 1669' and that 'tobacco and sugar re-exports in the 1660s cannot have been of very large dimensions as compared with the 1699–1701 figures'.[14] Unfortunately the 1671/2 Bristol Port Book does not record re-exports, so tobacco shipments from the 1678 Searcher's Book have instead been sampled to establish the growth of the trade.[15] This shows more than 1.5 million lb of tobacco being re-exported from Bristol, an exponential growth from the 42,400 lb shipped in 1661/2. The spread of markets remained similar, with Ireland taking 60 per cent of the total. More than 100,000 lb, though, was shipped to both Spain and the Netherlands, 75,000 to France and 32,000 to the Baltic. Due to the difficulty of estimating a reliable price for re-exported tobacco, it is hard to gauge exactly

12   Davis, 'English Foreign Trade', p. 89.
13   *Ibid.*
14   *Ibid.*, p. 89.
15   1678 Port Book. I am grateful to Dr Jonathan Harlow for providing me with these figures.

how important this new trade was to Bristol.[16] Clearly, however, it had become highly significant to maintaining the growth of Bristol's trade with Ireland and the continent, demonstrating the significant extent to which trade with the Americas had become interlinked with Bristol's commercial world as a whole.

Sources of Goods

Coastal and River Trade

The name Bristol comes from the Anglo-Saxon 'Brig Stowe', meaning 'place by the bridge'. At its heart, Bristol is and always has been a place where road and river networks meet, the ideal place for a market. In the long term, Bristol's proximity to the sea, and thus access to international trade, determined its fortunes. Yet its connections to roads and particularly rivers remained crucial. It was through these arteries that Bristol sourced many of the goods it then sent to all parts of the world, and in return distributed the foreign wares it received to a wider market. Walter Minchinton described Bristol as the 'Metropolis of the West' (a phrase oft-quoted because it is so apt).[17] Minchinton was writing about the eighteenth century, but this chapter suggests that Bristol was performing this entrepôt role for the West Country long before that.

The core dataset behind this book is the Overseas Port Books, providing a detailed record of all the goods that passed through the port of Bristol bound to or from ports in other countries. Fortunately, Port Books also exist for the coastal trade, as, while they were not taxable, it was necessary for the Customer and Controller to keep track of goods moving along the coast to make sure they were not being smuggled overseas.[18] 'Coastal' also includes riverine trade, with the port of Gloucester upriver from Bristol, and recognised creeks for unloading and loading of goods as far up the Severn as Shrewsbury. Fully analysing the Coastal Port Books for Bristol and its region would be a monograph-length study in itself. Fortunately, although focusing predominantly on the very late seventeenth and early eighteenth centuries, such a study has already been carried out by David Hussey. This chapter, therefore, will simply analyse the exports from Gloucester to Bristol recorded in Gloucester's 1666 Coastal Port Book to give an overall impression of the types of goods being brought to Bristol by river in the mid-seventeenth century. As much of the riverine trade passed through Gloucester, with the port acting as something of an entrepôt in its own

---

16   A rough calculation based on the import duty for tobacco suggests that the 1678 re-exports (£123,600) were worth more than twice as much as all recorded exports in 1661/2 (£61,600). This, however, is likely to be a significant overestimate.

17   W. E. Minchinton, 'Bristol, Metropolis of the West in the Eighteenth Century', *Transactions of the Royal Historical Society*, 4 (1954), pp. 69–89.

18   Hussey, *Coastal and River Trade*, p. 7.

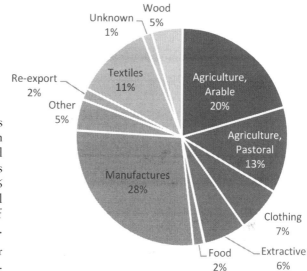

Figure 36. Shipments of goods from Gloucester to Bristol by commodity type, as recorded in the 1666 Gloucester Coastal Port Book (number of shipments).

Source: Gloucester Coastal Port Books.

right, and as more than a third of all coastal voyages bound for Bristol left from Gloucester, this dataset provides a fair indication of the types of goods passing along the Severn to Bristol.[19] Hussey's findings, then, provide an understanding of the flow of goods into Bristol from the region more broadly.

As they were not tax records, and thus contain no financial valuation of the goods, the Coastal Port Books are harder to analyse than most of their Overseas counterparts. Indeed, the Books of Rates do not seem to have been used at all when compiling them, resulting in a wide variety of units of measure that it is not possible to standardise for comparative purposes. 'Apparel' for example (a label which itself could include all kinds of goods) was recorded in baskets, boxes, packs, trunks, and trusses. The broad unit of 'the shipment' has thus been adopted here. While this does not give any indication of either the volume or importance of particular types of goods in Bristol's coastal trade, it at least gives an indication of the regularity with which they appeared.[20] In all, 1,424 shipments of goods from Gloucester into Bristol were recorded in 1666, covering many of the key classes of Bristol's overseas exports. Manufactured goods of all shapes and sizes were the most common, with 395 shipments making up 28 per cent of the total. These included 31 shipments of bellows, 25 of paper, 9 of scythes, as well as trunks, boxes, brass pots, ironware, earthenware, and even greater variety hidden within broad labels such as the 16 shipments of

---

19   *Ibid.*, p. 18.
20   This is similar to the approach taken by Hussey's study, which used 'the voyage' as its unit of measure. Hussey, *Coastal and River Trade*, p. 23.

'household goods'. A wide array of craftsmen from the surrounding region were clearly feeding their goods into the Bristol market, and from thence to consumers overseas. Given the ongoing importance of cloth to Bristol's trade, unsurprisingly a wide range of textiles were also shipped from Gloucester. Amongst these were 53 shipments of linen, 21 of Kidderminster stuff and 12 of cottons. Clothing was also prominent, with hats and stockings, at 31 shipments each, amongst the most common goods. As these were recorded in a diverse assortment of bags, baskets, boxes, packs, trusses and trunks, it is impossible to calculate how many hats, stockings, and other items of clothing came down the Severn to Bristol. Again, however, it is likely that many of these garments were eventually bound overseas, and particularly to the American colonies, with around 10 per cent of Bristol's overseas exports at this time consisting of clothing.

While textiles and other manufactured goods made up 46 per cent of shipments from Gloucester to Bristol in 1666, less heavily processed goods were also important. Agricultural goods featured prominently, split between pastoral produce (182 shipments) and arable (292). This included large quantities of calf-skins (71 shipments), probably to be tanned in Bristol, and also malt and hops for use in brewing (94 and 66 shipments). Foodstuffs such as cheese, cider, bacon and peas were much more common than in the overseas trade, suggesting that these were destined to feed the city itself and its ships, rather than for export. According to this method of calculating trade, mined goods did not feature particularly prominently, making up just 6 per cent of shipments. This figure, however, is misleading, as individual shipments of these goods could be much greater in volume than was the case with other commodities. There were, for example, more than 360 tons of iron in various forms, along with 145 tons, 778 pigs and 440 bars of lead. With just sixteen shipments of bar iron recorded, each one would have on average consisted of more than 11 tons, enough to make up most of the cargo of one of the Severn trows responsible for carrying this trade.[21] Coastwise shipments were the source of much of the metal that made up around a fifth of Bristol's overseas exports in the 1660s and 1670s, as well as the raw materials for many of the goods manufactured in the city. Indeed, such was the importance of metal from Bristol's hinterland to its overseas trade that many of the city's merchants invested in its production. For example, Walter Sandy was amongst the founders of the Ynyspenllwch ironworks in the Swansea Valley; in the 1640s John Taylor and John Gonning purchased shares in ironworks in the Forest of Dean (Gloucestershire); and in the 1650s John Stone was investing in an experimental iron smelting works

21 C. Green, *Severn Traders: The Westcountry Trows and Trowmen* (Gloucestershire, 1999).

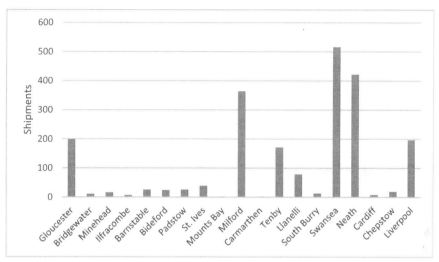

Figure 37. Shipments of 'extractive' goods from Bristol Channel ports.

Source: Hussey, *Coastal and River Trade*, p. 62.

near Bristol.[22] As Figure 37 shows, considerable amounts of extractive goods were shipped coastwise from the ports of South Wales, such as Milford Haven, Tenby, Llanelli, Swansea and Neath. This included considerable quantities of coal, which was sent all around the region, and a great deal of lead, much of which fed the burgeoning shot industry in Bristol.[23]

As Hussey remarked, 'even with the aid of computerised techniques, no work can ever do complete justice to the complexity and diversity of the total sum of commodities traded' within Bristol and its region.[24] While more may be possible with extensive transcription of the Coastal Port Books, ultimately the patchy and inconsistent nature of the data, with its bewildering array of non-standardised weights and measures, simply defies analysis. Unfortunately, most historical records were not created to meet historians' needs. Nonetheless, a few further broad observations about the contribution of Bristol's hinterland to the city's overseas trade can be made based on Hussey's data.[25] Each of the coastal and river ports in Bristol's extensive hinterland sent a different blend of goods to the city, based in turn on the makeup of trade and agriculture in

22   H. E. Nott, *The Deposition Books of Bristol, Volume 1: 1643–1647*, Bristol Record Society Vol. 6 (Bristol, 1935), p. 254; P. V. McGrath, *Merchants and Merchandise in Seventeenth Century Bristol*, Bristol Record Society Vol. 19 (Bristol, 1955), pp. 110–11, 114–15.

23   Hussey, *Coastal and River Trade*, pp. 79, 96–9.

24   *Ibid.*, p. 102.

25   The following observations are based on Hussey, *Coastal and River Trade*, pp. 90–103.

their own hinterlands. Up the River Severn, Bewdley served as a redistribution point for the hardware manufacturers of Birmingham and the Black Country, sending all manner of iron and ironware to Bristol, along with some salt and Kidderminster cloth. Worcester sent arable goods, especially hops, along with salt from the Droitwich brineries. Shrewsbury focused on agricultural goods, while Ironbridge and Bridgnorth sent both coal and ironware (linked to Bristol, of course, through the investment in Abraham Derby's furnaces). Gloucester was an entrepôt in its own right, sending a broad array of goods downriver, as well as to the other ports of the region. Turning to the Somerset coast, Minehead and the riverine port of Bridgwater focused on agricultural produce, both crops and garden produce from the rich lands of Taunton Deane, and livestock from the Somerset Levels, Brendan Hills and Exmoor. In North Devon, Barnstaple and Bideford were noteworthy international ports in their own right, focusing especially on Ireland and Newfoundland. Fish thus feature regularly amongst their coastwise trade, along with the produce of the region's increasingly commercialised agriculture (both pastoral and arable). Forty per cent of their coastal voyages featured craft and manufactured goods, in particular the great quantity of earthenware produced in their hinterlands. Ilfracombe's coastal exports, on the other hand, were much less diverse, consisting primarily of fish. The Cornish ports were different in character again, sending a variety of metals and extractive goods, particularly copper ore, tin, and pewter wares. As noted above, the Welsh ports Milford, Carmarthen, Tenby, Swansea and Neath shipped great quantities of extractive goods, with coal particularly dominant. At Neath and Swansea trade mainly consisted of coal, but the other ports also sent some low-grade cloth and clothing, as well as sizeable quantities of agricultural goods. The trade of Cardiff and Chepstow was predominantly agricultural in character, with rich agricultural hinterlands in South Wales, and, in the case of Chepstow, the cider orchards of Herefordshire.

Overland Trade

While many of the goods exported by Bristol doubtlessly came to the city by river or along the coast, some came overland. Unfortunately, however, as they were not subject to the scrutiny of the customs officials in the same way as goods put aboard ships, Bristol's overland trade is much more difficult to trace. A hint that this trade was substantial, however, comes from the city's Burgess Books. All of those who registered as a freeman of the city would record their trade here, giving a good indication of the types of employment in Bristol. In the 1650s, five men registered as couriers, and another eleven as hauliers. In the 1670s these numbers were even higher, with thirteen new couriers and twenty-one hauliers recorded.[26] While far short of the 181 mariners and seamen

---

26   *Index to the Bristol Burgess Books, Volumes 1 to 21: 1557–1995* (Bristol, 2005).

recorded in the 1670s, this makes it clear that significant amounts of goods were brought to and from Bristol by road as well as by water. The names of some of the goods being exported from Bristol also show the breadth of the region from which the city sourced its export goods. Types of cloth included, for example, Norwich stuffs from East Anglia, as well as Manchester and Northern cottons, and Kidderminster stuffs from the Midlands. A final hint at the role of overland trade comes from a variety of re-exported goods that simply do not feature amongst Bristol's imports. These include commodities such as coffee, and spices such as mace, pepper and nutmeg. Originating in the monopoly-protected trades, these goods had almost certainly come into England via London. Given the long trip around the south coast, and their high value in relation to bulk, road transport is by far the most likely way for them to have come to Bristol.

The ledger of Bristol merchant Thomas Speed gives a further indication of the source of one of Bristol's key export goods: stockings. The stocking-knitting industry had developed rapidly over the course of the sixteenth and seventeenth centuries, and found a market in all parts of Europe, with Pauline Croft's study of stockings in the London Port Books showing them being sent to destinations as far apart as Sweden and Sevilla.[27] The Burgess Books suggest very few stocking-makers were in Bristol itself, with just one stocking-maker and one hosier registering as freemen in the 1650s and only two hosiers in the 1670s.[28] Stocking-knitting was a craft practised principally in the countryside surrounding Bristol. Speed had around a dozen regular suppliers for his stockings, who brought in large consignments of up to 180 pairs at a time. Rather than those knitting the stockings themselves, these were larger-scale manufacturers, putting out the raw materials to hand-knitters to work at home, and collecting the finished stockings. Speed's stockings were produced in Somerset, in particular around the cathedral city of Wells (more akin to a small town in terms of size) where stocking-making was a principal industry.[29]

Manufacturing in Bristol

Bristol itself was an important manufacturing centre, and doubtlessly many of the exported goods were made within the city itself. The seventeenth century lacks a trade directory like those used to examine later Bristol businesses, but the registering of freemen under particular crafts in the Burgess Books can to an extent take its place.[30] These are substantial records, containing tens of

27   P. Croft, 'The Rise of the English Stocking Export Trade', *Textile History*, 18(1) (1987), pp. 3–16.
28   *Index to the Bristol Burgess Books.*
29   J. Harlow (ed.), *The Ledger of Thomas Speed, 1681–1690*, Bristol Record Society Vol. 63 (Bristol, 2011), p. xxxv.
30   Kenneth Morgan, for example, used Sketchley's *Bristol Directory* from 1775. See K. Morgan, *Bristol and Atlantic Trade in the Eighteenth Century* (Cambridge, 1993), p. 97.

1650s

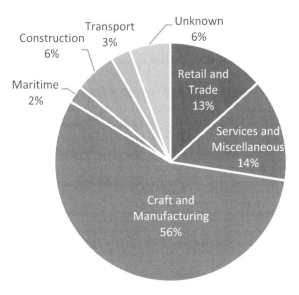

1670s

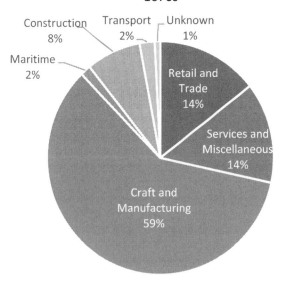

Figure 38. Occupation of freemen registered in the Bristol Burgess Books, 1650s and 1670s.

Source: *Index to the Bristol Burgess Books.*

thousands of entries from the mid-sixteenth century to the twentieth century, so two key decades have been sampled to establish the impact of developments in overseas trade on employment in the city: the 1650s and the 1670s (see Figure 38 and Table 6). While not a complete record of employment in the city, registrations in the Burgess Books still represent a considerable proportion of Bristol's workforce. Of Bristol's population of 15,000–20,000 in the mid-seventeenth century, more than 1,200 freemen registered in the 1650s, and almost 1,800 in the 1670s.[31]

Table 6. Occupation of freemen registered in the Bristol Burgess Books, 1650s and 1670s.

Occupation	1650s	1670s
Apothecary	5	21
Baker	32	43
Barber surgeon	8	33
Blacksmith	16	15
Brewer	20	12
Butcher	23	34
Carpenter	25	32
Cooper	100	136
Cordwainer	6	20
Gentleman	17	21
Glazier	2	16
Grocer	35	57
Hallier	11	21
House carpenter	4	19
Joiner	15	42
Linnen draper	13	18
Mariner	57	169
Mercer	25	23
Merchant	57	86
Milliner	18	13

31   For a discussion of Bristol's population in the seventeenth century, see J. Barry, 'The Hearth Tax and Bristol Population Estimates', in R. Leech, J. Barry, A. Brown, C. Ferguson and E. Parkinson (eds), *The Bristol Hearth Tax, 1662–1673*, Bristol Record Society Vol. 70 (Bristol, 2018), pp. 314–19.

Table 6 *continued*

Occupation	1650s	1670s
Pewterer	12	22
Pin-maker	4	16
Shipwright	23	72
Shoe-maker	51	42
Silk-weaver	8	27
Soap-boiler	42	56
Soap-maker	10	20
Tailor	71	69
Tiler	6	30
Vintner	9	26
Weaver	19	29
Whittawer	16	20
Other retail and trade	40	44
Other services	59	75
Other manufacturing	277	327
Other maritime	9	15
Other construction	11	27
Other transport	18	18
Unknown	71	14

Source: *Index to the Bristol Burgess Books.*

According to the Burgess Books, by far the biggest employment sector in Bristol in the post-Civil War decades was manufacturing. In both the 1650s and the 1670s, more than half of all new freemen enrolled declared their occupation to be some type of craft or manufacturing. No one trade dominated, however, with 104 different manufacturing professions given in the 1670s, and 88 in the 1650s. Perhaps unsurprisingly in a port city such as Bristol, the most common types of manufacturing were those associated with the sea. Both decades saw 100 or more coopers enrolled, who would have made and maintained the many barrels needed to move around the goods which Bristol was trading. There were also large numbers of shipwrights, with 72 registered in the 1670s and 23 in the 1650s. Large numbers of people also worked directly in shipping and trade, with the 1670s seeing 169 mariners and 86 merchants, the largest and third-largest professions respectively.

The range of goods produced in Bristol was diverse, with no one craft dominating. In the 1650s and 1670s there were large numbers of tailors (71 and 69), soap-boilers (42 and 56), shoe-makers (51 and 42) silk-weavers (8 and 27) and pewterers (12 and 22). Clearly much of their trade would have catered for domestic demand in both Bristol and its hinterland. These were already common professions in the city when records of enrolling freemen began in the 1520s.[32] Given the importance of such goods to Bristol's overseas trade, however (and particularly that with the Americas), it certainly seems that the export market was providing a significant additional outlet for craftsmen in the city. Although not as dominant as once it had been, there were also still noteworthy numbers of people employed in the various stages of cloth production. The 1670s, for example, saw ninety-seven of the new freemen working in textiles. This made up less than 6 per cent of the total, although it still would have been a very visible occupation in the city, with Millerd's map of 1673 showing a large 'Rack Close' in the Temple district, and Brandon Hill reserved 'for the use of drying cloaths'.[33] The types of cloth made in Bristol too had shifted to meet the demands of the overseas markets. Rather than the traditional heavy woollen broadcloth, the city now housed 18 linen-drapers, 27 silk-weavers, and 6 serge-makers. Other types of manufacturing were as diverse as Bristol's exports. The city held saddlers, trunk-makers, gunsmiths, upholsterers, periwig-makers, glass-makers, pin-makers, and even a maker of mathematical instruments. The output of most of these crafts features amongst Bristol's exports. Notably, though, some key types of goods that Bristol was shipping do not seem to have been produced in the city in significant quantities, suggesting that they were brought in from the region. There were, for example, comparatively few makers of felt hats (fourteen in the 1650s and five in the 1670s) and even fewer stocking-makers (just one in the 1650s). A final point is the sheer increase in the number of people employed in Bristol as its engagement with the Atlantic economy began to boost its economy. The first three decades of the Burgess Books (1557–87) saw an average of just 573 new freemen enrolled per decade, and the first half of the seventeenth century (1607–51) an average of 983. This compares to 1,245 registrations in the 1650s, and 1,780 in the 1670s.

32   R. Price, *Bristol Burgesses: 1525–1557, Calendared from the Corporation's Great Audit Books* (Bristol, 2010).
33   J. Millerd, *An Exact Delineation of the Famous Citty of Bristoll and Suburbs Thereof* (Bristol, 1673).

Goods for the Colonies

In the ongoing debates on the relationship between slavery and the Industrial Revolution, the role of the colonies in spurring development by providing a market for manufactured goods is one of the most enduring arguments. Many of the arguments proposed by Eric Williams in *Capitalism and Slavery* have been persuasively challenged by subsequent scholarship.[34] Profits from the transatlantic traffic in enslaved people, for example, have been shown to be much lower than Williams believed, and are unlikely to have provided sufficient capital to finance industrialisation.[35] Much recent scholarship has, however, further developed the broader arguments of the Williams thesis. In particular, Joseph Inikori has reinvigorated the debate by highlighting close links between the colonies and the development of industry in the northern regions of Britain that became the heartlands of the Industrial Revolution in the nineteenth century. This included both the key role of American cotton as a raw material for English industry, and the significant market for English manufactured goods in the Caribbean and North America.[36] Examining the role of Bristol's early colonial trade in the expansion of manufacturing in the city and the region, as above, thus makes an important contribution to these discussions.

As Figure 38 shows, Bristol's exports to the American colonies were broadly similar in makeup to the city's exports more broadly, although with a greater emphasis on cloth and other types of manufactured goods, and less on agricultural products. Textiles and clothing were the most important exports to Chesapeake Bay, making up 76 per cent of exports in 1661/2, and 51 per cent in 1671/2. Given that many garments did not incur export duty, this is likely to be a significant underestimate. They were less prominent in the Caribbean trade, making up just 46 per cent of exports in 1661/2 and 26 per cent in 1671/2. This may reflect the greater extent of enslaved labour in the Caribbean, resulting in less expenditure on clothing the workforce. Textiles, however, were not the only manufactured goods sent to the colonies, with a broad range of manufactured items forming the other major component of Bristol's American export trade. These rose considerably in importance over the decade between the two Port Books, rising from 17 per cent of exports to the Chesapeake in 1661/2 to 46 per cent in 1671/2, and from 14 per cent of exports to the Caribbean to 56 per cent. Like the Irish trade discussed in Chapter 2, these manufactures were bewildering in their variety, so much so that the customs officers simply lumped them together under the collective label 'wares'. Over £1,500 worth of

---

34 E. Williams, *Capitalism and Slavery* (London, 1964).

35 For a summary of the debates, see K. Morgan, *Slavery, Atlantic Trade, and the British Economy, 1660–1800* (Cambridge, 2000), pp. 41–8.

36 J. Inikori, 'Atlantic Slavery and the Rise of the Capitalist Global Economy', *Current Anthropology*, 61 (2020), p. 166.

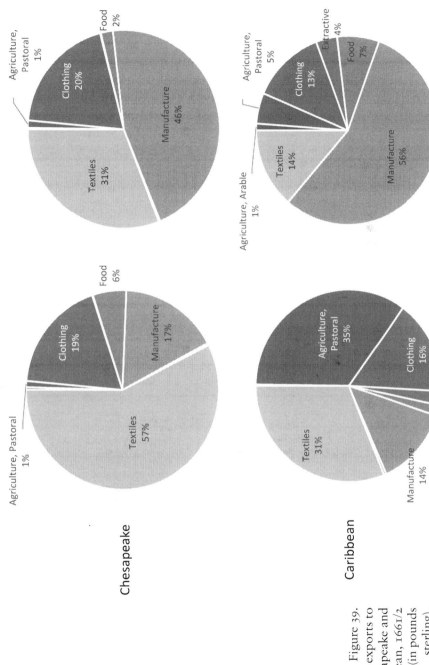

Figure 39.
Bristol's exports to
the Chesapeake and
Caribbean, 1661/2
and 1671/2 (in pounds
sterling).

Sources: 1661/2 Port
Book, 1671/2 Port Book.

1670s

Agriculture,
Pastoral
1%

Food
2%

Clothing
20%

Manufacture
46%

Textiles
31%

1650s

Food
6%

Clothing
19%

Manufacture
17%

Textiles
57%

Agriculture, Pastoral
1%

Chesapeake

Agriculture,
Pastoral
5%

Extractive
4%

Food
7%

Clothing
13%

Manufacture
56%

Textiles
14%

Agriculture, Arable
1%

Agriculture,
Pastoral
35%

Clothing
16%

Extractive
2%

Food
2%

Manufacture
14%

Textiles
31%

Caribbean

goods labelled as wares were sent to both the Caribbean and the Chesapeake in 1671/2, making up between a quarter and a third of recorded exports. Among the manufactured goods sent to the plantation colonies that can be identified from the customs records can be found a mixture of high- and low-status goods. These included mundane items such as large quantities of ironware and nails, which were staples of trade with both regions, and a wide range of household items and furniture, from books to feather beds, and saddles to tobacco pipes.

While Chapter 6 deals with Bristol's 'export' of human labourers to the New World, the large number of horses shipped to the Caribbean is also worthy of mention when discussing Bristol's role in supplying labour to the colonies. Indeed, at times this equine trade formed a key part of Bristol's trans-atlantic exports. In 1661/2 more than 300 horses were shipped from Bristol to the Caribbean, comprising 117 geldings and 202 'naggs'. Valued at more than £2,000, these shipments of horses made up more than 30 per cent of Bristol's exports to the Caribbean (they appear under 'Agriculture, Pastoral' in Figure 39). Indeed, these exports of horses were in fact more valuable than Bristol's exports of indentured servants that year. Contrastingly, very few horses appear in the 1671/2 export account, which features just one horse, and a few nags (possibly small horses or ponies). There were, however, many saddles and other horse furniture, suggesting that horses still formed an important part of the New World labour force. The more northerly colonies, which could not make a living from cash crops in the same way as their more southerly counterparts, also increasingly developed farming enterprises focused on supplying the Caribbean. They eventually became the main suppliers of food, timber and horses to the sugar plantations, so it may well be that the decline of Bristol's horse trade was caused by the emergence of a closer source of supply in New England and elsewhere.[37]

By the 1670s, goods shipped to the colonies still made up a relatively small proportion of both the value and volume of Bristol's exports, with £5,300 worth sent to the Caribbean in 1671/2 and £4,300 worth to the Chesapeake, making up around 16 per cent of Bristol's total recorded exports. Nonetheless, their focus on cloth, clothing, and manufactures (with less agricultural and extractive produce) means their economic impact on Bristol and its region should not be underestimated. It would be too much to argue that demand from the colonies was driving a revolution in industry at this point. As Chapters 1 and 2 have shown, manufacturing was already developing by the early seventeenth century as a result of demand from Ireland and continental Europe, and (as will be shown in the following section) this continued alongside the growth of the continental trade. Nonetheless, the sheer variety of wares consumed by the

37   R. Davis, *The Rise of the English Shipping Industry in the Seventeenth and Eighteenth Centuries* (Liverpool, 2018), pp. 279–80.

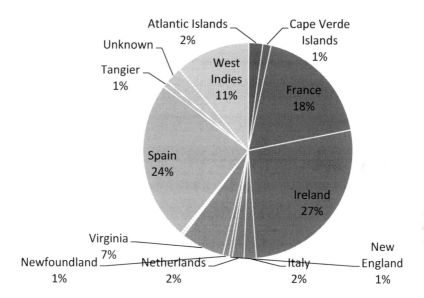

Figure 40. Bristol's exports by market according to the 1662 Port Book (in pounds sterling).

Source: 1662 Port Book. Valuations of goods have been adjusted to account for alterations to the Book of Rates valuations. See Technical Appendix for a full explanation.

colonies, alongside the increased demand that they presented, certainly played a part in fuelling increased manufacturing in both the city of Bristol and its region, as observed above.

European Trade

It would be easy to assume that, following the spectacular growth of Bristol's new North American and Caribbean trades, the city's trades with Europe began to wither. This, however, was not the case. While not continuing the impressive rate of growth seen in the late sixteenth and early seventeenth centuries, Bristol's trade with France and the Iberian nations remained significant in the latter half of the seventeenth century (see Figure 41). These trades were merely overshadowed, rather than crowded out, by the new transatlantic commerce. Indeed, as Figure 40 shows, on the export side European markets remained very significant to Bristol, with goods sent to the continent surpassing those sent to the New World. The £11,000 worth of exports sent to France in 1662 made up 20 per cent of the trade, and the £15,000 worth that went to Spain and Portugal, 24 per cent. With much longer voyages, transport costs were much higher in

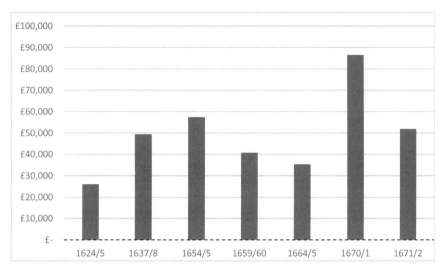

Figure 41. Bristol's Iberian imports as recorded in the Port Books and Wharfage Books, 1624/5–1671/2 (in pounds sterling).

Sources: D. H. Sacks, *The Widening Gate: Bristol and the Atlantic Economy 1450–1700* (Berkeley, 1991), pp. 42–3; TNA PRO E190/1136/10, E190/1137/3, E190/1138/1; BRO SMV/7/1/1/1; SMV/7/1/1/2. Figures prior to 1654/5 have been doubled to account for increases in the customs valuations.

the transatlantic trades, and thus the goods themselves formed a much smaller percentage of the initial capital outlay than in the nearby trades. While the Americas thus provided an additional market for English manufactures, in the mid-seventeenth century more goods produced in Bristol and its region were still being marketed on the continent.

Iberian Peninsula
Although it fluctuated, on the whole Bristol's trade with the Iberian Peninsula continued the prosperity of the half-century before the English Civil War. Even adjusting for increases in the customs values, the £57,000 worth of Iberian goods imported in 1654/5 shows continued growth since 1637/8. The figures from 1659/60 and 1664/5 show a drop-off in Spanish trade, almost certainly as a result of the tensions surrounding the Anglo-Spanish War (1654–60). Even so, with imports of £41,000 and £35,000 respectively, these years still saw more goods coming from the Peninsula than at any time before the 1630s. By the 1670s it is clear that trade was once more booming, with the value of imports as high as £86,000 in 1670/1. Imports in 1671/2 were again down, although this can be accounted for by the disruption to European shipping caused by the outbreak of the Third Anglo-Dutch War.

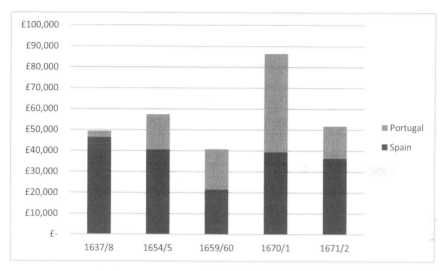

Figure 42. Bristol's Iberian imports by country of origin, 1637/8–1671/2 (in pounds sterling).

Sources: TNA PRO E190/1136/10, E190/1137/3, E190/1138/1; BRO SMV/7/1/1/1; SMV/7/1/1/2. The value for 1637/8 has been doubled to take account of changes in the customs rates. All other values were calculated using the '1675 Book of Rates', with wine given a nominal value of £16 per ton.

Key to the success of Bristol's Iberian trades in the second half of the seventeenth century was growing commercial links with newly independent Portugal. Trade with Portuguese ports had been fairly minimal in 1637/8, but in 1654/5 reached nearly £17,000, already making up more than a quarter of Iberian imports (see Figure 42). By 1659/60 this trade had become even more significant, with imports worth £19,000 from Portugal not far off the £21,500 from Spain. Although it was affected by the outbreak of the Anglo-Dutch War in 1672, the Port Books clearly show the growing importance of Portuguese trade after the Restoration. Bristol's imports from Portugal had grown to more than £47,000 in 1670/1, easily surpassing the value of Spanish imports in that year (£39,400). The vast majority of Bristol's Portuguese trade was centred on Lisbon, Portugal's monopoly port for transatlantic trade.[38] In 1654/5, for example, Lisbon accounted for £15,000 of Bristol's £16,000 worth of imports from Portugal. Although 1659/60 also saw £6,000 worth of goods come in from Faro, it seems likely that this port was being used during the Anglo-Spanish War as an entrepôt for trade with Sevilla, which lies just across the Gulf of

38 P. O'Flanagan, *Port Cities of Atlantic Iberia, c. 1500–1900* (Aldershot, 2008), pp. 129–54.

Cadiz.[39] As throughout the previous century, Bristol's Spanish trade remained focused on southern Andalusia, and in particular the outports of Sevilla. This continued focus of Bristol's Iberian trade around the two official centres for transatlantic commerce shows that, even once the city had its own direct trade with American colonies, it continued to benefit indirectly through the impact of New World silver on the Spanish economy (see Chapter 1).

Far from being superseded by Bristol's growing trade with the American colonies, the Iberian links that had been the backbone of its late sixteenth- and early seventeenth-century expansion continued to prosper alongside the new trades. Indeed, some merchants continued to favour 'traditional' commercial links with the continent, and there is even some evidence that they may have been more profitable than the new transatlantic trades. Surviving merchants' private records are unfortunately rare, with only two complete ledgers existing from Bristol for the period covered by this book. One of these is that of the Quaker merchant Thomas Speed, covering 1681–90. This ledger has been examined in depth by Jonathan Harlow, who combined it with other records such as the Wharfage Books to establish Speed's trading activities over the course of his long career.[40] From the 1650s onwards Speed combined transatlantic and European trade. In the initial boom years of the American trades Harlow's figures suggest that this was relatively balanced, with tobacco and sugar making up 48 per cent of Speed's imports. Later, however, when the prices for colonial goods had begun to wane, Speed shifted towards European trade. Between 1675 and 1694, wine, oil and dried fruit made up more than 60 per cent of his import trade.[41] It seems that Speed found European trade more profitable than that with the colonies: the ledger shows that in the 1680s Speed made an average profit of 17 per cent on his trade in wine, and over the same period, a loss of 2 per cent on his sales of sugar, and did not trade regularly in tobacco. Profits on raisins were less spectacular than wine at 2.5 per cent, but even so the shorter voyages meant that capital was not tied up for long, allowing re-investment and thus greater overall profits.[42] These figures provide a valuable, salutary lesson, that a new trade expanding significantly in volume does not necessarily mean a significant expansion in profits for the merchants concerned. As was the case with Speed, the steady transactions of the older forms of commerce could, in the long run, prove more profitable. Equally, however, it is important to note that Speed's surviving ledger comes from a

---

39   This is an interesting development from the latter sixteenth century, when the French ports of La Rochelle and Saint Jean de Luz were used to facilitate trade with Spain throughout the Armada War. See Chapter 1 of this volume; and P. Croft, 'Trading with the Enemy 1585–1604', *The Historical Journal*, 32(2) (1989), pp. 281–302.

40   J. A. S. Harlow, 'The Life and Times of Thomas Speed' (unpublished PhD thesis, University of the West of England, 2008).

41   Harlow, *The Ledger of Thomas Speed*, pp. xxx–xxxi.

42   *Ibid.*, pp. xxxi–xxxii.

period when the price for sugar was depressed.[43] Unfortunately no comparable records survive from the earlier period, but it seems probable that in the 1650s, 1660s and 1670s (and indeed much of the eighteenth century) Bristol merchants' profits on colonial sugar and tobacco would have been much greater than those realised by Speed in the 1680s.

As Table 7 shows, Thomas Speed was far from unique in dividing his trading activities between the new transatlantic trades and the traditional European ones. Of Bristol's twenty leading import merchants in 1671/2, all imported some goods from the colonies, and fifteen declared imports from Europe. In most cases, though, American trade dominated, with the two leading importers, Edward Fielding and Richard Crumpp, focusing almost exclusively on colonial commerce. John Speed, elder brother of Thomas, also imported £5,500 worth of goods from the New World and just £250 from the continent. Even at this stage, though, some were more balanced, with William Hayman, for example, importing £5,100 worth of goods from the colonies and £4,700 worth from European markets. Although not exclusively the case, those more heavily involved in European trade tended to be members of the Society of Merchant Venturers, while some of the biggest American merchants did not join Bristol's 'merchant guild'. In 1671/2, only two of Bristol's leading twenty importers focused more heavily on European trade: Edward Jones, who imported £6,100 worth of European goods and just £150 worth from the Americas; and William Colston (father of the now notorious Edward) who imported £5,200 worth of goods from Europe compared to less than £400 worth from across the Atlantic. The activities of the city's leading merchants, then, reinforce the conclusion that the expansion of Bristol's new colonial trades was not to the detriment of the city's more established links in Europe. Many of Bristol's most successful merchants, and the most prominent members of its civic society, continued to split their interests between old and new branches of trade.

Table 7. Trading activities of Bristol's leading merchants in 1671/2.

Merchant name	Total imports	Joined Merchant Venturers	Colonial imports	European imports	Irish imports
Edward Fielding	£21,881.25		£21,006.67	£–	£874.58
Richard Crumpp	£17,885.38		£17,217.08	£86.25	£582.04
William Yeamans	£14,743.21	1646	£12,915.54	£1,827.67	£–
Robert Yate	£12,969.38	1639	£8,036.58	£4,932.79	£–

43   J. J. McCusker and R. R. Menard, *The Economy of British America, 1607–1789* (London, 1991), p. 157.

Table 7 *continued*

Merchant name	Total imports	Joined Merchant Venturers	Colonial imports	European imports	Irish imports
John Luffe	£12,074.83		£10,876.00	£1,198.83	£–
Richard Pope	£10,370.75		£10,020.83	£334.92	£15.00
William Hayman	£10,005.92	1665	£5,100.08	£4,727.50	£178.33
William Crabb	£8,750.79		£8,031.63	£700.00	£19.17
William Bullocke	£7,624.21	1650	£7,624.21	£–	£–
John Walter	£7,548.08		£7,548.08	£–	£–
John Sanders	£7,288.92		£6,506.42	£780.00	£2.50
Samuel Wharton	£7,050.08		£7,036.75	£–	£13.33
Gabriel Deane	£6,379.88	1665	£4,712.88	£1,667.00	£–
Edward Jones	£6,302.00	1680	£166.67	£6,135.33	£–
Reginald Tucker	£5,935.54		£5,795.54	£140.00	£–
William Davis	£5,798.38		£4,158.25	£773.58	£866.54
John Speede	£5,718.13	1660	£5,477.29	£240.83	£–
William Colston	£5,557.08	1634	£386.67	£5,170.42	£–
William Rogers	£5,509.17	1667	£5,394.25	£8.00	£106.92
John Dudlestone	£5,428.92		£5,396.92	£32.00	£–

Source: 1671/2 Port Book; P. V. McGrath, *Records Relating to the Society of Merchant Venturers of the City of Bristol in the 17th Century*, Bristol Record Society Vol. 17 (Bristol, 1952), pp. 27–33, 261. Where an entry lists multiple merchants, the value of the goods has been divided equally between them. Where the records show one merchant importing on behalf of another, the value has been attributed to the intended owner of the goods. It is likely that some of the recorded trade represented one merchant acting as factor for others, but has not been recorded as such.

France

France had been one of the bastions of Bristol's commercial world for more than three centuries, and as late as 1637/8 still accounted for 35 per cent of Bristol's imports. Unlike the ongoing prosperity in the Iberian trades, however, by the end of the seventeenth century the city's French commerce had experienced a steep decline. The middle years of the seventeenth century were particularly tough, with imports from France falling to as little as £11,200 in 1654/5. After adjusting for inflation of the customs rates, this is a fifth of the size of the trade just sixteen years earlier (see Figure 43). These doldrums continued throughout the 1650s and 1660s and, while the early 1670s appear to have seen something

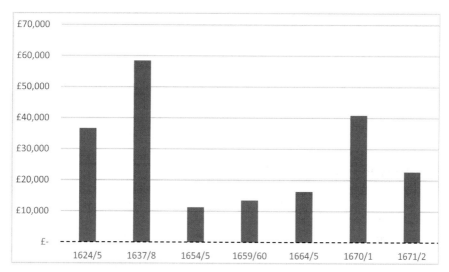

Figure 43. Bristol's French imports as recorded in the Port Books and Wharfage Books, 1624/5–1671/2 (in pounds sterling).

Sources: Sacks, *Widening Gate*, pp. 42–3; TNA PRO E190/1136/10, E190/1137/3, E190/1138/1; BRO SMV/7/1/1/1, SMV/7/1/1/2. Figures prior to 1654/5 have been doubled to account for increases in the customs valuations.

of a recovery, imports from France still fell well short of their level before the Civil War. Throughout the 1650s, 1660s and 1670s, imports from France never made up more than 6 per cent of Bristol's total, and in some years as little as 3 per cent: a far cry from the fifteenth century, when Bristol's commercial world had been defined by its symbiotic links with Bordeaux.

The reasons for the apparent decline of Bristol's trade with France are complex. An increase in smuggling may have played some part. William Culliford's investigation into corruption in the Bristol customs house revealed that considerable quantities of linen were being smuggled into Bristol in the 1680s. He did not, however, uncover many cases of illicit trade in wine. It seems that the decline in recorded trade was thus genuine, not simply a shift to smuggling. Perhaps more significant is aggressive economic legislation. Seeking to curb the economic expansion of a competing power, both France and England introduced measures to restrict imports of goods produced by their nearest rival. In 1649–50, for example, English cloth was excluded from France, and in retaliation the English government placed an embargo on imports of French wine, wool, and silk.[44] Relations remained tense, with France signifi-

44   W. B. Stephens, *Seventeenth-Century Exeter: A Study of Industrial and Commercial Development, 1625–1688* (Exeter, 1958), p. 69.

cantly raising the duty on English cloth in 1654; the English embargo on French goods was not finally lifted until 1656.[45] Even when a full embargo was not in place, restrictively high tariffs were placed on trade in goods deemed not in the national interest, leading to high taxes on imported goods that were seen as luxuries, and low taxes on exports of manufactures. The aim was to keep as much gold and as much economic activity in England as possible. Indeed, serious attempts were even made by the Royal Society and others to develop English cider production as a replacement for French wines![46] Whether or not they had the desired economic effect, these attempts at fiscal engineering through the customs system seem to have been relatively effective in terms of restricting trade.

This discussion of Bristol's commercial links with France does not sit comfortably within the broader narrative of the development of the city's trade, however. Generally, the story was one of spectacular growth, but in the case of France a previously prosperous trade declined drastically in just over two decades. This is a valuable reminder that, while on the whole the rise of the Atlantic economy meant good times for England's merchants, this was not uniformly the case. Trade remained vulnerable to external factors, and in particular needed a favourable political environment. Even short of outright war, governments could still significantly hinder trade with perceived rivals through restrictive legislation.

A Transatlantic Material Culture?

While exports to the new American and Caribbean colonies tend to attract the lion's share of attention, Bristol's exports to its old continental markets were of greater value in the 1660s and 1670s. The 1661/2 Port Book shows almost £23,000 worth of goods sent to France and the Iberian Peninsula, compared to £12,100 worth crossing the Atlantic. In 1671/2 the margin is narrower, with just under £10,000 worth of transatlantic exports and £11,000 worth to Europe, but this account does not include re-exports, and reflects likely disruption of continental trade due to the outbreak of the Third Anglo-Dutch War. As Figure 44 shows, while the proportions of particular commodity types varied, the makeup of Bristol's European and American trades was broadly similar. Cloth and clothing featured heavily in both branches, as did the produce of pastoral agriculture. The biggest difference is that unworked metals were more important in the continental trades, whereas with the colonies manufactures featured more heavily. The other significant difference is the much more limited range of goods sent to France and the Iberian Peninsula. In 1661/2, for example, Bristol sent 72

45 *Ibid.*, p. 70.
46 See, for example: J. Evelyn (ed.), *Pomona, or, An appendix concerning fruit-trees in relation to cider the making and several ways of ordering it* (London, 1670); J. Worlidge, *Vinetum Britannicum: Or a Treatise of Cider...* (London, 1678).

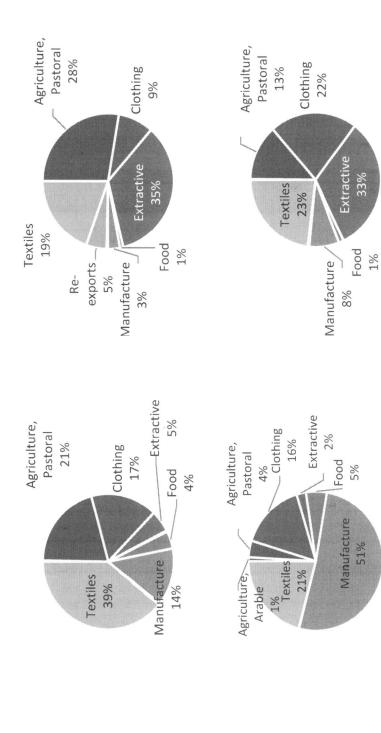

Europe

Americas

1661/2

Europe 1661/2
- Agriculture, Pastoral 28%
- Clothing 9%
- Extractive 35%
- Food 1%
- Manufacture 3%
- Re-exports 5%
- Textiles 19%

Americas 1661/2
- Agriculture, Pastoral 21%
- Clothing 17%
- Extractive 5%
- Food 4%
- Manufacture 14%
- Textiles 39%

1671/2

Europe 1671/2
- Agriculture, Pastoral 13%
- Clothing 22%
- Extractive 33%
- Food 1%
- Manufacture 8%
- Textiles 23%

Americas 1671/2
- Agriculture, Pastoral 4%
- Clothing 16%
- Extractive 2%
- Food 5%
- Manufacture 51%
- Agriculture, Arable 1%
- Textiles 21%

Figure 44. Bristol's exports to Europe and the Americas by category, 1661/2 and 1671/2 (in pounds sterling).

Sources: 1661/2 Port Book, 1671/2 Port Book.

different types of goods to the Peninsula and 52 to France, compared to 278 to the Chesapeake and 270 to the Caribbean. This is likely because the European regions with which Bristol traded had manufacturing sectors of their own, and thus were both less reliant on manufactured goods from England and more inclined to import raw materials for their own industries.

Table 8. Bristol's principal exports to the continent, 1661/2 and 1671/2.

| | Iberia | | France | |
	1661/2	1671/2	1661/2	1671/2
Butter	£1,295	£197	£1,153	£32
Calf-skins and leather	£3,233	£1,235	£1,985	£406
Cloth, bayes	£900	£1,865	£50	£44
Cloth, cotton	£56.00	£168	£1,225	£482
Cloth, serge	£977	£533	£43	£6
Cloth, shortcloth	£310	£37	£210	£16
Lead and shot	£3,919	£4,643	£4,972	£1,390
Stockings, worsted	£1,176	£2,692	£258	£419
Tobacco	£1,267	n/a	£237	n/a
Other	£1,797	£455	£1,211	£729
Total	£14,928	£11,823	£11,344	£3,524

Sources: 1661/2 Port Book, 1671/2 Port Book.

In many respects, Bristol's exports to Europe in the post-Restoration period were similar to those in the first half of the seventeenth century (see Table 8 and Chapter 1). Cloth was much less dominant than it had been in the Middle Ages, and the new, lighter types of cloth had now almost completely eclipsed the heavier broadcloths. The surge in manufactured exports in the 1630s accounts had somewhat abated, but Spain, Portugal and France continued to take noteworthy quantities of English manufactures. The agricultural and extractive trades that began to develop in the late sixteenth and early seventeenth centuries also continued to play an important part, with 1661/2 seeing £5,000 worth of calf-skins and leather, and nearly £9,000 worth of lead and shot sent to the continent. These markets, then, continued to facilitate increased market orientation in both farming and mining in Bristol and its region.

Comparison of Bristol's exports to markets all around the Atlantic basin raises the intriguing thought that elements of a shared material culture were beginning to emerge. The Port Book data affirms the long-held understanding that the American colonies, even after their breakaway to form the United

States, were reliant on manufactures from England, and thus had a distinctly Anglophile material culture.[47] A child in late seventeenth-century Virginia may thus have worn woollen stockings, hose and a coat all manufactured in the English countryside (the 1671/2 Port Book records all of these items of clothing being exported to Virginia in specifically children's sizes).[48] More disturbingly, an enslaved person in the Caribbean could well have been wearing a felt hat made in Gloucestershire, clothes made from low-grade Welsh cloth, and shoes crafted in Bristol. Susan Flavin has also shown that Ireland imported a wide range of consumer wares in the late sixteenth century, and very much followed the fashions of London.[49] As Chapter 2 showed, Ireland's 'consumer revolution' continued apace in the seventeenth century. Manufactures sent to France and the Iberian Peninsula were, by the latter seventeenth century, both less numerous and less varied than those destined for other markets. Nonetheless, they regularly featured small articles such as nails, glass bottles, felt hats, and tallow candles. A batch of small metalware items made by a blacksmith in Bristol or its region may thus have been sold to consumers in Jamestown, Virginia, Cadiz or Wexford. The consumer revolution has increasingly been recognised as an important driver of economic and industrial development in Britain, with demand-led growth spurring manufacturers to increase production. This tends to be treated as an internal driver of development. However, the findings presented here show that by the late seventeenth century the Atlantic market-place was increasingly integrated, and consumers all around its shores were equally desirous of a growing range of manufactured wares. Growing demand for manufactures and the resultant drive to increase production thus came from both in and outside Britain.

Conclusions

Explanations of the expansion of England's trade in the latter seventeenth century have tended to take an import-led approach, focusing on the soaring demand for colonial tobacco and sugar as prices fell, and the quest for luxury imports in the Mediterranean and beyond. As Nuala Zahedieh has observed based on her study of London's customs accounts, however, the role of exports has been unduly overlooked, with the colonies being valued as much as markets as they were sources of raw materials.[50] This observation is certainly borne out

---

47   C. Shammas, *The Pre-Industrial Consumer in England and America* (Los Angeles, 2008), pp. 4–5.
48   1671/2 Port Book.
49   S. Flavin, *Consumption and Material Culture in Sixteenth Century Ireland: Saffron, Stockings and Silk* (Woodbridge, 2014).
50   Zahedieh, *Capital and the Colonies*, p. 289.

at Bristol, where the Port Books show a diverse range of manufactures, agricultural and extractive produce being sent to Ireland, continental Europe, and the Americas. Re-exports certainly played some part and merit further study, but this was very much secondary to the shipping of English produce. As with the earlier period, then, when merchants' accounts have shown that the export trades could be more profitable than imports, we might well ask whether it was demand for English exports, rather than English demand for foreign wares, driving the growth of trade. This substantial demand for all manner of wares to load onto Bristol ships was also clearly having a significant effect on English economic development. As shown in Chapter 1, as early as the late sixteenth century Bristol's overseas markets were already providing a considerable outlet for the increasingly commercialised agriculture and innovative mining ventures of the region. The first half of the seventeenth century also saw an increasingly large amount of manufactured wares. This growth of production continued in the mid- to late seventeenth century, with the Burgess Books showing more and more people engaged in manufacturing in Bristol itself, and the Coastal Port Books revealing a plethora of agricultural goods, minerals, and manufactures flowing in from the city's hinterland. At this stage it might be a bit much to call this an industrial revolution, but nonetheless it is clear that by the second half of the seventeenth century the Atlantic economy (and by extension the slavery on which the American colonies relied) was already driving economic development and market orientation in England and Wales.

6

Servants and Enslaved People

On 17 February 1662, two Bristol merchants, John Juce and Thomas Colston (younger brother of the infamous Edward Colston), began loading goods onto a ship named the *Endeavour* of Bristol. Over the next four days, the customs officers recorded an assortment of cloth, clothing, and other commodities to stow on the *Endeavour*.[1] On the face of it, this was nothing unusual. Most of these goods were of a kind with those that filled the hulls of Bristol's ships on the main routes. Her declared destination, however, was rather different: the Cape Verde islands, an archipelago off the coast of West Africa noted for its association with the Atlantic slave trade, and not a common trading partner for Bristol's merchants.[2] Precisely, Cape Verde was the *Endeavour*'s initial destination. Most of the entries in the customs ledgers state that she was bound for Cape Verde. When a consignment of felt hats, belonging to a Richard Newman, were loaded onto the *Endeavour*, she was instead mysteriously said to be going to Barbados.[3] This could simply be an administrative error, but other evidence hints at something more intriguing. Ten months later, just before Christmas 1662, the *Endeavour* returned to Bristol carrying a cargo of sugar.[4] Unfortunately by this stage the Wharfage Books no longer record the last port of call, but this sugar was clearly not grown in the Cape Verde islands. It thus seems, as Richard Newman suggested, that after leaving Cape Verde the *Endeavour* headed across the Atlantic to Barbados or one of the other Caribbean islands. In the eighteenth century, such a triangular transatlantic voyage would be nothing unusual. In 1662, however, it was unprecedented. Historians usually begin their accounts of Bristol's involvement in the slave trade in 1698, with the lifting of the Royal African Company monopoly that

---

1   1661/2 Bristol Port Book, TNA PRO E190/1240/6, ff. 12r–13r.
2   M. João Soares, 'The British Presence on the Cape Verdean Archipelago (Sixteenth to Eighteenth Centuries', *African Economic History*, 39 (2011), pp. 129–46; W. Rodney, 'Portuguese Attempts at Monopoly on the Upper Guinea Coast, 1580–1650', *The Journal of African History*, 6(3) (1965), pp. 307–22.
3   1661/2 Bristol Port Book, f. 13r.
4   'Wharfage Book 1659–1666', Bristol Archives, SMV/7/1/1/2, p. 255.

formally excluded Bristol's merchants from trading to Africa.[5] But the 1662 voyage of the *Endeavour*, and an assortment of others like it over the next three and a half decades, suggest that Bristol may in fact have been trading in enslaved people for much longer than previously thought.

In terms of demand, that Bristol ships were carrying enslaved labourers to the New World colonies as early as the 1660s is not that surprising. In addition to the provisions and manufactures detailed in the last chapter, the early colonies were also highly reliant on English shipping to bring them labourers. By the end of the seventeenth century, most of the English colonies with which Bristol was trading already had substantial populations. The population of Virginia, for example, was more than 35,000 in 1670, and by the end of the century it had passed 58,500.[6] But significant numbers of settlers did not necessarily equate to sufficient labour. Wages in the colonies were high. The plentiful supply of land for colonists to set up on their own, and the high costs of emigration, meant that those in the Americas who were free to sell their services were unlikely to do so cheaply.[7] A constant supply of bound (rather than waged) labour was thus needed to keep cash crop production going. This situation was further exacerbated by the harsh work regimes of the plantations, in particular in sugar production, and the resultant high mortality amongst the workforce.[8] With a considerable excess of deaths over births, the colonial labour pool needed constant replenishing.

In the seventeenth century, bound labour in the English American colonies took two forms. Initially the colonists favoured 'indentured servants': labourers bound by a written contract (known as an indenture) to serve a particular master for a fixed period, typically four to seven years. Although they still had some rights, and certainly more than enslaved Africans, for the duration of this contract the indentured servant was considered the chattel property of their master, and could be bought and sold, moved around, and instructed at will.[9] Some indentured servants were the victims of abduction or coercion by shadowy recruiting agents known as 'spirits'. But, unlike enslaved labourers, the

5   See, for example: D. Richardson, *Bristol, Africa, and the Eighteenth-Century Slave Trade to America, Volume 1: The Years of Expansion, 1698–1729*, Bristol Record Society Vol. 38 (Bristol, 1986); K. Morgan, *Bristol and the Atlantic Trade in the Eighteenth Century* (Cambridge, 1993), p. 129.

6   https://www.census.gov/library/publications/1975/compendia/hist_stats_colonial-1970.html, p. 1168.

7   J. J. McCusker and R. R. Menard, *The Economy of British America 1607–1789* (Chapel Hill, 1991), p. 135.

8   K. Morgan, *Slavery and the British Empire: From Africa to America* (Oxford, 2007), pp. 90–6.

9   K. Morgan, *Slavery and Servitude in North America, 1607–1800* (Edinburgh, 2000), pp. 8–9.

vast majority signed up willingly.[10] Potential servants would enter an indenture for a variety of reasons. For some the motivation may have been opportunity. Once their term was served, they might establish themselves as landowners in a way which simply was not possible in England.[11] Probably more important, however, was unemployment in the home country. Indentured servants were drawn from a fairly wide area within England, many having already migrated from their homes one or more times (often to urban areas) in search of work.[12] Bristol has better records for the shipment of indentured servants than any other port, with the city's Register of Servants to Foreign Plantations giving details of over 10,000 servants embarking at the port of Bristol between 1654 and 1686.[13] The register also gives an insight into how this 'trade' in indentured servants was organised: potential emigrants would bind themselves to a master before leaving England, who would then pay for their passage to the colonies and sell them on to a landowner on their arrival.

In the Chesapeake tobacco colonies, indentured servants remained the core of the labour force until late into the seventeenth century. By 1670 there were only 2,500 African enslaved people in Virginia and Maryland, making up just 6 per cent of the population, and enslaved labour only slowly established itself as the norm over the period 1680–1720.[14] In the sugar islands of the Caribbean, however, slavery provided the core of the workforce almost from the outset. As early as 1653, Barbados had 20,000 enslaved people compared to 8,000 indentured servants, and by 1680 the enslaved accounted for almost 70 per cent of the island's population.[15] While the Portuguese had been trading in African enslaved people since the mid-fifteenth century, England had been relatively slow to become involved. Sir John Hawkins's three slave-trading voyages in the 1560s were both highly prestigious and very profitable, but resistance from the Spanish, who were highly protective of their monopoly on New World trade, meant that such ventures did not become a regular feature

---

10   D. H. Sacks, *The Widening Gate: Bristol and the Atlantic Economy, 1450–1700* (Berkeley, 1991), p. 253; D. Souden, '"Rogues, Whores and Vagabonds"? Indentured Servant Emigrants to North America, and the Case of Mid-Seventeenth-Century Bristol', *Social History*, 3(1) (1978), p. 38.

11   R. R. Menard, 'From Servant to Freeholder: Status Mobility and Property Accumulation in Seventeenth-Century Maryland', *The William and Mary Quarterly*, 30(1) (1973), pp. 37–64.

12   Morgan, *Slavery and Servitude*, p. 14.

13   'Register of Servants to Foreign Plantations', Bristol Archives: 04220/1-2. The dataset used here was extracted from a digital version available from: http://www.virtualjamestown. org/indentures/search_indentures.html. See Morgan, *Slavery and Servitude*, p. 12, for details of other surviving sets of records.

14   McCusker and Menard, *Economy of British America*, pp. 134–7.

15   Morgan, *Slavery and the British Empire*, p. 27.

of English commerce until almost a century later.[16] Indeed, when a Company of Adventurers to Guinea and Benin was set up in 1618, its charter did not list enslaved people amongst the goods it was looking to acquire.[17] When the English did finally establish a significant slave trade in the 1660s, it was in the form of joint stock monopoly companies with a royal monopoly: the Company of Royal Adventurers Trading to Africa (founded 1660) and its successor the Royal African Company (founded 1672). Until the Royal African Company surrendered its exclusive monopoly rights in 1698, it was not possible for private traders to legally acquire enslaved people on the African coast.[18] While Bristol was to become a leading centre for the slave trade in the eighteenth century, its merchants were thus not legally allowed to trade in enslaved people until after 1698. Indeed, Bristol's most infamous slave-trader Edward Colston was not in fact a Bristol slave-trader. Colston moved from his native Bristol to London where he became an investor and leading player in the Royal African Company.[19] As already mentioned, however, the Thomas Colston involved in the *Endeavour* voyage described at the start of this chapter was Edward's younger brother, and Edward inherited his business when he died in 1683.[20] So the Colston family may indeed have been among the pioneers of Bristol's involvement in the transatlantic slave trade after all.

This chapter examines the role Bristol played in supplying labour to the early North American and Caribbean colonies, and also the significance of this trade to Bristol's commercial development. With Bristol's later rise to ascendancy in the slave trade, these are crucial questions, as for many in the city today the legacy of this history is still very much a live issue. The chapter opens with a discussion of Bristol's indentured servant trade. By comparing the approximate financial value of servants shipped from Bristol to other exports to the New World, it shows that the servant trade was much less commercially significant to the city than has previously been supposed. Finally, it turns to the much-debated question of whether Bristol was illegally engaging in the slave trade prior to the end of the royal monopoly in 1698. While many previous authors have speculated on this question, with some suggesting that a significant illicit trade existed, none have previously been able to address it in light of such

16   M. Kaufman, *Black Tudors: The Untold Story* (London, 2017), pp. 56–89. I am grateful to Miranda Kaufman for sharing with me a forthcoming article in which she discusses the subject of England's involvement in the slave trade between Hawkins's voyages and the foundation of the Company of Royal Adventurers in more depth.

17   M. Kaufman, 'English Involvement in Slave Trading, 1530–1663' (unpublished draft article, 2011); K. G. Davies, *The Royal African Company* (London, 1957), p. 41.

18   Davies, *Royal African Company*, pp. 41–4, 97–8, 132–5.

19   K. Morgan, *Edward Colston and Bristol*, Bristol Historical Association Pamphlets no. 96 (Bristol, 1999), pp. 2–3.

20   *Ibid.*, pp. 2–3; K. Morgan, 'Colston, Edward', *Oxford Dictionary of National Biography* (Oxford, 2004).

detailed evidence for Bristol's trade as that offered by the Port Books and Wharfage Books. For the first time, therefore, it is shown that Bristol definitely was engaging in the slave trade before 1698, in the process identifying the city's two earliest recorded slave-traders in 1662. This trade, however, is shown to have been on a limited scale, with no more than one or two ships a year going on slave-trading voyages. Overall, it is shown that the trade in labour was of limited direct commercial significance to Bristol in the seventeenth century, and the manufactures and provisions discussed in the last chapter formed a much greater proportion of its exports to the New World. The significance of the labour trades was, rather, that they facilitated the production of the cash crops in which the wealth of the Atlantic economy truly rested.

Indentured Servants

Much has been written about the shipment of indentured servants from Bristol. This analysis, however, has tended to be from a migration perspective, considering the types of people who populated the early American colonies and what drove them to leave England.[21] The only author to consider the shipment of servants from a commercial perspective has been D. H. Sacks. For Sacks, the trade in indentured servants was central to Bristol's early involvement with the Americas. He suggested that we should 'consider trans-Atlantic commerce as a two-way traffic, with each shipment of servants resulting in a return cargo of sugar or tobacco'.[22] Opening his discussion of the growth of the New World trades, Sacks stated that 'some historical processes of this magnitude are captured in a single source [that can] let us see a whole world in a grain of sand'.[23] For Sacks, the Register of Servants to Foreign Plantations was just such a document, and he thus centred his analysis of Bristol's American trade around it. There is no doubting that Bristol carried out substantial 'trade' in indentured servants, especially during the first decades of its involvement with the New World. The analysis presented below, however, suggests that the shipment of indentured servants was not as central to the business of American trade as Sacks suggested. When a monetary value is given to shipments of indentured servants, and this value is compared to the other goods involved in Bristol's early American trade, it emerges that the trade in labour in fact only accounted for a relatively small percentage of Bristol's New World exports. Furthermore, analysis of the people responsible for the shipment of servants shows that these were not, on the whole, the big players of Bristol's merchant

21 See, for example, Souden, '"Rogues, Whores and Vagabonds"?', pp. 23–41.
22 Sacks, *Widening Gate*, p. 260.
23 *Ibid.*, pp. 251–2.

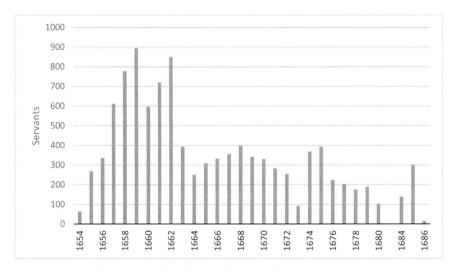

Figure 45. Bristol's exports of indentured servants by year.

Source: Register of Servants to Foreign Plantations.

community. Instead, the indentured servant trade was mostly an occasional sideline for mariners and other members of Bristol's maritime community.

As with the rise of American trade recorded in the Wharfage Books, the trade in indentured servants almost certainly pre-dated record-keeping in 1654. In all, the shipment of almost 10,600 servants is recorded in the Bristol register between 1654 and its end in 1686 (see Figure 45). The peak was in the late 1650s and early 1660s, with as many as 4,450 servants leaving Bristol between 1657 and 1662 (42 per cent of the total). After this, the trade petered out, averaging 340 servants per annum for the rest of the 1660s, 250 in the 1670s, and just 110 in the 1680s. As a significant trade, therefore, shipping indentured servants from Bristol was relatively short-lived.

The timing of the rise and fall of Bristol's trade in indentured servants suggests that it was not as central to the success of the city's New World commerce as Sacks has supposed. While there is no doubt that the peak years of indentured servant shipments coincide with Bristol's initial entrance into the American trade, thereafter their paths diverge (see Figure 46). Bristol's servant trade declined significantly from the mid-1660s, but the city's imports from Virginia and the Caribbean continued to expand rapidly. By the time Bristol's American trade had reached its highest seventeenth-century levels, in the 1670s, indentured servant exports had fallen to less than half their peak levels. As the city's New World connections continued to thrive while the passage of servants declined, it seems highly unlikely that the trade in indentured labour was amongst the main drivers of Bristol's 'American Revolution'.

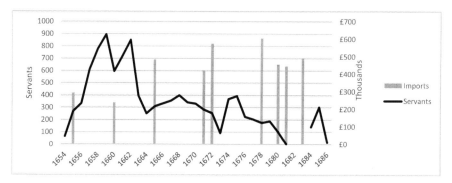

Figure 46. Comparison of Bristol's recorded imports and indentured servant exports.

Sources: *Ibid.*; 1654/5 Wharfage Book; 1659/60 Wharfage Book; 1664/5 Wharfage Book; 1670/1 Port Book; 1671/2 Port Book; 1678/9 Port Book; 1680/1 Port Book; 1681/2 Port Book; 1682/3 Port Book.

As people were not a taxable commodity, shipments of indentured servants were not listed in either the Port Books or Wharfage Books. While the Register of Servants provides a vast amount of detail regarding the servant trade, including information about both the servants themselves and the masters responsible for their shipment, it does not give any information about their financial value. To allow comparison with other types of goods and establish the relative significance of the servant trade, a value must thus be added from elsewhere. It has not been possible to find a price from Bristol, although the cost of indentured servants in the 1670s would certainly not have exceeded the £20 fine imposed on shipmasters who received unauthorised persons on their vessels as bound servants.[24] If the price had been higher than £20, this fine would not have been considered a sufficient deterrent. Evidence from elsewhere suggests that it would cost something in the region of £10–14 to buy a male indentured servant in the colonies.[25] The price in Bristol, however, is likely to have been substantially lower than this, as the cost of passage alone amounted to around £5 or £6.[26] Indeed, figures from London suggest that those wishing to export indentured servants would pay as little as £2 per head to the agent who sourced them.[27] Although the price in Bristol may have been higher, or the

24   C. M. MacInnes, *Bristol: A Gateway of Empire* (Newton Abbot, 1968), p. 161.
25   H. McD. Beckles, *The First Black Slave Society: Britain's 'Barbarity Time' in Barbados, 1636–1876* (Jamaica, 2016), p. 35.
26   Morgan, *Slavery and Servitude*, p. 17.
27   N. Zahedieh, *The Capital and the Colonies: London and the Atlantic Economy 1660–1700* (Cambridge, 2010), p. 244.

merchants involved may have ascribed a greater value to servants, £2 still seems an appropriate nominal value to use for comparison with other exports. It must, after all, be borne in mind that the Book of Rates valuations used elsewhere in the analysis were often significantly lower than the actual value of the goods.[28]

Examining the trade in indentured servants in financial terms, it becomes increasingly clear that it was not of great significance to Bristol, at least directly. As Figure 47 shows, if a nominal price is assigned to the shipments of indentured servants, they make up a fraction of Bristol's export trade. Bristol's exports of goods that paid customs duties to North America and the Caribbean in 1661/2 were worth a total of £12,100.[29] That year saw 850 indentured servants shipped, which, if they are valued at £2 each, gives a nominal value of £1,700. This was the second-highest annual total for indentured servants leaving Bristol recorded in the Register. Even at the height of the indentured servant trade, it thus accounted for just 12 per cent of Bristol's exports to the Americas. The next year where a comparison with other exports is possible shows indentured servants to have been even less significant. In 1671/2 Bristol exported just under £10,000 worth of goods to the American colonies. The 254 indentured servants who accompanied them, therefore, made up just 5 per cent of total exports by value (£508). While not totally insignificant, the trade in indentured servants was thus a long way from being, as Sacks suggested, the key component of Bristol's New World commerce. Even at their height, shipments of indentured servants were just a small part of the value of the cargo of ships crossing the Atlantic, and as the servant trade declined they became even less central.

Analysis of what is known about the people responsible for conducting Bristol's indentured servant 'trade' further points to it being peripheral to Bristol's main mercantile business with the colonies. As Table 9 shows, in the year 1661/2 393 different people appeared in the Register of Servants as the 'Agents' responsible for a servant's journey. Of these, the vast majority registered just one (243) or two (66) servants. There are exceptions; for example, the mariner John Haskins sent twenty-two servants, and merchant Henry Bankes sent twenty-three. Interestingly, both men were involved in the trade on a significant scale over several years. Haskins registered thirteen servants between 1656 and 1658, and Bankes was the biggest player in the early years of the trade, sending 108 servants between 1654 and 1660.[30] Broadly, though, the findings from 1662 fit with Souden's analysis of the first six years of Bristol's indentured servant trade. He showed the trade to have been spread over more than a thousand different masters, of whom 44 per cent shipped just one servant,

28   See Technical Appendix for a discussion of this deficit between customs valuations and wholesale prices.
29   This value is after adjusting to account for revisions to the customs rates. See Technical Appendix for a full explanation of the methodology.
30   Souden, "'Rogues, Whores, and Vagabonds'", p. 35.

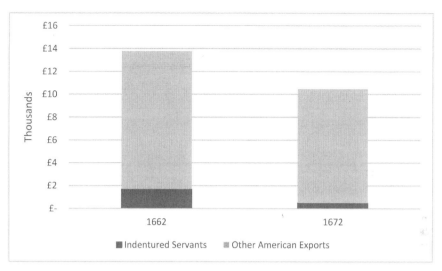

Figure 47. Indentured servants as a proportion of Bristol's transatlantic exports.

Sources: Register of Servants to Foreign Plantations; 1661/2 Port Book; 1671/2 Port Book.

with an average of just 3.49 servants per person. A third of the servants were sent by big operators who registered ten or more over the six years.[31] Souden was not, however, right to suggest that 'the whole Bristol trading community appears to have been involved in the trade of sending servants to the colonies'.[32] As Table 10 shows, of the 553 people whom the Bristol Port Book records as exporting goods in 1662, just 139 also shipped servants. Bristol's leading merchants do not seem to have been involved in the servant trade to any great extent. Indeed, of the fifty-three people who shipped more than £250 worth of other goods, just two (John White and Henry Gough) were also involved in the servant trade, registering one servant apiece. The vast majority of people shipping both servants and goods were those involved on a lesser scale. Around a quarter of those shipping between £25 and £250 worth of goods also sent servants. Of these, a third sent less than £25 worth of other commodities. The vast majority of those responsible for shipping indentured servants, however, were not involved in the commodity trade at all, with only around one in three of those registered as agents in 1662 also recorded in the Port Book.

31   *Ibid.*, pp. 34–5.
32   *Ibid.*, p. 35.

Table 9. Number of servants exported per agent (1661–62).

Servants exported	Number of agents
1	243
2	66
3	26
4	20
5	11
6	7
7	4
8	5
9	2
10	1
11	1
12	3
13	1
17	1
22	1
23	1
Total	393

Source: Register of Servants to Foreign Plantations.

Table 10. Bristol's American exporters by value of goods and number of servant agents (1661–62).

Value of exports	Number of merchants	Number of servant agents
Over £2,000	2	
£1,000–£2,000	7	
£750–£1,000	8	1
£500–£750	14	
£250–£500	34	1
£100–£250	77	24
£50–£100	100	29
£25–£50	79	8
Under £25	232	76
Total	553	139

Source: *Ibid.*; 1661/2 Port Book.

If they were not the city's leading merchants, then who were those responsible for Bristol's indentured servant trade? In addition to the few large-scale agents, Souden has highlighted that 'mariners, particularly on Virginia voyages, would often take one or two servants, in order to make a quick profit on the side on their own account'.[33] Sacks defined them slightly more broadly, suggesting that 'a broad spectrum of crafts was represented among the hundreds of individuals who indentured servants', although he did note that 'members of the shipping industry appear to have taken the largest share of the business' at 54 per cent.[34] Unfortunately the level of recording in the Register of Servants had declined by 1662, so it is not possible to analyse the occupations of those sending servants in that year.[35] The record from 1654–58, however, is much more complete, allowing the identification of the occupation of the agents shipping the servants in all bar 335 out of 2,056 cases (see Table 11 and Figure 48).[36] By far the largest group was mariners, responsible for shipping more than a third of all servants from Bristol during this period (701). Given the large numbers exported by mariners (such as Thomas Haskins and Richard Storme, 13; Henry Russell, 16; and David Warren and Hugh Jones, 23), this is likely to have been a fairly broad definition, incorporating both well-paid shipmasters and poorer ordinary seamen. Most, however, were relatively small-scale operators shipping one or two servants as a sideline. Of the 258 mariners appearing in the Register of Servants during these four years, 145 (including my namesake Richard Stone) shipped just one servant, and 38 just two. On average, mariners shipped 2.8 servants each. The next largest group was merchants, sending 487 servants, although, as noted above, these seem to have been the smaller players in the merchant community. As many as 159 servants were registered to individuals listed as planters, suggesting that some in the New World sourced their servants directly.[37] The servant trade was not, as Sacks has suggested, a 'shoemakers' holiday', providing an opportunity for those from the world of manufacturing and other crafts to become involved in overseas trade.[38] This was clearly part of Bristol's maritime world, with 84 per cent of the servants for whom the agent's occupation is known being sent by mariners, merchants, planters or other people connected to the business of shipping.

33   Souden, '"Rogues, Whores, and Vagabonds"', p. 36.
34   Sacks, *Widening Gate*, pp. 258–60.
35   Souden, '"Rogues, Whores, and Vagabonds"', p. 25.
36   Using a spreadsheet to cross-reference the data has filled in many of the blanks in the dataset. It was not uncommon for the occupation of an agent to be listed when shipping one servant but omitted with another. The figures used here are thus much more accurate than those available to Sacks and Souden. Where previously the occupations of the agents were unknown for 895 out of 2,056 servants (44 per cent) only 336 are now unknown (16 per cent).
37   A further thirty-one servants are likely to have been shipped by planters. These are cases where, while no occupation for the agent is listed, their place of origin is given as one of the colonies. These were: Barbados, 20; St. Kitts, 3; and Virginia, 8.
38   Sacks, *Widening Gate*, pp. 251, 259, 267.

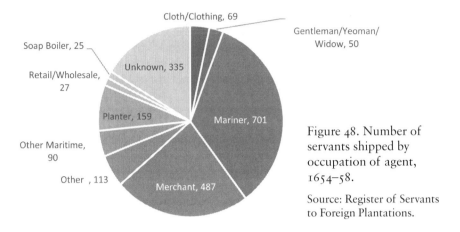

Figure 48. Number of servants shipped by occupation of agent, 1654–58.

Source: Register of Servants to Foreign Plantations.

Table 11. Number of servants shipped by occupation of agent, 1654–58[39]

Agent's occupation	Number of servants
Apothecary	2
Baker	4
Block-maker	1
Butcher	1
Carpenter	4
Chandler	1
Clerk	4
Clothier	3
Cooper	46
Cordwainer	2
Cutler	1
Draper	14
Fellmonger	1
Felt-maker	1
Gentleman	23
Grocer	17
Haberdasher	4
Hosier	1

39   *Ibid.*

Agent's occupation	Number of servants
Innholder	5
Ironmonger	5
Mariner	622
Mariner/Blacksmith	16
Mariner/Cooper	20
Mariner/Draper	8
Mariner/Merchant	19
Mariner/Shipwright	6
Mercer	14
Merchant	487
Merchant/Mariner	10
Painter	11
Pipe-maker	1
Planter	160
Pump-maker	1
Shipwright	8
Shoe-maker	7
Smith	13
Soap-boiler	25
Spinster	5
Surgeon	79
Tailor	3
Upholsterer	35
Victualler	1
Vintner	3
Widow	17
Yeoman	10
Unknown	335
Grand total	2,056

Previous work on Bristol's indentured servant trade has, then, tended to misunderstand its significance. Even at its height in the late 1650s and early 1660s, the indentured servant trade was just a sideline to the main business of Bristol's transatlantic commerce. It made up little more than a tenth of the value of Bristol's exports to the Americas in the 1660s, and by the 1670s just a twentieth. It was also not Bristol's merchants who were responsible for the movement of indentured servants. Neither was it, as Sacks suggested, tradesmen from other crafts who wanted to get a foothold in overseas trade. Instead, this was predominantly carried on by Bristol's maritime community alongside their day-to-day activities. People were not bought as commodities in huge numbers in order to be sold on by wealthy merchants (unlike in the slave trade itself). Regardless of whether or not indentured servants were property, they (for the most part) entered into the engagement willingly, looking for work and opportunities that a new life in the Americas would bring. David Souden's analysis has already challenged the prevailing myth that indentured servants were the dregs of society, shipped off forcibly to labour in the colonies. Instead, he showed that the servants sent from Bristol came from two main groups: craftsmen with skills that would prove valuable in the colonies (with such individuals thus being given favourable terms) and agricultural labourers from wood-pasture regions, often at a significant distance from Bristol. With unemployment in such regions relatively high, it was common for labourers to travel great distances in search of work. If opportunities were lacking in the city, or the prospect of a better life in the colonies proved tempting, it was not a particularly great leap for those who had already travelled far from their homes to take one more step across the Atlantic. Souden has shown that those appearing in the Register of Servants to Foreign Plantations represent the general pattern of rural to urban movement in southern England, and thus that indentured servants were 'part of the general system of migration'.[40] Rather than a 'trade' in indentured servants, it might be better to think of this as assisted migration, with those involved in Bristol's maritime world using their connections to relocate labourers to the colonies (and make a profit on the side).

Rather than a branch of trade in its own right, the significance of indentured servants to Bristol lay in establishing a labour force in the colonies, and particularly Virginia. As has already been shown (see Chapters 4 and 5), the flow of tobacco back to Bristol from Chesapeake Bay, and the wide range of manufactured goods sent in return, revolutionised Bristol's commercial world in the middle of the seventeenth century. This simply would not have happened had thousands of indentured labourers not migrated to the colonies to labour on the plantations. This also explains why Bristol's American trade flourished long after shipments of indentured servants from the city declined. Mortality on the tobacco plantations, unlike in the sugar fields of the Caribbean, was comparatively low.[41] Once a workforce was established in Virginia, a much lower supply of new servants was needed, but the business of growing and harvesting tobacco continued apace.

40   Souden, '"Rogues, Whores, and Vagabonds"?', p. 38.
41   Morgan, *Slavery and the British Empire*, pp. 85–7.

The Slave Trade

Although many thousands of words have been written about Bristol's involvement in the slave trade, its early history has received comparatively little attention. While several scholars have discussed the question of whether, and to what extent, Bristol was trading in enslaved people prior to the ending of the Royal African Company's monopoly in 1698, this has usually been confined to a few pages, or even sentences, in longer works. Their conclusions have varied wildly, with one author suggesting that, in spite of the prohibition on participation by non-Company members, Bristol was a major player in the slave trade by the 1660s, while others have suggested that it is unlikely that its merchants were involved on any great scale before the turn of the century. This lack of agreement is partly due to an absence of clear evidence. Breaking the Royal African Company monopoly was, after all, illegal, so merchants would have been keen to keep any such activities out of official records. The following discussion, therefore, seeks to re-examine previous arguments for a pre-1698 Bristol-based slave trade, and, through some detective work with the surviving customs records, to substantiate the extent to which Bristolians did indeed trade in enslaved people in the latter seventeenth century.

Previous Arguments for a Pre-1698 Bristol Slave Trade
Speculation that Bristol may have been breaking the Royal African Company monopoly dates back to at least the late nineteenth century. In his monumental *The Annals of Bristol* John Latimer highlighted Bristol merchants' displeasure at the granting of the Royal African Company's monopoly, a proclamation that they 'quietly ignored' and that was 'unable to prevent the steady development of African trade in Bristol'. He later elaborated that, 'although positive evidence on the point has perished, it is certain that they, and others, sent vessels to the Slave Coast, and carried out a large contraband business'.[42] The first modern historian to think seriously about the question of whether Bristol was involved in the slave trade during the Company era was the University of Bristol's great professor of imperial history, Charles MacInnes. Between the 1930s and 1950s MacInnes addressed this question in a variety of works on England's role in the slave trade, and Bristol's role in the British Empire. For MacInnes, there was no doubt that Bristol merchants were breaking into the monopoly on a significant scale. In his 1934 work *England and Slavery*, for example, he stated that, '[a] fter the Restoration [in 1660] Bristol threw itself with great energy into the slave trade', and that a 1673 royal command for non-members to cease trading 'fell on deaf ears, for the city of Bristol steadily developed its connection with Africa

---

42   J. Latimer, *The Annals of Bristol in the Seventeenth Century* (Bristol, 1900), pp. 368, 485.

throughout the remainder of the century'.[43] In a later book, *Bristol: A Gateway of Empire*, MacInnes argued that 'in spite of the Royal Prohibition, [Bristol's merchants] not only continued to carry on their trade with the [African] coast, but, in the twenty years after the Company received its charter, they expanded their African connections at a rapid rate'.[44] By 1696, MacInnes suggested that 'the African trade was the largest carried on by Bristol' and that 'everyone in the city at that time … appreciated the rich and growing triangular trade which had developed between Bristol, the west coast of Africa, and the Plantations'.[45] This certainly fits with the views of the aforementioned and oft-cited Bristol annalist from the reign of Queen Anne, who remarked that 'the bricks of Bristol are baked in the blood of slaves'.[46]

It is easy to see why MacInnes argued so strongly that Bristol was a significant centre for the slave trade prior to 1698. The extent of interlopers into the Royal African Company's monopoly was well-known, even to contemporaries. MacInnes cited an estimate that 'the company exported 140,000 negroes from the coast, and the free traders 160,000'.[47] Given that Bristol became a leading player in the slave trade in the early eighteenth century once the monopoly was lifted, and that new phases of grand building work in the city showed it to have been prospering in the latter seventeenth century, it must have seemed reasonable to assume that Bristol was the source of many of these illicit slave-traders. As MacInnes remarked, however, 'statistics relating to the trade at this time are notoriously unreliable'.[48] Unfortunately, as was still common with many historians of the first half of the twentieth century, MacInnes included no references to cite his sources of information. However, he stated in the introduction to *England and Slavery* that his research was 'largely based upon hitherto unpublished material and books and pamphlets of the eighteenth and early nineteenth century which are now rare'.[49] It seems that many of MacInnes's assumptions were based on the vehemence with which Bristolians opposed the Royal African Company monopoly, expressed through both petitions to Parliament, and published pamphlets.[50]

By 1963, when he published a pamphlet on *Bristol and the Slave Trade*, MacInnes had tempered his arguments slightly, while still firmly believing that Bristol was already significantly involved in the slave trade as early as the 1660s. He now argued that 'it seems *fairly evident* … that increasing numbers of ships

43   C. M. MacInnes, *England and Slavery* (Bristol, 1934), p. 27.
44   MacInnes, *Bristol: A Gateway of Empire*, p. 179.
45   MacInnes, *England*, p. 28; MacInnes, *Bristol: A Gateway of Empire*, p. 181.
46   Morgan, *Bristol and the Atlantic Trade*, p. 131.
47   MacInnes, *England*, p. 28.
48   *Ibid.*
49   *Ibid.*, p. 7.
50   *Ibid.*, pp. 28–9.

resorted to the African coast' (my emphasis).[51] One influence on the softening
of MacInnes's arguments for Bristol interloping into the slave trade may have
been the work of his colleague Patrick McGrath. McGrath was principally a
historian of the seventeenth century, with a particular interest in the port of
Bristol and its merchant community. His early work consisted of a detailed
study of the previously un-examined records of Bristol's Society of Merchant
Venturers, along with other records, both local and national, relating to Bristol
and its mercantile business in the seventeenth century.[52] With an approach to
research firmly rooted in a detailed study of the surviving evidence, perhaps
to an extent reflecting the 'revisionist' turn in English historical studies of the
1950s and 1960s, McGrath was less prone to making broad assumptions than
scholars of MacInnes's generation.[53] His interpretation of Bristol's pre-1698
involvement in the African slave trade was, therefore, much more cautious.
While stating that 'the period saw the beginning of Bristol's connection with the
slave trade', he added that 'it seems doubtful, however, whether the trade was
of any great importance until after 1698'. Like MacInnes, McGrath's analysis
of Bristol's seventeenth-century involvement in the slave trade was rooted in
analysis of its interactions with the Royal African Company's monopoly.[54]
Rather than the city's protests against the monopoly, however, McGrath focused
on direct examples of ships penalised for illicitly participating in the trade. He
identified two such examples: the *Society* of Bristol, seized in Virginia in 1688
with a cargo of both enslaved Africans and ivory from Guinea, and the *Betty*
of Bristol, prosecuted for violating the Company's monopoly.[55] McGrath had
also clearly discussed the matter with K. G. Davies, the leading historian on the
Royal African Company, from whom he learned that 'no Bristol ships appear in
the register kept by the Royal African Company of ships seized while attempting
to trade illegally'.[56] For McGrath, this was evidence that, while occasional
Bristol ships were interloping into the African trade, there was no reason to
suppose that they were doing so on a significant scale. This does, however, leave
the perpetual problem for historians of illicit trade: absence of evidence does
not equate to evidence of absence. In other words, while confirming that illegal
slave-trading ventures were indeed carried out by Bristol vessels, such evidence

---

51   C. M. MacInnes, *Bristol and the Slave Trade*, Bristol Historical Association Pamphlets
(Bristol, 1963), p. 2.
52   P. W. McGrath, *Records Relating to the Society of Merchant Venturers of the City of
Bristol in the 17th Century*, Bristol Record Society Vol. 17 (1952); P. V. McGrath, *Merchants
and Merchandise in Seventeenth Century Bristol*, Bristol Record Society Vol. 19 (1955)
53   See Ronald Hutton's chapter on 'Revisionism' in R. Hutton, *Debates in Stuart History*
(Basingstoke, 2004), pp. 6–31.
54   McGrath, *Merchants and Merchandise*, p. xxii.
55   *Ibid.*, p. xxii.
56   *Ibid.*

only shows us those voyages where something went sufficiently wrong for the ship to be caught, so we have no idea of the number of successful ventures.

The most detailed study of Bristol's involvement in the slave trade is without doubt David Richardson's four-volume *Bristol, Africa and the Eighteenth-Century Slave Trade to America*, published by the Bristol Record Society between 1986 and 1996. Drawing together evidence from a wide range of sources, Richardson provided details of every known Bristol slave-trading voyage between 1698 and 1807. Perhaps tellingly, Richardson chose the ending of the Royal African Company's monopoly in 1698 as the beginning point for his study. For him, '[t]he ending of the [monopoly] in 1698 permitted Bristol merchants to enter the trade on a regular basis for the first time', and Bristol's merchants had 'very limited experience of it before 1698'.[57] Beyond this, Richardson did not further address the question of pre-1698 Bristolian involvement in the slave trade, simply referring the reader to McGrath's research. For more recent writers who have focused on the economic aspects of Bristol's involvement with the slave trade, such as Kenneth Morgan, the question of pre-1698 involvement simply does not figure.[58] For them, what was important was the expansion, operation, and ultimately decline of Bristol's involvement in the slave trade. What, as McGrath had shown, was probably minimal involvement prior to 1698 was merely a precursor to this story.

The most recent study to address the question of whether Bristol merchants were trading in enslaved people prior to 1698 shows greater confidence. While falling far short of MacInnes's claims, Madge Dresser has suggested that 'it seems reasonable to suppose that some Bristolians were involved in this illicit commerce'.[59] Dresser also identified several further examples of Bristol ships likely to have been involved in slave trading during the monopoly era.[60] These include the *Isabella*, which was seized in 1681 for illegally trading to Guinea. Dresser also notes a further vessel that the State Papers record as being seized the following year, although as this had come direct to Bristol from Guinea it is unlikely to have been a slave-trader. Perhaps most intriguing is an example that potentially shows one of the strategies used by Bristol merchants to conceal their illicit slave trade: three vessels recorded as leaving Bristol for Madeira in 1679 (the *Mary*, the *Hopewell*, and the suggestively named *Blackamore*). As Dresser points out, 'it was a common fiction for ships going to Africa to slave to state their destination as Madeira or the Cape Verde Islands'.[61] The name of the *Blackamore*, along with the cargoes of the three vessels (which included

57   Richardson, *Bristol, Africa, and the Eighteenth-Century Slave Trade*, pp. xiv–xv.
58   Morgan, *Bristol and the Atlantic Trade*, pp. 128–51.
59   M. Dresser, *Slavery Obscured: The Social History of the Slave Trade in Bristol* (Bristol, 2007), p. 14.
60   *Ibid.*, pp. 15, 43.
61   Dresser, *Slavery Obscured*, p. 15.

types of cloth and felt hats, which were common components of slave-trading cargoes), suggest that this may well have been the case with these vessels.

New Evidence

As stated above, that there have been varying opinions on the extent of Bristol's pre-1698 involvement in the slave trade is predominantly a result of a lack of clear evidence. Prior to this study, evidence had only been found for three Bristol ships that were certainly interloping into the slave trade, along with a further three that circumstantial evidence suggests may have been doing so. Not only were the surviving Bristol trade records too dense to be subjected to detailed analysis, but non-Company slave trading was illegal at this time, so merchants would not be expected to leave a paper trail that could lead to their conviction. Thus, the majority of vessels identified as participating in this trade are the unlucky few who were caught and prosecuted, and any attempts to gauge the total number involved have rested on speculation and back projection. Standards of criminal investigation in the seventeenth century were, however, low. Although merchants would, as described, declare a false destination for any Africa-bound ships, this was about the extent of their subterfuge in the customs records. When the same vessel returned carrying sugar from the Caribbean or tobacco from Virginia, they would not attempt to hide it. There was virtually no risk of anyone going back to the customs books to check the declared destination upon departure from Bristol. With the aid of modern technology, however, such investigations are relatively straight-forward. By comparing the return cargoes of ships that look like they may have been declaring a false destination to cover a trip to Africa, it is possible to identify whether they had made a triangular voyage. Opportunities to do this are unfortunately limited, as only relatively few export Port Books survive for Bristol from the latter half of the seventeenth century. Fortunately, however, as the Wharfage Books record imports in a continuous run from the 1650s to the 1680s, wherever export records survive it is possible to check the return of the ships. As a result of this new methodology, several previously unknown early Bristol slave-trading voyages have been uncovered.

The *Blackamore*, 1672

One of the Madeira-bound ships that Dresser identified as suspicious in 1675 also appears in the export side of the 1671/2 Port Book. The *Blackamore* was once again declared as being bound for Madeira, carrying an assorted cargo of cloth and other wares that certainly could have found a market on the Slave Coast.[62] Even more interestingly, she returned to Bristol on 7 July 1673 carrying a cargo of tobacco, which almost certainly meant that she had come from

62   TNA PRO E190/1138/1, ff. 114r–116r.

the American colonies.[63] Although declaring Madeira as a destination was certainly a tactic used to cover an illicit African voyage, it must be added that it was common practice for ships to genuinely stop at Madeira en route to the American colonies, both to re-supply, and to pick up a cargo of wine (as Madeira wine had a specific exemption from the Staple Act). Indeed, in 1686 at least forty ships called at Madeira on their way to the colonies, and it has been estimated that as much as 80 per cent of wine consumed in the colonies originated in the Atlantic islands.[64]

The identity of the merchants shipping goods on the *Blackamore* may also lead us to ask whether this was a slave-trading voyage. Comparison with other records has shown that the majority of those involved were Quakers. In 1676, the noted Quaker (and close acquaintance of many of the Bristol Friends) George Fox published a pamphlet that read,

> if you were in the same condition as the Blacks are ... now I say, if this should be the condition of you and yours, you would think it hard measure, yea, and very great Bondage and Cruelty. And therefore consider seriously of this, and do you for and to them, as you would willingly have them or any other to do unto you ... were you in the like slavish condition.[65]

It is thus certainly possible that Bristol's Quaker merchants could have avoided the slave trade on religious and moral grounds. Equally, however, it was not until 1761 that the Quakers formally prohibited slave ownership, and such a move was only necessary because many Quakers had become heavily involved.[66] Even at the time Fox was writing his pamphlet, other leading Quakers were involved in the buying, selling, and holding of enslaved people. William Penn, for example, both owned and traded in enslaved people in his Pennsylvania colony. Penn was a descendant of a Bristol family, and maintained close ties to the city, as shown by his marriage to Bristol Quaker Hannah Callowhill.[67] The exports on the *Blackamore* were declared in the names of three individuals: William Yeamans, John Speed and Harculas Hodges, with Yeamans accounting for the vast majority. On the return voyage, both Yeamans and Speed again

---

63   BRO SMV/7/1/1/5.

64   Zahedieh, *Capital and the Colonies*, pp. 254–5.

65   G. Fox, *Gospel Family-Order, Being a Short Discourse Concerning the Ordering of Families, Both of Whites, Blacks and Indians* (1676).

66   J. Jennings, 'Mid-Eighteenth-Century British Quakerism and the Response to the Problem of Slavery', *Quaker History*, 66(1) (1977), p. 25.

67   J. McNeill, *The Life and Family of William Penn: 260 Years of Bloody Colonial History*, Bristol Radical Pamphleteer No. 18 (Bristol, 2012); E. R. Turner, 'Slavery in Colonial Pennsylvania', *The Pennsylvania Magazine of History and Biography*, 25(2) (1911), pp. 141–51; M. L. Geiter, 'Penn, William', *Oxford Dictionary of National Biography* (Oxford, 2004).

declared goods, and they were joined by John Speed's brother Thomas and a Thomas Gouldney. It is well attested that the Speed family were Quakers,[68] as was the grocer Thomas Gouldney, who was imprisoned three times for his faith.[69] Hodges has proved impossible to trace and this is his only recorded shipment, possibly implying he was a mariner conducting a limited amount of trade in his own name. William Yeamans is also difficult to identify, as two related merchants of the same name were active in Bristol in the early 1670s. One was certainly a leading member of the Quaker community, and indeed married the stepdaughter of George Fox, but discussion with Jonathan Harlow suggests that the William Yeamans involved in this voyage is likely to be the older of the two, who, although probably not a Quaker, was a regular trading partner of John Speed. Being a Quaker in the 1670s certainly did not prohibit being involved in the slave trade, or indeed slave ownership. The links to the Friends of many of those involved in the *Blackamore* voyage do at least, however, give pause for thought when considering whether she was indeed trading in enslaved people in 1672.

The *Blackamore* remained active in Bristol's colonial trade for at least another decade, with the last record of her in the Port Books examined to date coming in October 1684, when she set sail for Barbados. In this time, the records show at least another ten transatlantic voyages, and there are doubtless others for which no records survive. Frustratingly, it may not be possible to prove conclusively whether these were slave-trading voyages. One to and from Virginia in 1678/9 that took just six months seems unlikely to have been. Others, however, seem much more plausible. Twice more she declared Madeira as a destination. In 1679 she left Bristol for Madeira and Nevis and returned nine months later from Barbados. In 1681 she once more recorded her destination as Madeira, not appearing in the Bristol Port Books again until her return nearly thirteen months later.[70] Whether or not she can conclusively be proven to have been a slave-trader, however, the name of the *Blackamore* certainly shows that Black Africans were increasingly on the minds of Bristol's merchants and shipowners by the 1670s and 1680s.

The *Endeavour* and *Mary Fortune*, 1662

While the *Blackamore*'s 'Madeira' voyages may or may not be slave trading, the 1661/2 Searcher's Export Port Book from Bristol contains two further examples of potential slave-traders that leave less room for doubt. These are the *Endeavour*, which was loading goods at Bristol in 1662 (with the last entry

---

68   J. A. S. Harlow, 'The Life and Times of Thomas Speed' (unpublished PhD thesis, University of the West of England, 2008).
69   R. Mortimer (ed.), *Minute Book of the Men's Meeting of the Society of Friends in Bristol 1667–1686*, Bristol Records Society Vol. XXVI (1971), p. 201.
70   1678/9 Port Book; 1681/2 Port Book; 1682/3 Port Book.

on 21 February), and the *Mary Fortune*, the last consignment for which was declared on 6 September.[71] Both vessels declared their destination as the Cape Verde islands, and these are the only examples of this destination being listed in any of the pre-1698 Bristol Port Books examined to date. It is also interesting because both of Bristol's first two 'legal' slave-traders after the end of the monopoly in 1698 declared themselves as bound initially for Cape Verde. According to Richardson's detailed listing of all known Bristol slave-trading voyages after 1698, the aptly named *Beginning* left Bristol, bound initially for Cape Verde, on 18 January 1698. No other African destination for her is known, but she returned to Bristol from Jamaica on 30 June 1699. Similarly, in Bristol's second post-monopoly slave-trading voyage, the *Betty of Exon* left on 10 February 1698, bound again for Cape Verde, although her ultimate African destination was Guinea. She then returned (to Plymouth) from Barbados on 6 April 1699.[72] The exact timing of these two 1698 voyages, not remarked on by Richardson, is interesting, as they both left England *prior to* the official end of the Royal African Company monopoly. While the monopoly was increasingly under fire, with discussions ongoing in Parliament, and the Company itself was coming to realise that it was no longer sustainable, it was still in force in January and February 1698.[73] Any non-Company vessels leaving to trade to Africa at that point, therefore, did so illegally. The Bill bringing the monopoly to an end was not passed by the House of Commons until 23 May 1698, and received royal assent on 5 July, although the African slave trade was officially opened from 24 June.[74] While the trade was probably made legal whilst the *Beginning* and the *Betty* were on the African coast, their investors cannot have been certain that this would happen when they left Bristol. It seems, therefore, that they declared Cape Verde to the customs officers as their destination as a cover for their true intentions. Cape Verde, crucially, not being on the African mainland, was not covered by the Royal African Company monopoly. As Cape Verde was used by Bristol merchants as a false destination to cover illicit slave-trading voyages to Africa in the dying days of the monopoly-protected trade in 1698, it thus seems likely that they may have been using the same ruse at the beginning of the monopoly period in 1662.

However, these voyages may genuinely have been bound for the Cape Verde islands, which in the early eighteenth century were a regular stopping-off point for slave-trading voyages. David Richardson concluded that 'the practice of exporting goods to Africa via Madeira and Cape Verde was commonplace

---

71   1661/2 Port Book. As remarked in the introduction to this chapter, one consignment on the *Endeavour* in fact had Barbados as its stated destination.

72   Richardson, *Bristol, Africa and the Eighteenth-Century Slave Trade*, p. 1.

73   Davies, *Royal African Company*, pp. 132–3.

74   *Ibid.*, pp. 133–4; E. Donnan, *Documents Illustrative of the History of the Slave Trade to America, Volume I: 1441–1700* (Washington, 1930), pp. 421–9.

among outport merchants in the 1710s and 1720s'.[75] While in the first decade post-1698 Bristol's slave ships normally declared themselves bound for the coasts of Africa, post-1712 Richardson's figures show a change, with significant numbers declaring Cape Verde or Madeira instead as their destination. Of the 219 ships involved in Bristol's African trade between 1712 and 1721, 111 declared destinations in the Atlantic islands, with seventy of these clearing for Cape Verde.[76] That the *Endeavour* and *Mary Fortune* were genuinely using Cape Verde as a staging post for voyages ultimately bound for Africa is thus very much a possibility.

If the 'Cape Verde' declared destination of the 1662 *Endeavour* and *Mary Fortune* voyages looks suspiciously like slave trading, the same is certainly true of their export cargoes. In the eighteenth century, the goods sent on Bristol's slave-traders consisted of assorted textiles, beads, liquor, metalware and firearms, with East Indian textiles in particular making up 27 per cent of the total.[77] Variety was important, as was the right mix of goods, as customers on the African coast were sophisticated and would not buy goods they did not want. The Invoice Books of the Royal African Company show a similar pattern. In 1674, for example, cloth made up 74 per cent of their exports, with just under a third of this being East Indian. Manufactured goods and metals made up much of the remainder, with iron bars (7 per cent) and copper bars (8 per cent) particularly prominent.[78] Both ships left Bristol with their holds filled with goods looking very like those of a typical Bristol slave-trader (see Figure 49). As with the Royal African Company's ships, the most important component of both cargoes was cloth, making up 50 per cent of the *Endeavour*'s lading, and 64 per cent of that of the *Mary Fortune*. Both vessels also contained considerable quantities of felt hats (just under 10 per cent of the value of both cargoes), a regular and important feature of Bristol's eighteenth-century slave trade.[79] The cargo of the *Mary Fortune* also featured small quantities of a couple of commodities that are diagnostic of African trade: 60 lb of glass beads, and 28 yards of Indian cloth.[80] That there is not a higher proportion of Indian cloth makes the cargo makeup of these vessels rather different from that of the Royal African Company's slave-traders, but this is likely to have been due to

75   D. Richardson, 'Cape Verde, Madeira and Britain's Trade to Africa, 1698–1740', *The Journal of Imperial and Commonwealth History*, 22(1) (1994), p. 4.
76   *Ibid.*, pp. 3–4.
77   Morgan, *Bristol and the Atlantic Trade*, pp. 133–4.
78   Davies, *Royal African Company*, pp. 350–7.
79   Chris Heal, 'The Felt Hat Industry of Bristol and South Gloucestershire, 1530–1909' (unpublished PhD thesis, University of Bristol, 2012), pp. 201–2.
80   Morgan, *Bristol and the Atlantic Trade*, pp. 133–4. £542 worth of glass beads made up 1.5 per cent of the Royal African Company's exports in 1674 (Davies, *Royal African Company*, p. 357).

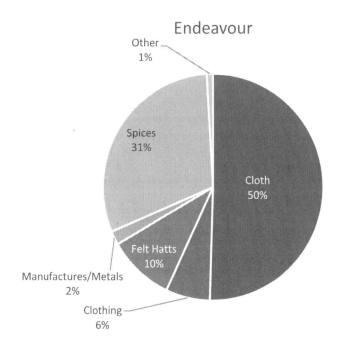

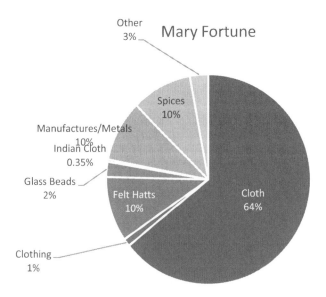

Figure 49. Cargoes of the *Endeavour* and *Mary Fortune* (in pounds sterling).
Source: 1661/2 Port Book.

the fact that Bristol's merchants would not have had such easy access to goods imported by the London-based East India Company. A little more perplexing is the spices that both ships carried, including considerable amounts of pepper on both ships, and smaller amounts of cinnamon, mace, and nutmegs on the *Mary Fortune*. Although relatively small in volume, these were very valuable goods, making up 10 per cent of the value of the *Mary Fortune*'s cargo, and more than 30 per cent of the *Endeavour*'s. These were not particularly common on later slave-trading voyages, perhaps suggesting that here we are seeing the slave trade at a formative stage, where the merchants were still trying to work out the best balance of goods to sell in Africa.

The most convincing evidence that the *Endeavour* and *Mary Fortune* were on slave-trading voyages comes, as with the *Blackamore* in 1671/2, from tracing their return to Bristol the following year. Once again there is no surviving Port Book for the period when the ships came back to Bristol, but we can gain some information about this from the Society of Merchant Venturers' Wharfage Books. The *Endeavour* returned to Bristol on 20 December 1662, ten months after the last of her outward-bound cargo was entered.[81] The *Mary Fortune* returned to Bristol in May 1663, eight months after her departure. Both of these seem a little swift for slave-trading voyages, but not impossibly so. It is generally accepted that slave-trading voyages took twelve to eighteen months, with Richardson having suggested a figure of around fifteen months for voyages from Bristol.[82] Analysis of the data for Bristol slave-trading voyages held in the 'Transatlantic Slave Trade Database', however, suggests that this might be an overestimate (see Figure 50). This shows that in the first decade of Bristol's official involvement in the slave trade, voyages took an average of 11 months 21 days from their departure from Bristol to their return to England. Voyages extended as Bristol's involvement in the slave trade reached its peak, reaching an average of sixteen months in the 1730s, perhaps reflecting increased competition resulting in it taking longer to assemble a full cargo of enslaved people on the African coast. There was also a great deal of variation in the length of voyages, with a standard deviation from the mean of around two months over the first fifty years of the eighteenth century. As is shown by the error bars on Figure 50, much shorter voyages were regularly recorded. One vessel that left Bristol in 1706 returned just 7 months 25 days later, and the fastest recorded over the whole century returned in 6 months 16 days. At eight

81   1662 Wharfage Book. Although falling within the same customs year as her departure, unfortunately only an export Port Book survives from 1662, so the Wharfage Book is the only available record of imports and thus the *Endeavour*'s return.
82   D. Richardson, 'The British Empire and the Atlantic Slave Trade, 1660–1807', in P. J. Marshall (ed.), *The Oxford History of the British Empire, Volume II: The Eighteenth Century* (Oxford, 1998), p. 447; D. Richardson, *The Bristol Slave Traders: A Collective Portrait* (Bristol, 1985), p. 5.

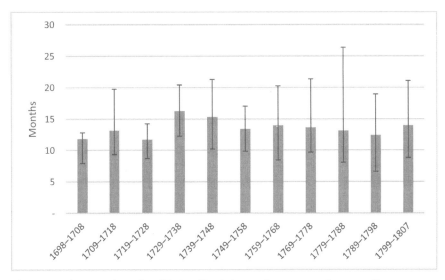

Figure 50. Average length of Bristol's eighteenth-century slave-trading voyages (with shortest and longest voyage error bars).

Source: https://www.slavevoyages.org/voyage/database (accessed 27/10/21). The dataset includes all voyages on the database for which both the date of departure from Bristol and date of arrival back in England are known.

and ten months, the voyages of the *Endeavour* and the *Mary Fortune* in 1662 thus fit well with being slave-trading voyages. This is particularly true given that sailing time in fact made up a relatively small proportion of the duration of slave-trading voyages. Ships would typically take around a month to reach Africa, the notorious middle passage four to six weeks, and the return leg to Britain took a further month.[83] Shorter voyages could thus easily be achieved if a supply of enslaved people was available on the African coast, or if (as is likely to have been the case with both these ships) their arrival in the colonies coincided with the harvest, and thus a return cargo was readily available.

While the timing of the return of the *Endeavour* and the *Mary Fortune* to Bristol perhaps leaves some doubt about where they had been in between, the cargoes that both ships declared when they returned to Bristol clearly show that they had been on a triangular transatlantic voyage. Unfortunately, the later Wharfage Books do not list the ship's last port of call, but on her return to Bristol the *Endeavour* was carrying 61.5 tons of sugar, along with 12 casks of tallow, a ton of trayne oil, 70 rolls of tobacco and a hogshead of ginger. The goods carried by the *Mary Fortune* were very similar: 26.5 tons of sugar, 22

83   Morgan, *Slavery and the British Empire*, p. 54.

bags of cotton wool, a hundredweight of indigo and 5 bags of ginger.[84] This cargo dominated by sugar with a smattering of other goods fits perfectly with the pattern for Bristol's late seventeenth-century Caribbean trade discussed in Chapter 4. Indeed, there is no other region from which a ship carrying this commodity makeup can have come. The only oddity is the trayne oil and tallow on the *Endeavour*, goods not normally seen from the Caribbean. These are much more characteristic of trade with New England, suggesting that she may have stopped there en route home, an interesting hint at potential early attempts to sell enslaved people beyond the plantation colonies. This aside, however, there is no doubt that these two vessels, which left Bristol declaring a destination off the coast of Africa, sailed on to the Caribbean before returning to the city. This is most likely to have been Barbados, as one consignment of felt hats on the *Endeavour* (declared by Richard Newman) listed Barbados rather than Cape Verde as the destination. This is certainly the same ship, as the master (William Simmonds) is the same, and the hats were declared on 19 February, right in the middle of the five-day period when the goods for Cape Verde were entered.[85]

With the new evidence of the *Blackamore* in 1672, and the *Endeavour* and *Mary Fortune* a decade earlier, it is now possible to say with a fair degree of certainty that Bristol merchants were participating in the transatlantic slave trade more than thirty-five years before the end of the Royal African Company's monopoly in 1698. The traditional start date for studies of Bristol's involvement with this form of commerce, therefore, needs to be moved back to at least the early years of the reign of Charles II. Indeed, it may be that it stretches even further back than this. Unfortunately, the administrative breakdown of the Civil War and Interregnum means that no Bristol Port Books survive for the period 1639–62. The Wharfage Books fill this gap to some extent, but as these only record goods being imported into Bristol (not exports), all we see is the returning tobacco and sugar, so it is virtually impossible to detect vessels that may have been to Africa en route. The two voyages in 1662, therefore, are Bristol's first *recorded* slave-traders, not necessarily Bristol's *first* slave-traders, although it seems highly unlikely that evidence will ever substantiate earlier voyages.

The Significance of Bristol's Seventeenth-Century Slave Trade

Overall, then, it is now possible to offer a clear assessment of the extent of Bristol's involvement in the slave trade prior to the end of the Royal African Company monopoly in 1698. Bristol merchants and vessels certainly participated in this trade as interlopers. Table 12 lists all ten voyages so far identified as either known or strongly suspected to have been participating in the slave trade.

84   1662 Wharfage Book, pp. 255–9, 292–5.
85   1662 Port Book, f. 13r.

Given that identifying these has relied on the uncommon occurrences of having customs records for successive years, or of a vessel being caught and seized by the Royal African Company, it is almost inconceivable that there would not have been more. It is highly unlikely, however, that this ever amounted to more than a few vessels in any given year. While some voyages can almost certainly be identified as slave trading, the majority do not arouse such suspicions. That Bristol's early involvement in the slave trade was modest is perhaps best proved by the development of the trade in the years after the lifting of the monopoly. David Richardson's survey of all Bristol slave-trading voyages between 1698 and 1807 shows that, even after the monopoly was lifted, Bristol sent out only a few slave ships a year. Just two slave-trading voyages are recorded in 1698, three in 1699, 1700 and 1702, and four in 1701.[86] With the monopoly abolished, Bristolians had no reason to conceal their slaving voyages, but still declared just two or three a year. It thus seems highly unlikely that they had been carrying out a trade on a more significant scale than this prior to the ending of the monopoly.

Table 12. Known or suspected pre-1698 Bristol slave-trading voyages.

Date	Ship name
1662	Endeavour
1662	Mary Fortune
1672	Blackamore
1679	Blackamore
1679	Hopewell
1679	Mary
1681	Isabella
1686	Unknown
1688	Society
1688	Betty

Sources: 1661/2 Port Book; Wharfage Books; 1671/2 Port Book; Dresser, *Slavery Obscured*, pp. 15, 43; McGrath, *Merchants and Merchandise*, p. xxii.

With an estimate of the number of slave-trading voyages Bristol was conducting in the second half of the seventeenth century, it is possible to estimate both the number of enslaved people that they carried, and the significance of this branch of trade within Bristol's broader commerce. From David Richardson's detailed investigation, we have good knowledge of the number

---

86   Richardson, *Bristol, Africa, and the Eighteenth-Century Slave Trade*, pp. 1–4.

of enslaved people carried by Bristol ships in the eighteenth century. Although the number varied according to the size of the vessel, there was a general trend towards larger enslaved 'cargoes' as the trade developed. Thus, while slave vessels in the mid-eighteenth century were carrying 250 or more enslaved people on average, those in the first decade averaged around 160.[87] Taking a conservative estimate of 150 enslaved people per vessel, the one or two triangular voyages sent out from Bristol per year in the last four decades of the seventeenth century would thus have shipped between 150 and 300 slaves each year. By the 1670s the slave trade may thus have already become more significant to Bristol than that in indentured servants. While, at this time, many more ships carried servants from Bristol than went to Africa for enslaved people, the number of servants on any given ship was comparatively small. In the 1670s Bristol's servant exports averaged just 242 people a year, falling to 110 in the 1680s.[88] It is certainly a chilling thought that, even before Bristol officially entered the slave trade in 1698, its vessels may have been responsible for carrying more than 10,000 enslaved people from Africa to the New World.[89]

This estimate also allows us to gauge Bristol's potential contribution to the British slave trade as a whole in the seventeenth century. The Transatlantic Slave Trade Database shows that almost 160,400 enslaved people were loaded onto British slave ships between 1661 and 1698, with a peak of 72,500 in the 1680s.[90] A putative Bristol contribution of 10,000 enslaved people over the period would thus represent around 6 per cent of the total British slave trade. However, the database is, of course, reliant on the surviving sources, and thus omits the vast majority of enslaved people shipped by illegal interlopers. Of the enslaved people recorded, 22,890 were on ships of the Company of Royal Adventurers Trading to Africa, and 127,706 on Royal African Company vessels. Although impossible to quantify, there is no doubt that the number of interlopers was significant. Between 1679 and 1682, for example, the Royal African Company agents in the Caribbean reported thirty-two interlopers, of which only four were seized and thus have left any mark on the records.[91] Davies has suggested that 'while the interlopers were delivering fewer slaves to the Plantations than the company the margin between them at this time was not as great as might be

87   Calculated from D. Richardson, 'The Eighteenth-Century British Slave Trade: Estimates of Its Volume and Coastal Distribution in Africa', *Research in Economic History*, 12 (1989), pp. 185–95.
88   Register of Servants to Foreign Plantations.
89   If 150 slaves per year on average were shipped in the thirty-six years between the first recorded Bristol slave-trading voyages in 1662 and the opening of the trade in 1698, this would mean 5,400 slaves were carried. An average of 300 slaves per year would give a total of 10,800. The Register of Servants to Foreign Plantations records 10,573 indentured servants shipped from Bristol between 1654 and 1686.
90   https://www.slavevoyages.org/voyage/database#tables (accessed 03/11/21).
91   Davies, *Royal African Company*, p. 113.

supposed'.[92] Nuala Zahedieh has similarly suggested that private slave trading was worth at least half that of the Royal African Company.[93] Bristol's share of the slave trade, therefore, is likely to have been lower than the figures suggest. It seems that the days in the 1720s and 1730s when Bristol was England's leading slave-trading port were still a long way off in the latter seventeenth century, with the city at this stage specialising instead, as it was to do in the second half of the eighteenth century, in reaping the rewards of trade in the produce grown by the enslaved.[94]

In terms of the economic significance of Bristol's seventeenth-century slave trade, its role in providing labour for the broader Atlantic slave economy was more significant than the profits of the slave trade itself. The 1661/2 Port Book shows 49 voyages leaving Bristol bound for the New World, of which 21 were declared as heading to the Caribbean and 20 to Virginia. The two slave-trading voyages of the *Endeavour* and *Mary Fortune* thus represented just 4.65 per cent of Bristol's trade with the cash crop colonies by the rough measure of shipping, or 8.7 per cent of ships headed ultimately for the Caribbean. In financial terms, they also played a relatively small part in the trade. Between them the *Endeavour* and *Mary Fortune* were carrying around £220 worth of goods when they left Bristol. While clearly the use of these goods to purchase enslaved people would have increased the value of their cargo, this is just 3 per cent of the total value of Bristol's recorded exports to the Caribbean in that year (£7,000). As with Bristol's trade in indentured servants, it was thus its role in driving the production of cash crops that was most significant, not the profits of the slave trade itself. As discussed in Chapter 4, by the time of Bristol's first recorded slave-trading voyages in the 1660s, trade with the tobacco colonies of Chesapeake Bay and the Caribbean sugar plantations had already revolutionised Bristol's commercial world. Enslaved people formed a crucial part of the workforce that produced both these crops. While, as noted above, it was only over the period 1680–1720 that enslaved labour became the norm in Virginia, in the Caribbean colonies it dominated the workforce from the outset.[95] The profits of seventeenth-century slave-trading voyages themselves were thus perhaps not of massive significance to Bristol (the profitability of the slave trade in the eighteenth century is a significant debate in its own right), but there would have been no 'American Revolution' in the city's trade were it not for the forced labourers carried by the slave ships of Bristol and London.

92   *Ibid.*
93   Zahedieh, *Capital and the Colonies*, p. 105.
94   Morgan, *Bristol and the Atlantic Trade*, p. 132.
95   McCusker and Menard, *Economy of British America*, pp. 134–7; Morgan, *Slavery and the British Empire*, p. 27.

Conclusions

Bristol's two seventeenth-century 'trades' in human beings were, then, in many respects polar opposites. That in indentured servants provided small sums of money to large numbers of people; that in the enslaved provided a small number of people with large sums of money. The profits of both, however, were marginal compared to Bristol's broader involvement in transatlantic commerce. It was rather the role this supply of labour played in facilitating an economy that generated significant import and export markets which was to truly revolutionise the city. Ultimately, it was for those sent across the Atlantic by Bristol's traders that the impact of Bristol's two trades in people was most significant. Here too these two trades were, in many ways, polar opposites. For the indentured servants, the journey to America was one which, while full of toil and danger, also presented the possibility of great opportunities. One young Welshman who left Bristol as an indentured servant in 1656, for example, may well have ended his days as one of the wealthiest men in Jamaica, owning three plantations and 122 enslaved people.[96] For those carried across the Atlantic by the *Endeavour* and Bristol's other slave-trading vessels, however, there was no such prospect of success at the end of suffering.

Bristol's seventeenth-century indentured servant and slave trades show once again the importance of using the most detailed data available to assess the importance of a branch of trade. As a result of the relatively scanty evidence base accessible to previous generations of scholars, wildly different conclusions have been arrived at as to the significance of both of these trades. These vary from seeing them as negligible to suggesting that they were the mainstays of Bristol's emerging transatlantic commerce in the seventeenth century. Detailed investigation of the Port Books, Wharfage Books, and Register of Servants to Foreign Plantations, combined crucially with the ability to link these different sets of records together, provides a much clearer and more certain set of conclusions. Due to both its multi-leg nature and illicit status, Bristol's early slave trade will always retain an element of uncertainty, but it is now clear that this should be seen as a small but regular part of Bristol's trade as early as the 1660s. The early 'trades' in both African and British labourers can thus be clearly understood as crucial to the seventeenth-century Atlantic

96   Little is known of the Henry Morgan who went on to become a successful privateer, pirate, and eventually Deputy Governor of Jamaica prior to 1665. One common suggestion is that he arrived in the Caribbean as an indentured servant, and the dates of the Henry Morgan of Abergavenny who left Bristol in February 1656 on a three-year indenture would certainly fit. Register of Servants to Foreign Plantations, http://www.virtualjamestown.org/indentures, Record Identification Number = 478; N. Zahedieh, 'Morgan, Sir Henry c. 1635–1688', *Oxford Dictionary of National Biography* (Oxford, 2008).

economy more for the labour they provided than the profits they generated. Nonetheless, given the unimaginable impact that they had on the lives of those who formed their main 'commodity', this economic perspective can only ever be a small part of the story.

Conclusion

One last ship. On 18 January 1698 the aptly named *Beginning* left Bristol. She was initially bound for the Cape Verde islands, and, like the *Endeavour* and *Mary Fortune*, she was a slave-trader. She arrived at Jamaica more than a year later, on 13 February 1699, and was back in Bristol by 30 June. She was to set sail on her second slave-trading voyage just four months later. We have no record of how many people the *Beginning* carried to a life of enslavement, but when the identically-sized *Betty of Exon* left Bristol in February 1698 it was to transport ninety-seven souls from Africa.[1] In some respects this *Beginning* is not significant. After all, this book has shown that Bristol had already been trading in African enslaved people for almost fifty years, and had been benefiting from slavery for at least a hundred and fifty. Yet, the monopoly of the Royal African Company on all trade with Africa had just been lifted, and this was thus Bristol's first legal slave-trading voyage. It was to open the floodgates. By the early 1730s Bristol was sending out nearly fifty slave-trading voyages a year, making it Britain's most notorious slave-trading port.[2] Over the 109 years between 1698 and the abolition of the trade in 1807, 2,114 slave-trading voyages left Bristol, carrying more than half a million enslaved people.[3] Through the blood, sweat, and suffering of these forced labourers, Britain's plantations were able to produce ever-growing amounts of sugar. Bristol's sugar trade grew exponentially, from 7,400 hogsheads in 1671/2 to a peak of almost 23,000 in 1785.[4] This boom in trade, and all the economic activity which came with it, was to see Bristol's population double, from around 25,000 in 1700 to 50,000 by the middle of the eighteenth century.[5] It financed the construction of many of

1 D. Richardson, *Bristol, Africa, and the Eighteenth-Century Slave Trade to America, Volume 1: The Years of Expansion 1698–1729*, Bristol Record Society Vol. 38 (Bristol, 1986), p. 1.
2 K. Morgan, *Bristol and the Atlantic Trade in the Eighteenth Century* (Cambridge, 1993), p. 132.
3 D. Richardson, 'Slavery and Bristol's "Golden Age"', *Slavery and Abolition*, 26(1) (2005), p. 36.
4 Morgan, *Bristol and the Atlantic Trade*, p. 191.
5 K. Morgan, 'The Economic Development of Bristol, 1700–1850', in M. Dresser and P. Ollerenshaw (eds), *The Making of Modern Bristol* (Bristol, 1996), p. 49.

the finest buildings and streets that are still a valued part of the city's aesthetic today.[6] It is sobering, though, that to double in size and increase its fortunes, Bristol's ships condemned more than ten times the city's population to a life enslaved and far from home. The *Beginning* ushered in a period often referred to as Bristol's 'Golden Age', but which was also its darkest hour.

In some respects, then, this book ends part way through the story. Between 1500 and 1700 Bristol's commercial world changed almost beyond all recognition. Yet much more was to come in the eighteenth century. The developments that followed were very much of the same character as those of the sixteenth and seventeenth centuries. In the most detailed study to date of Bristol's eighteenth-century trade, Kenneth Morgan characterised the development of the port's overseas activities as a process of 'Americanisation'.[7] As this study has shown, this process began in the 1650s with the first rise of a significant trade in colonial tobacco and sugar, and continued throughout the second half of the seventeenth century. The eighteenth century also saw Bristol continue its role, as discussed in Chapter 5, as 'Metropolis of the West', sourcing manufactured wares, agricultural produce and extractive goods from the region and shipping them on to the colonies.[8]

It is no exaggeration to say that the Port Book data has significantly rewritten our understanding of the state of the trade of Bristol, England's second-biggest port, in the sixteenth and seventeenth centuries. The sixteenth century was an era of depression and decay for Bristol, first overwhelmed and outcompeted by powerful London merchants, and then sharing in the overall malaise that characterised England's trade after the fall of the Antwerp mart.[9] But this study has shown that trade was in fact expanding from at least the middle of the century, with the Iberian markets flooded with New World silver providing high prices for a diverse range of English wares. Furthermore, the exact origins of the city's trade with the American and Caribbean colonies have always been uncertain. That it developed in the second half of the seventeenth century has always been known, but it was thought to account for less than a sixth of Bristol's trade in the 1650s and 1660s, rising to between a quarter and a third in the 1680s.[10] The data presented in this book shows that New World trade

6   M. Dresser, *Slavery Obscured: The Social History of the Slave Trade in Bristol* (Bristol, 2001), pp. 96–128; R. Leech, J. Barry, A. Brown, C. Ferguson and E. Parkinson (eds), *The Bristol Hearth Tax, 1662–1763*, Bristol Record Society Vol. 70 (Bristol, 2018), pp. 55–65.

7   Morgan, *Bristol and the Atlantic Trade*, p. 2.

8   *Ibid.*, pp. 89–127; W. E. Minchinton, 'Bristol, Metropolis of the West in the Eighteenth Century', *Transactions of the Royal Historical Society*, 4 (1954).

9   J. M. Vanes, *The Port of Bristol in the Sixteenth Century*, Bristol Historical Association Pamphlets no. 39 (Bristol, 1977), pp. 22–3.

10   P. V. McGrath, *Merchants and Merchandise in Seventeenth-Century Bristol*, Bristol Record Society Vol. 19 (Bristol, 1968), p. xxi.

already accounted for more than half of Bristol's much-expanded imports by the middle of the century, and continued to expand rapidly until at least the 1680s. This increased commercial activity was not confined to merchants and overseas trade, with the need to both provide a diverse range of exports and process the large volumes of imports shown to have driven a great deal of activity and innovation in manufacturing, agriculture, and mining in Bristol and beyond.

Arguably one of the key reasons Bristol's commercial developments in the sixteenth and seventeenth centuries have been underestimated is that scholars have tended to assume that trends observed at London would be reflected in the outports. Thus, Bristol's successes and failures have often been measured, for example, by looking at broadcloth exports, when, as this book has shown, these made up an increasingly small part of its trade.[11] This study has shown that it is rash to rely on information from one port to explain developments elsewhere. Equally, however, all that has been written about the development of English overseas trade in the sixteenth and seventeenth centuries is based on relatively little data. The statistics from Bristol analysed here thus represent a considerable proportion of the currently available evidence for the development of England's overseas commerce in this period. It would therefore be equally foolhardy not to consider whether the evidence from Bristol sheds fresh light on how we understand both the factors driving the development of overseas trade, and its impact on English economic development.

The first aspect that we may need to reconsider is the widely cited 'three phases' model for the development of English overseas trade during the Commercial Revolution. Separated by periods of near stagnation, Ralph Davis suggested that overseas trade grew in three bursts: 1475–1550, as a result of soaring demand for English broadcloth; 1639–89, due to the opening up of new markets in the south, and across the Atlantic; and finally the mid-eighteenth century, driven by increased production of manufactures and colonial demand.[12] Robert Brenner has already proposed modifications to this model. In particular, he suggested that Davis's second phase should be split in two, with the rise of long-distance import- and re-export-driven trades with the Near East beginning as early as 1550, followed by the development of plantation trades in tobacco and sugar from the early seventeenth century.[13] This model simply does not fit with the trends observed at Bristol, which experienced growth driven by the Atlantic economy relatively continuously from the 1550s to the 1680s, first through the Iberian Peninsula and then direct trade with the colonies. Due to

11   W. B. Stephens, 'The Cloth Exports of the Provincial Ports, 1600–1640', *Economic History Review*, 2nd ser., 22(2) (1969), pp. 228–48.

12   R. Davis, *English Overseas Trade 1500–1700* (London, 1973), p. 7.

13   R. Brenner, *Merchants and Revolution: Commercial Change, Political Conflict, and London's Overseas Traders, 1550–1653* (London, 2003), p. xi.

the dominance of London, which accounted for between two-thirds and three-quarters of England's trade in the early seventeenth century, the discontinuous phases model may still be appropriate for discussing the extent of the nation's trade.[14] That the second-largest port was showing a completely different pattern, however, suggests that it is not appropriate to explain what was driving trade. Instead, I would propose a model based not on time periods, but on economies. Until the 1550s the dynamics of English overseas trade were driven by the northern European economy centred on the London–Antwerp axis. This was then superseded by new dynamic forces in two different economies: the emerging Atlantic economy, driven principally by demand for a new range of English exports; and new attempts to break into markets in the Mediterranean and further east, driven by demand for imported wares and a desire to cut out Antwerp to get directly to the source of supply. While Bristol merchants may have aspired to be part of this eastern economy as well as the Atlantic one, the findings of this book show that they were largely unsuccessful.

The Bristol evidence also challenges the long-held crisis-driven explanation for the development and diversification of English overseas trade in the sixteenth and seventeenth centuries, instead proposing that change was driven by opportunity. The core argument here is very straightforward: Bristol never had any significant trade with the Netherlands and thus the expansion of its trade with southerly markets cannot have been motivated by a need to replace lost Antwerp trade. The growth of Bristol's trade with the Iberian Peninsula, mirrored by similar developments at London, was instead driven by demand and high prices for English exports in Spain and Portugal as a result of the influx of New World bullion, and broader prosperity brought by the colonial trades.[15] As Chapter 3 shows, experimentation and innovation were not confined to periods of crisis. The Port Books and other records show Bristol's merchants to have committed small amounts of capital to occasional voyages to new markets, or other ventures such as voyages seeking out new routes, from the middle of the fifteenth to the mid-seventeenth century, when the American colonies became established. Even at this point they continued to seek to innovate and find further potentially profitable avenues, such as the attempts to break into the transatlantic traffic in enslaved Africans discussed in Chapter 6.

There is also another lesson to be taken from Bristol's repeated experimental ventures: there was nothing inevitable or continuous about the development of new trades. The city's merchants would regularly cut their losses and abandon a venture if it was not profitable. They or another generation of merchants might pick up interest in it in the future, but equally they might not. This, for

---

14   B. E. Supple, *Commercial Crisis and Change, 1600–1642: A Study in the Instability of a Mercantile Economy* (Cambridge, 1949), p. 7; F. J. Fisher, 'London's Export Trade in the Early Seventeenth Century', *Economic History Review*, 2nd ser., 3(2) (1950), p. 152.
15   Fisher, 'London's Export Trade', pp. 154–5.

example, happened with the American trades, which were discarded by Bristol after several false starts spanning the late fifteenth to the early seventeenth century. It was only when, by the middle of the seventeenth century, the profitability of colonial commerce had been proven that they committed on a large scale. Equally the development of trade did not occur along predictable paths, suggesting there was no grand plan or dreams of empire as the writers of Whig histories liked to believe. Indeed, for the majority of the period covered here, Bristol's merchants showed as much interest in developing trade with the Mediterranean as they did with the Americas, and it was only the monopolies established by the London companies that prevented this becoming a more significant focus. As late as the 1630s (perhaps less than a decade before the city's trade was revolutionised by the growth of American commerce), Bristol merchants thought the Mediterranean as or more likely than the Americas to be the next big thing.

Much of the work on England's new trades in the seventeenth century has suggested that it was driven by imports. This is true of both the expanding trades in the Mediterranean and the East, where merchants are said to have been seeking to get closer to the source of supply for luxury wares, and the transatlantic trades, where exponential increases in production of tobacco and sugar, and the resultant dramatic fall in their price, created new markets for these cash crops in both Britain and, through the re-export trade, Europe.[16] This work does not seek to challenge the role of imports as a driver of the expansion of overseas trade. It does, however, build on Nuala Zahedieh's work on the London Port Books to suggest that overseas demand for English exports has been unduly overlooked.[17] In the sixteenth and early seventeenth centuries, the flow of New World silver into the Iberian Peninsula drove an expansion of trade by creating a profitable market for English wares. Ireland, too, from the late sixteenth century consumed an increasingly diverse range of English manufactures. Once England established its own overseas colonies, their exclusive focus on cash crop production meant that they were reliant on English vessels to provide them with all manner of goods, from food, clothing and tools to luxury goods.

This greater emphasis on export-led demand has significant implications for the relationship between slavery and English economic development, and in particular the causation of the Industrial Revolution.[18] Davis and others have suggested that the diversification of English exports, moving away from

---

16   Brenner, *Merchants and Revolution*, pp. 39–45; Davis, *English Overseas Trade*, p. 7; N. Zahedieh, *The Capital and the Colonies: London and the Atlantic Economy 1660–1700* (Cambridge, 2010), p. 15.

17   Zahedieh, *Capital and the Colonies*, p. 289.

18   E. Williams, *Capitalism and Slavery* (London, 1964); K. Morgan, *Slavery, Atlantic Trade, and the British Economy, 1660–1800* (Cambridge, 2000); J. E. Inikori, 'Atlantic Slavery

an almost exclusive focus on broadcloth, occurred in the late seventeenth and early eighteenth centuries.[19] The Bristol Port Books, however, show England's largest outport to have already diversified its exports by the mid-sixteenth century. Initially, this was focused on the produce of an increasingly market-oriented agricultural sector, as well as the increased output of mines adopting new technologies.[20] Increasingly, though, this was alongside a wide range of manufactured 'wares', sent to Ireland, continental Europe, and, from the mid-seventeenth century, North America and the Caribbean. Analysis of the Burgess Books shows that growing numbers of people were employed in an increasing range of manufacturing roles in mid-seventeenth-century Bristol. This included both processing the huge volumes of tobacco and sugar that flowed into the city, and producing the array of goods for export. The Coastal Port Books show that this economic development was not confined to the city, with manufactures and agricultural and extractive produce flowing into Bristol from all parts of the coastal and riverine hinterland. The links to slavery here are clear. From the outset, the colonies in the Caribbean were reliant on enslaved labour, as were those of Chesapeake Bay as the seventeenth century progressed. This book's findings on the development of Iberian trade also push English economic benefit from slavery back to the sixteenth century, where slave-mined gold and silver provided a market for the output of increasingly market-oriented agriculture, crafts, and industry in England.

A final point is the increasing extent to which an Atlantic economy was emerging in the sixteenth and seventeenth centuries. This idea was championed by Immanuel Wallerstein's work on world systems theory, and, despite several challenges, has recently won greater acceptance in light of Kenneth Pomeranz's work on the question of the 'Great Divergence'.[21] The role of Atlantic markets in providing demand that drove commercial and industrial development has already been discussed. That this long pre-dated England's own colonies, with English development being shaped by the New World through its impact on Spanish and Portuguese prices, is a perfect illustration of why one needs to understand what is happening *everywhere* in the Atlantic world to interpret developments in a particular location. It is also worth noting some of the

and the Rise of the Capitalist Global Economy', *Current Anthropology*, 61(supplement 22) (2020).

19   Davis, *English Overseas Trade*, p. 9.

20   Brenner, *Merchants and Revolution*, pp. 39–45; J. U. Nef, 'The Progress of Technology and the Growth of Large-Scale Industry in Great Britain, 1540–1640', *Economic History Review*, 5(1) (1934), pp. 9–11.

21   I. Wallerstein, *The Modern World-System II: Mercantilism and the Consolidation of the European World-Economy, 1600–1750* (London, 2011); K. Pomeranz, *The Great Divergence: China, Europe, and the Making of the Modern World Economy* (Princetown, 2000).

more complex interconnections that have emerged from this research, the most interesting of which is Ireland. Far from being merely another 'colony', it was an independent actor, with a web of connections to different parts of the Atlantic. In the late sixteenth century, Ireland imported an increasingly wide range of consumer wares from Bristol (even though the absolute value of Ireland–Bristol trade was in steep decline) because Ireland had its own trade connections with the same Spanish markets driving Bristol's prosperity at the time. There were many more such interconnections: for example, the role of Irish provisions in feeding the enslaved on the Caribbean plantations, or the role of Newfoundland cod in Bristol's Spanish trade. This research very much supports Pomeranz's suggestion that the 'ghost acres' of the New World fuelled English economic development (and indeed had done so for much longer than previously supposed).[22] In turn, we must recognise the complexity of the system, with the American colonies relying on their own 'ghost acres' growing provisions in England and Ireland, and European trades being closely tied to those across the Atlantic.

Perhaps the biggest lesson of this research, however, is how misleading partial or summary statistics can be. In many instances, such as the extent of Bristol's American trade in the second half of the seventeenth century, detailed research based on the Port Books has shown previous estimates to be a long way short of the mark. In others, based on sources that look at only part of the picture (for example estimates of imports based on the New Impositions returns, or of exports based solely on broadcloth), deeply flawed conclusions can be reached. Fortunately, the advent of computer technology means we now no longer need to rely on sampling techniques such as simply counting the number of ships, or easy-to-access sources that just give totals for trade (or even trade in specific commodities). Once transcribed, it is possible to examine the entirety of a port's trade for a given year, based on the value of the goods and their volume, and thus get the most complete and accurate picture possible of the state of trade. These more detailed sources are admittedly not without their problems. For example, transcription is still hugely time-consuming: it took me around three months to transcribe each of the late seventeenth-century Bristol Port Books. Poor survival means we do not have a continuous series, and thus risk basing conclusions on an incomplete year; and goods that were either smuggled or duty-exempt can be overlooked. Nonetheless, as this book has sought to do, carrying out source-linkage with the imperfect but more continuous data series, and other more qualitative records that point to gaps in the data, can help to address and compensate for these problems. Furthermore, the pace at which computer technology is developing points to a bright future for such rich sources, and also potential remedies for some of the issues with

22 Pomeranz, *Great Divergence*, pp. 264–85.

using them. The E190 series contains as many as 20,000 Port Books spanning the years 1565–1799, and the Particular Accounts contained in the E122 series take the coverage back to as early as 1272.[23] Machine reading technology is developing at a significant rate, and it seems likely that computers will be able to automatically transcribe early modern handwriting in the near future. This has the potential to make the Port Books a much larger data series, if still not a continuous one, and also to facilitate studies that go beyond a single port. In the meantime, there are attempts underway to crowdsource transcriptions of the Port Books, and some have already been transcribed by commercial family history companies.[24] Furthermore, this book has used just one piece of software to examine the Port Book data, but there are significant possibilities to gain new insights via other technology such as Geographical Information Systems, Social Network Analysis Software, and relational databases. This book has aimed to act as a torch shining a light on the so-called 'dark ages' of English economic history, but in the future there is the potential to add a more powerful battery, and a much brighter bulb.[25]

---

23   http://www.nationalarchives.gov.uk/records/research-guides/port-books.htm.
24   https://portfolio.winchester.ac.uk/ (accessed 01/04/22); https://search.findmypast.co.uk/search-world-records/devon-port-books (accessed 01/04/22).
25   F. J. Fisher, 'The Sixteenth and Seventeenth Centuries: The Dark Ages in English Economic History', *Economica*, New Series, 24(93) (1957), pp. 2–18.

Technical Appendix

Analysing the figures contained in the Port Books is an extremely technically demanding process. To convert raw data into meaningful information, a great many calculations and conversions need to be performed; after all, these records were not created with the needs of those performing in-depth statistical analysis in mind. Indeed, such an analysis as is presented here would have been inconceivable in the sixteenth and seventeenth centuries! For the sake of transparency and verifiability, it is necessary to explain how these calculations have been made, and any decisions taken in interpreting the data. To do so in the main body of the book, however, would greatly disrupt the flow of the argument, and make the text very difficult for a non-specialist to follow. Therefore, this appendix both removes technical explanations from the core chapters and gives them the space to be explored fully. This approach also allows issues to be explored across the whole period and all branches of trade, rather than facing the chronological and geographical restrictions that considering such issues within the chapters would impose. Finally, consolidating all the information in one place provides a guide for anyone carrying out future research on the Port Books.

Inputting the Data

To facilitate the detailed analysis that forms the backbone of this project, eleven seventeenth-century Port Books and three years of Wharfage accounts were transcribed into Excel. These were supplemented by thirteen Particular Account and Port Book datasets from the sixteenth century, previously transcribed and published by the ESRC-funded project 'Ireland-Bristol Trade in the Sixteenth Century'.[1] To ensure consistency, the transcription conventions adopted by the Ireland-Bristol project were followed. In particular, as the analysis relies heavily

---

[1] Digital versions of the Ireland-Bristol Trade datasets are available here: http://www. bris.ac.uk/Depts/History/Ireland/datasets.htm (accessed 20/06/22). The transcriptions have also been published in print as Susan Flavin and E. T. Jones (eds), *Bristol's Trade with Ireland and the Continent: The Evidence of the Exchequer Customs Accounts* (Dublin, 2009).

on using alphabetical sort and search functions, the spelling of commodities was standardised and modernised. Modern names for the ports were also added, along with their nation, to allow regionalised analysis of trade patterns. An additional column was also added to decimalise pounds, shillings and pence, again to facilitate easy analysis; £1 13s. 4d. thus becomes £1.67.

In an ideal world all the surviving Port Books and Wharfage Books would have been fully transcribed and analysed. Transcription of a whole year of accounts is, however, a very time-consuming process, and so, even though survival is patchy, some choices have had to be made about which accounts were transcribed. The Port Books that are in best condition, and thus yield the most complete dataset, were favoured. The accounts transcribed in full were supplemented by more continuous data from the less detailed Enrolled Accounts and New Imposition returns, which only provide total figures for duty collected in a given year. The total duty collected has also been extracted from a number of additional Port Books, giving the total value of trade in those years. The majority of the Port Books transcribed were produced by the Customer and Controller, as these record the poundage paid, from which the value of goods can be calculated. The export account from 1662, however, is a Searcher's account. As the Searcher did not record the duty paid, these values have had to be added by hand, calculated from the volume of goods. There are a few cases where it has not been possible to ascribe a value, either due to differences in the unit of measurement or no valuation existing for that commodity. The impact of this on the validity of the dataset is minimal, however, as it has been possible to ascribe values to 7,070 out of 7,137 individual consignments (99 per cent), and those which are lacking tend to be for obscure or unusual goods. The Customer and Controller's accounts also, in many cases, did not list consignments of goods on which no duty was payable. In particular, consignments of re-exported tobacco are not listed in the 1671/2 export account. Fortunately, these goods were recorded by the Searcher, as his role was to check what goods were loaded on the ship, not what duty they paid. This is generally not an issue, as such goods only made up a relatively small percentage of trade. Some caution is, however, needed in years when it is necessary to rely entirely on a non-Searcher's account for exports. For example, while no tobacco re-exports are recorded in 1671/2, this is unlikely to have been the case, as the Searcher's account from ten years earlier shows substantial trade.

Weights and Measures

Since at least the time of Magna Carta, attempts have been made to standardise the plethora of weights and measures in use in England.[2] More than four hundred years later, however, there was still a great deal of inconsistency, with the capacity of numerous containers varying significantly according to time, place and commodity.[3] To allow consistent analysis, this study has standardised the capacity measures of the key shipping containers to those listed in Table 13. This may, therefore, result in some slight discrepancies, although it will certainly not undermine the broad trends shown by the data. These measures have also been used by several other studies of Bristol's sixteenth- and seventeenth-century trade, so will allow for easy comparison.[4]

Table 13. Capacity of shipping containers.

	Tons
Barrels	8
Tierces	6
Hogsheads	4
Puncheons	3
Butts/Pipes	2

Where possible, measures listed in the Book of Rates in use at the time have been used. When conversions have been necessary, it has been assumed throughout that 2,240 lb = 1 ton. The Book of Rates lists a hundredweight on most goods as 112 lb (resulting in exactly 20 cwt per ton) so it seems likely that this was the definition most commonly in use at the time. The values stated in the Book of Rates in use at the time were adopted for all other weights and measures.

2   The 35th clause of Magna Carta (first issued in 1215) demanded the introduction of standardised weights and measures for several important commodities, including grain, wine, beer and cloth. https://www.bl.uk/magna-carta/articles/the-clauses-of-magna-carta (accessed 29/06/18).
3   See J. J. McCusker, 'Weights and Measures in the Colonial Sugar Trade: The Gallon and the Pound and Their International Equivalents', *The William and Mary Quarterly*, 30(4) (1973), pp. 599–624.
4   See Flavin and Jones (eds), *Bristol's Trade with Ireland*, pp. 943–66; J. Harlow (ed.), *The Ledger of Thomas Speed, 1681–1690*, Bristol Record Society Vol. 63 (Bristol, 2011), p. 524.

Valuing Goods

To make comparisons between different types of goods, and between different branches of trade, it is essential that all commodities are assigned a financial value. Some conclusions can certainly be drawn from volume-based compar-isons, and observing increases or decreases in the volume of goods being shipped often provides a valuable verification of trends observed from the value of trade. The significant variation of different types of goods in relation to their bulk, however, makes volume-based measures unreliable for examining the overall picture of trade. A ton of sheepskins, for example, was worth considerably less than the same volume of wine. Branches of trade that consisted predomi-nantly of high-volume low-value goods (such as that with Ireland), therefore, will appear much more prominently in a tonnage-based study than reflects their true economic importance. In the Middle Ages, when overseas commerce consisted predominantly of the shipment of particular staple goods to and from a narrow range of markets, volume can perhaps to an extent be used as a cipher for the value of trade. In the fifteenth century, for example, across all branches of trade, 98 per cent of the value of Bristol's exports consisted of woollen cloth.[5] With the increasingly diverse range of both goods and trade routes that characterised the sixteenth and seventeenth centuries, however, such an approach is not suitable. Assigning a monetary value to the goods is thus key to facilitating meaningful analysis.

Fortunately, as taxation is inherently a financial process, monetary values were applied to goods as they passed through the customs house and were recorded in the Port Books. In the main, these values are used in this study. Under the early modern English customs system, overseas trade goods paid one of two basic types of duty. Some, such as wine, leather and broadcloth, paid 'specific' duties, which meant that the duty was dependent on the volume of goods shipped: broadcloth, for example, paid 6s. 8d. per cloth. All other goods paid poundage, an *ad valorem* tax of one shilling in the pound. Poundage thus amounted to a 5 per cent tax on the recorded value of the goods. This meant, for example, that a barrel of honey valued at 30s. in the Port Book would be liable to pay 1s. 6d. poundage. It is important, however, to understand that the values recorded in the Port Books were based neither on the market value of the goods nor on the merchant's own declaration. Instead, valuations were based on an official list known as the 'Book of Rates' that recorded the nominal value of every type of commodity known to the customs service. Therefore, even if

---

5   R. Stone, 'Bristol's Overseas Trade in the Later Fifteenth Century: The Evidence of the "Particular" Customs Accounts', in E. T. Jones and R. Stone (eds), *The World of the Newport Medieval Ship: Trade, Politics, and Shipping in the Mid-Fifteenth Century* (Cardiff, 2018), p. 183.

the market value of the aforementioned barrel of honey was known to be 60s., it would still be valued by the customs at 30s.

While the poundage valuation provides a monetary value for the vast majority of goods appearing in the Port Books, for those that paid specific duties, based on their volume, an alternative solution has to be found. Unfortunately, this includes two of the key commodities for Bristol's trade: woollen 'broadcloth' and wine. One potential solution to this problem would be to simply apply current wholesale prices for these commodities. This was the approach taken by D. H. Sacks in his analysis of Bristol's late sixteenth- and early seventeenth-century trade. Sacks valued wine at £15 per ton and broadcloth at £8 per piece, based on early seventeenth-century wholesale prices.[6] However, this does not take account of the fact that the valuations in the Books of Rates rarely reflected current wholesale prices, and were often significantly lower than them. As Table 14 shows, comparison of the 1604 Book of Rates with known wholesale prices from the first decade of the seventeenth century reveals market values to have been two or three times higher than the customs valuations, with even greater disparities for agricultural products. For example, while lead was valued at £0.45 the hundredweight by the 1604 Book of Rates, its average wholesale price for the decade 1603–12 was 15s. 4½d. the hundredweight, 70 per cent more than the customs valuation. The difference for wheat was even more dramatic: the Book of Rates valued it at £0.33 the quarter, whereas its wholesale price was more than five times higher at £1.76 the quarter. Applying unadjusted wholesale prices to goods paying specific duties would, therefore, greatly exaggerate the importance of trade in these commodities. As discussed in Chapter 1, in Sacks's study, the artificially high valuation used for wine significantly impacted his conclusions. By over-valuing the importance of Bristol's southern import trades, Sacks's figures created an artificial deficit between imports and exports.

Table 14. Comparison of 1604 poundage valuations with contemporary wholesale prices.

			1603–12		1633–43	
Commodity	Quantity	Customs valuation (£)	Average wholesale price (£)	% difference	Average wholesale price (£)	% difference
Barley	quarter	0.25	0.97	388	1.21	484
Hops	cwt	1.00	3.32	332	4.11	411
Iron	cwt	0.35	1.63	466	2.33	666

6   D. H. Sacks, *The Widening Gate: Bristol and the Atlantic Economy, 1450–1700* (London, 1993), p. 41.

Table 14 continued

			1603–12		1633–43	
Commodity	Quantity	Customs valuation (£)	Average wholesale price (£)	% difference	Average wholesale price (£)	% difference
Lead	cwt	0.45	0.77	171	0.87	193
Nutmegs	lb	0.15	0.22	147	0.24	160
Prunes	12 lb	0.05	0.13	260	0.11	220
Raisins	12 lb	0.10	0.21	210	0.25	250
Rice	12 lb	0.09	0.3	333	0.22	244
Salt	quarter	0.27	0.94	348	1.34	496
Sugar	12 lb	0.40	1.01	253	1.08	270
Wheat	quarter	0.33	1.76	533	2.06	624

Source: Based on a comparison of James E. Thorold Rogers, *A History of Agriculture and Prices in England, Volume 5* (Oxford, 1887) and the 1604 Book of Rates. This table shows a comparison of the valuations found in the 1604 Book of Rates (in use throughout the early Stuart period) and known wholesale prices from the time (from Rogers's survey). Using the wholesale price from a specific year would run the risk of an atypical price, so a decennial average for the decade closest to the 1604 Book of Rates has been selected. The last decade before the Civil War is also reproduced to show any potential effects of price rises. To allow calculations, the values have been converted into decimals. The figure for '% difference' expresses the typical wholesale value as a percentage of the customs value. Although analysis of a wider range of commodities would be preferable, the lack of a detailed recent study of price data from the seventeenth century meant that it was only possible to find reliable data for eleven of the goods regularly involved in Bristol's trade.

This study has adopted the values for goods paying specific duties used by the ESRC-funded project Ireland-Bristol Trade in the Sixteenth Century. For the period 1558–1604, wine is valued at £8 per ton, cloths of assize at £4 the cloth, and leather at £2 the dicker.[7] As customs valuations were, on the whole, two to three times lower than current wholesale prices, and these figures are roughly half the wholesale prices employed by Sacks, these valuations should be roughly in line with those on commodities paying poundage. To account for inflation and the resultant increases in the poundage valuations, these nominal values for cloth, wine, and leather have been increased in line with each revision of the Book of Rates. A summary of the nominal values used throughout the period is provided in Table 15.

7   http://www.bris.ac.uk/Depts/History/Ireland/datasets.htm (accessed 15/06/12).

Table 15. Nominal values used for goods paying 'specific' duties.

Commodity	Unit	pre-1558	1558–1604	1604–42	post-1642
Wine	the ton	£4	£8	£9	£16
Broadcloth	the cloth	£2	£4	£4.50	£9
Leather	the dicker	£1	£2	£2.25	£4.50

Inflation and Adjustment

When conducting a study of trade that spans two centuries, one of the biggest problems is inflation. In an era when prices were rising rapidly, it is virtually impossible to compare figures across the whole period without making adjustments to balance out inflation. As set down in the Books of Rates, the poundage valuations used in this study did not fluctuate year-to-year in response to market forces. In the short term, therefore, any trends observed will be a result of developments in trade rather than changes in prices. Changes to the Books of Rates had to be approved by Parliament, and thus making adjustments to account for shifts in prices was not a simple process. The result was that significant revisions of the poundage variations were rare, with just four occurring in the sixteenth and seventeenth centuries (1558, 1604, 1642, 1660). Instead, the Crown was forced to resort to adding legally questionable 'Imposition' duties (recorded separately in the Port Books) to increase its revenues from overseas trade taxation. Large-scale re-assessments of the rates occurred predominantly at the beginnings of new reigns, when Parliament had to officially re-grant the right to collect customs duties to the new monarch. These revisions could be significant, and therefore could seriously distort the figures presented by the customs accounts. Some adjustment, therefore, is necessary to allow the direct comparison of poundage-derived figures from either side of these revisions.

The simplest way to establish the extent of the change, and thus the adjustment that needs to be made to the customs figures, is to compare the valuations in the old and new Book of Rates. T. S. Willan, for example, calculated that the revised Book of Rates issued in 1558 saw rates increase by an average of 118 per cent.[8] A simple doubling of all pre-1558 values, therefore, allows a fairly effective comparison with any figures from after this date. Comparing new values with old, however, is unfortunately not as straightforward as it initially appears. The extent of the revaluation varied markedly from commodity to commodity, so determining the exact level of increase is difficult. Moreover, for some goods, changes in the terminology used or the

8   T. S. Willan, *A Tudor Book of Rates* (Manchester, 1962), pp. xxvii–xxviii.

unit of measure make direct comparison virtually impossible. Nonetheless, when comparing the 1604 Book of Rates (the next significant revision) with that from 1558 examined by Willan there are still 780 commodities appearing in both the old and new Book of Rates where both the definition and unit of measure remain the same and thus a direct comparison is possible. This reveals that the official valuations of 553 commodities were unchanged in 1604; 52 goods had their valuations decreased; and 175 had their values increased. The overall impact of these changes was a mean rise of 13 per cent, far short of Willan's figure of 118 per cent for the previous revision. As this figure is based on the entire Book of Rates, it may be artificially low, as it will naturally include some commodities that were rarely traded and thus did not merit a revision. Restricting the comparison to the most commonly traded goods, however, reveals a similarly low figure. Looking at a selection of twenty-five of the most significant commodities for Bristol's trade (accounting for 65 per cent of the value of the goods paying poundage in Bristol in 1600/1), the mean rise in valuations is still only 20 per cent. As a final check, Bristol's trade in these twenty-five commodities for 1600/1 was recalculated using both the old and new rates of duty. This showed that, while the total value of these goods in the 1600/1 account was listed as £17,800, if the 1604 valuations had been in use that year, the total value of the goods would have been £19,000.[9] The revaluation would thus have resulted in a rise of just 7.23 per cent in the customs receipts collected on these goods. Comparison of poundage-based Port Book figures from the late sixteenth and early seventeenth centuries, therefore, is relatively unproblematic. No adjustment has thus been made in this study when comparing pre- and post-1604 figures.

New Books of Rates were issued on several occasions between 1604 and the outbreak of the Civil War, but crucially for the purposes of analysis based on the customs records, the poundage valuations remained largely unchanged.[10] There were some minor alterations, with a few commodities being removed from the book while others were either added to the list or were divided into subcategories. In the vast majority of cases where direct comparison can be made, however, the official values of goods in the 1635 Book of Rates (in use up to 1642) were identical to those listed in 1604.[11] With Parliament remaining uncooperative, the first Stuart monarchs resorted

9   Based on analysis of '1604 Book of Rates' and http://hdl.handle.net/1983/1308.
10   New Books of Rates were issued in 1609, 1610, 1635 and 1636. A. M. Millard, 'The Import Trade of London, 1600–1640' (unpublished PhD thesis, University of London, 1956), pp. 19–20.
11   In 1609 the subsidy for tonnage and poundage was revised on forty-nine commodities, with all but two of these being reductions. The changes in 1610 and 1635 were restricted to the addition of Imposition duties, and in 1636 tonnage and poundage were raised on six commodities. Millard, 'The Import Trade of London', pp. 19–20.

to further Imposition duties to expand their revenue from customs receipts, rather than revising the valuations in the Book of Rates. Impositions could be 'imposed' directly by royal prerogative without recourse to Parliament, whereas adjusting the Book of Rates required parliamentary consent. As tensions mounted between the King and Parliament, the political consequences of this policy for Charles I were catastrophic. For statistical purposes, however, it makes the situation much simpler: between 1558 and 1642 there was only one significant revaluation (the 1604 book), which resulted in a mean rise of no more than a fifth.

A significant overhaul of the customs valuations did, however, occur in 1642, with several new Books of Rates issued over the next two decades until the final 1660 form. Although new versions of the Book of Rates were issued regularly over the remainder of the seventeenth century, the poundage valuations themselves remained unaltered, with changes relating either to other types of duty, or the laws governing trade that were re-printed in the Books. In this study, the 1660 Book of Rates has been used for the whole period from 1642 onwards. Any figures from the last six decades of the seventeenth century can therefore be compared without adjustment. Some revision is needed, however, to compare these post-Civil War figures with those from earlier in the century. As with the 1604 revisions, the duties levied on many commodities had risen considerably during the Interregnum, although the scale of this increase was far from uniform, with many remaining unaltered. Comparison of the pre-1642 and post-1660 rates for a sample of twenty of the most important commodities for Bristol's trade (accounting for 84 per cent of total imports in 1654/5) shows an average increase in valuations of 74 per cent (see Table 16). The mid-seventeenth-century revisions, therefore, were more akin to the wholescale reassessment of 1558 than the minor adjustments of 1604. The situation is complicated somewhat, however, by the rates for tobacco and sugar which, as discussed below, fell in price considerably in the mid-seventeenth century. A significant reduction in their valuation, therefore, could in fact still represent an increase in relation to their wholesale price. Exclusion of these two commodities from the comparison shows an average increase of 92 per cent over the 1604 values. For the purposes of analysis, therefore, a simple doubling of any figures from prior to 1642 should permit a fairly accurate comparison with those from the latter half of the seventeenth century.

Table 16. Comparison of pre-1642 and post-1660 customs rates.

Commodity	Measure	pre-1642			post-1660			% increase
		£	s.	d.	£	s.	d.	
Aquavita	hogshead	4	0	0	4	0	0	100
Iron, battery	cwt (112 lb)	3	0	0	9	0	0	300
Canvas, vittery	100 ells (6 score)	3	6	8	5	0	0	150
Cloth, dowlas	peece (106 ells)	3	6	8	5	0	0	150
Cloth, frise	ell	0	0	16	0	5	0	375
Currants	cwt (112 lb)	0	30	0	6	0	0	400
Figgs	cwt (112 lb)	0	16	8	1	13	6	201
Fish, herrings white	last (12 barrels)	5	0	0	5	0	0	100
Hemp, rough	cwt (112 lb)	0	13	4	0	13	4	100
Honey	barrel	0	30	0	2	0	0	133
Oyle	ton	16	0	0	32	0	0	200
Paper, copy	ream	0	2	6	0	4	6	180
Prunes	cwt (112 lb)	0	10	0	0	15	0	150
Raisons, great	cwt (112 lb)	0	13	4	1	10	0	225
Raisons, of the sun	cwt (112 lb)	0	18	0	2	0	0	222
Soap, Castile	cwt (112 lb)	0	33	4	3	0	0	180
Sugar, brown/ muscovado (plantations)	cwt (112 lb)	3	6	8	1	10	0	45
Sugar, white (plantations)	cwt (112 lb)	3	6	8	5	0	0	150
Tallow	cwt (112 lb)	0	16	8	0	16	8	100
Tobacco	lb	0	5	0	0	1	8	33

Sources: '1635 Book of Rates'; '1675 Book of Rates'.

Tobacco and Sugar

While across-the-board adjustments to the valuations of goods are a reasonably good way of facilitating comparison of trade over extended periods of time, they become problematic when some goods went against the broader current of rising prices. In particular, the prices for tobacco and sugar fell rapidly during the middle of the seventeenth century, with increasingly efficient and well-established plantation production in the colonies flooding the market. The price of tobacco, for example, had fallen from more than 13s. per lb before the Civil War to 2s. (or even less for lower-quality leaf) by the end of the century.[12] Such was the speed of the decline that the Book of Rates valuations were constantly becoming out of date, and could thus lag considerably behind the actual value of tobacco and sugar. As these were such crucial commodities in the increasingly important New World trades, this presents a significant problem for analysing customs figures. Using artificially high valuations for these key commodities risks seriously overstating the importance of the new American trades. For example, in 1654 Bristol imported 1.9 million lb of tobacco. If this is valued according to the (then current) 1642 Book of Rates, it would be considered worth £311,000. However, if the slightly later 1660 Book of Rates is used, the same tobacco would be valued at £156,000. Given the rapid price falls during the 1640s and 1650s, the latter figure is likely to more accurately represent the current price for tobacco in 1654. In order to avoid exaggerating the growth of the American trades, and to facilitate easy comparison with the post-1660 Port Books, it was thus decided to apply the valuations from the 1660 Book of Rates to all accounts analysed from after 1642.

In the case of tobacco in particular, questions have been asked as to whether the tobacco valuation in the Book of Rates, even the later 1660 version, is so inaccurately high that it is rendered unusable. Ralph Davis, for example, commented that the customs valuation of 1s. 8d. the lb on colonial tobacco was 'absurd', as its first cost in the colonies was more in the region of 2d.[13] Customs valuations in the seventeenth century, however, were not based on first cost, instead being intended to reflect the value of the goods in the port. In a study of London's trade from slightly later in the seventeenth century, Zahedieh also adopted significantly lower values for tobacco of 6d. per lb for the period 1663/9, with an even lower value of 2.4d. the lb for 1686.[14] The earlier of these valuations is ultimately derived from the 'Book of Tables', a series of import statistics for the port of London compiled by the House of Lords from the customs records.[15] As Davis has shown, the valuations were only added to these statistics at a later date (probably 1678), and so probably represent much later prices.[16] Coming from the 1697 Inspector General's Ledgers, the latter figure is even later, and indeed is probably based on the colonial rather than the home

---

12   Rogers, *A History of Agriculture*, pp. 467–8.
13   R. Davis, 'English Foreign Trade, 1660–1700', in W. E. Minchinton (ed.), *The Growth of English Overseas Trade in the 17th and 18th Centuries* (London, 1969), p. 87.
14   N. Zahedieh, *The Capital and the Colonies: London and the Atlantic Economy 1660–1700* (Cambridge, 2010), p. 189.
15   Davis, 'English Foreign Trade', p. 84.
16   *Ibid.*, p. 85.

price.[17] These values again are likely to be too low. Davis suggests that the value of 6d. per lb was 'probably near the merchants' price for poorer qualities'.[18] Prices as low as 6d. can be found in the late seventeenth century, but there were in fact many different grades of tobacco at greatly varying prices. One price current from 1686, for example, lists thirteen varieties, varying in price from 7¼d. to 3s. the pound.[19] There is unfortunately no complete series of retail prices for tobacco from the seventeenth century, although Rogers has collected some examples from sources such as Pepys's diary and college accounts (see Table 17). These show that tobacco prices fluctuated, but certainly were significantly higher than the customs valuation, especially before prices fell in the 1670s. Although the Book of Rates valuations were often significantly lower than current retail prices, comparison of the figures for a selection of overseas trade goods suggests that the valuations of sugar and tobacco, in the 1670s at least, were not out of line with those for other commodities (see Table 18). It seems, therefore, that the Book of Rates valuation for tobacco was not particularly out of line with the other values contained within the Book of Rates, and so no adjustment is needed.

Table 17. Retail price for colonial tobacco, 1633–86 (per lb).

Year	Retail price	
	s.	d.
1633	12	3
1649	4	0
1655	8	0
1658	9	5
1662	8	0
1670	3	1.5
1674	2	6
1681	2	6
1684	1	8

Source: Rogers, *A History of Agriculture*, pp. 467–8. Rogers was careful to differentiate between colonial and the more expensive Spanish tobacco.

17   Zahedieh, *Capital and the Colonies*, pp. 12–13.
18   Davis, 'English Foreign Trade', p. 87.
19   Zahedieh, *Capital and the Colonies*, p. 205.

Table 18. Comparison of retail prices and Book of Rates valuations, 1663–72.

Commodity	Quantity	Book of Rates valuation (1675) (£)	Average retail price (1663–72) (£)	Retail price as % of Book of Rates value
Ginger	lb	0.07	0.05	75
Hops	cwt	1.50	4.48	299
Iron (wrought)	cwt	0.80	1.88	234
Lead (wrought)	cwt	1.00	1.15	115
Raisins	lb	0.01	0.03	194
Sugar (brown, coarse)	lb	0.01	0.04	280
Tallow	cwt	0.83	1.24	149
Tobacco	lb	0.08	0.11	131

Sources: Rogers, *A History of Agriculture*, pp. 467–8; '1675 Book of Rates'. Values have been decimalised to aid comparison.

Irish Trade

Although the general trend was for goods to have their valuations increased after 1642, to adjust for inflation, commodities traded with Ireland appear to have been an exception. Analysis of the customs rates for the goods most commonly involved in Bristol's Irish trade shows that on the whole they were not increased. This was largely due to the types of goods involved in this trade, which relied heavily on raw material imports and manufactured exports. Trade in these goods was seen as beneficial to the English economy, so those setting the customs rates kept their valuations low to encourage their shipment. As Table 19 shows, the vast majority of goods imported from Ireland saw no increase in their customs valuations between 1635 and 1675, with only tanned hides seeing their valuation doubled. The eight import commodities included in this table made up as much as 73.5 per cent of Bristol's imports from Ireland in 1671/2, so on the import side it can safely be concluded that the revision of the Book of Rates had only minimal impact on the figures for Irish trade. Recalculating the figures recorded in 1671/2 for these 73.5 per cent of commodities using both the old and new valuations shows an increase in value of just 1.5 per cent.[20] On the export side, the majority of goods sent to Ireland were manufactures (56.9 per cent of recorded exports by value in 1671/2) which, as discussed below, had their valuations halved, and other exports such as hops and lead saw only

20   Using the '1635 Book of Rates', recorded imports of these eight commodities would have been valued at £10,688.85. Using the post-1660 version, the valuation is only fractionally higher at £10,847.44.

modest increases. Although figures for Irish exports are thus likely to have been distorted by changes to the Book of Rates, it is unlikely that they will have been artificially inflated. Unlike other branches of trade, therefore, the figures for Irish imports and exports after 1642 do not need to be adjusted upwards to account for inflation, and thus should be directly compared with those before the Civil War. This does, however, mean that by the post-Restoration period, the valuations of goods involved in the Irish trades had not undergone any significant revision for more than a century.

Table 19. Comparison of customs valuations for Irish trade goods, 1635 and 1675.

Commodity	Unit	1635				1675				% increase
		£	s.	d.	£ [decimal]	£	s.	d.	£ [decimal]	
Cloth, frieze	yard	0	0	9	£0.04	0	0	9	£0.04	100
Fish, herring white	barrel	0	8	4	£0.42	0	8	4	£0.42	100
Hides, cow or horse in hair	piece	0	2	6	£0.13	0	2	6	£0.13	100
Hides, cow or horse tanned	piece	0	5	0	£0.25	0	10	0	£0.50	200
Hops	cwt (112 lb)	0	20	0	£1.00	1	10	0	£1.50	150
Lead, cast	fodder (20 cwt)	9	0	0	£9.00	20	0	0	£20.00	222
Oil, trayne	ton	6	0	0	£6.00	6	0	0	£6.00	100
Skins, goat in hair	dozen	0	6	8	£0.33	0	6	8	£0.33	100
Skins, sheep in wool	skin	0	0	3	£0.01	0	0	3	£0.01	100
Tallow	cwt (112 lb)	0	16	8	£0.83	0	16	8	£0.83	100

Source: '1635 Book of Rates'; '1675 Book of Rates'. Hops and lead are export rates; all others are import rates. The '% increase' figure expresses the valuation in use after 1660 (1675) as a percentage of the 1635 valuation of that commodity.

Exported Goods

Changes to the Book of Rates valuations for exported goods have also made Bristol's exports much more difficult to analyse for the second half of the seventeenth century. Here the relationship to wholesale price, tenuous at the best of times, appears to have been completely broken. In an age that produced the Navigation Acts and Staple Act, and with a tradition of manipulating customs valuations in the light of mercantilist principles dating back to at least James I's creation of Imposition duties, it is perhaps unsurprising to see poundage valuations being manipulated to suit the economic ideals of the time. In an attempt to foster domestic industry, and to stifle that of England's rivals, the duty on exports of English manufactured goods was halved in an effort to encourage trade. Alongside this, the valuations of many raw materials were increased significantly to discourage their export. With the growing importance of manufactures in the second half of the seventeenth century, the net result was that the recorded value of exports actually dropped after the Restoration, when the great expansion of imports suggests that exports too should have been growing. Recorded exports, for example, were £48,000 in 1636/7 but just £32,000 in 1671/2. While some of the deficit in 1671/2 may be explained by the absence of tobacco re-exports, even the Searcher's account from 1661/2 (which includes these) records exports valued at just £51,500.[21] This means that export figures from before and after the Civil War cannot be directly compared without significant revisions. This has the potential to seriously distort any analysis based on customs figures, potentially overstating the level of the deficit between imports and exports and underplaying the importance of manufactured goods in the makeup of export cargoes. Fortunately, however, the rate of adjustment seems to have been fairly uniform. Rather than tailoring the adjustment for each individual commodity, those altering the Book of Rates valuations simply halved the valuations on all manufactured goods. Looking at a prominent type of cloth, for example, single pieces of Barnstable Bays were valued at £2 in the pre-Civil War Books of Rates, but in the post-1660 version their valuation had been changed to £1.[22] It is thus fairly straightforward to 'correct' the Port Book data to give a balanced set of export figures. When processing the 1661/2 and 1671/2 export accounts, the values of manufactured exports have been doubled.

21   1636/7 Port Book; 1661/2 Port Book; 1671/2 Port Book.
22   1635 Book of Rates; 1675 Book of Rates.

Illicit and Invisible Trade

One of the most difficult factors for a historian of trade to account for is the impact of smuggling. Illicit trade was widespread in the early modern world and could thus potentially have a significant impact on the Port Book figures. Indeed, some historians have suggested that the early modern customs records are rendered useless by the uncertainties of potentially significant illicit trade.[23] As important recent work by Evan Jones has shown, however, merchants did not smuggle indiscriminately. By examining the available evidence and considering which branches of trade gave sufficient incentive to smuggle, it is thus possible to gauge the likely impact of illicit trade. Provided illicit trade is considered and accounted for, the trade figures from the Port Books can therefore be treated with confidence.

In the first half of the seventeenth century, Bristol's illicit trade appears to have followed much the same pattern as observed by Jones for the sixteenth century.[24] The high cost of licences meant that considerable quantities of prohibited goods such as calf-skins and Welsh butter were exported illicitly, and prohibitively high Imposition duties also led to the smuggling of luxury goods such as wine. Wartime embargoes on trade could also lead to some illicit commerce with restricted markets, and the growth of monopolies and other restrictions may also have led Bristol's merchants to conceal voyages to Greece and (right at the end of the period) the Americas. The principal conclusions about Bristol's trade in this period are not, on the whole, undermined. The main story is growth in Bristol's trade, and smuggling would only have added to this, although it may to some extent have exaggerated the level of decline in the 1560s and 1570s. Although towards the end of the period there may have been some illicit ventures into new markets, these remained peripheral, and on the eve of the Civil War the traditional trades remained the core of Bristol's commerce. As noted in Chapter 1, smuggling is likely to have had the most significant impact on Bristol's overseas commerce trade in terms of prohibited agricultural goods to the Iberian Peninsula in the mid- to late sixteenth century. The significant expansion in the quantities of such goods being recorded in the Port Books once licensing regimes were relaxed early in the following century, along with the large amount of qualitative evidence, suggests that this trade is likely to have been significant. As discussed in Chapter 1, therefore, Bristol's continental trade under the Tudors is likely to have been much more export-led than a straight reading of the customs data suggests.

---

23   E. T. Jones, *Inside the Illicit Economy: Reconstructing the Smugglers' Trade of Sixteenth-Century Bristol* (Farnham, 2012), pp. 8–11.
24   *Ibid.*

Marking a major watershed in terms of the development of Bristol's trade as a whole, the second half of the seventeenth century also saw significant shifts in Bristol's patterns of illicit trade. As a result of falling agricultural prices, export prohibitions were lifted in the early 1660s, removing the incentive for one of the principal branches of Bristol's illicit trade.[25] This, combined with the relatively low duty on manufactured exports, means that illicit exports would have been minimal in the second half of the seventeenth century. The export figures from the Port Books can thus be treated as reliable for this period. Import smuggling, on the other hand, remained rife. William Culliford's investigations into the Bristol customs service in the early 1680s revealed an administration every bit as corrupt as that of the sixteenth century.[26] As a result of the introduction of prohibitively high duties, considerable amounts of linen, and other luxury commodities such as wine and spirits, were smuggled in from France. The main branch of illicit trade, however, appears to have been tobacco imports. Estimates of the extent of this trade vary, but it seems that something between 3 and 17 per cent of Bristol's tobacco may have been smuggled in the late seventeenth century.[27] Again, this does not undermine the principal conclusions of this study. The decline of the French trade may have been slightly less marked than suggested by the figures, but overall the American colonies had replaced the traditional European commerce at the heart of Bristol's overseas trade. Regardless of the level of smuggling, there is no doubt that Bristol's American trades had expanded greatly, and additional smuggled tobacco would only serve to accentuate this trend.

The Wharfage Books
The three datasets derived from the Society of Merchant Venturers' Wharfage Books (1654/5, 1659/60 and 1664/5) form an invaluable part of this study, providing information on a crucial period for the development of Bristol's trade from which, unfortunately, no Port Books survive. Wharfage, however, was a duty based on the volume, rather than the value, of goods. Turning the Wharfage Books into a usable dataset that can be compared to those from the Port Books thus poses an additional technical challenge.

Wharfage was a duty, first imposed in 1606, on all goods imported into Bristol. Officially the money was designated for the repair of Bristol's port facilities, but as early as 1610 the Society of Merchant Venturers was collecting

25   L. A. Clarkson, 'English Economic Policy in the Sixteenth and Seventeenth Centuries: The Case of the Leather Industry', *Bulletin of the Institute of Historical Research*, XXXVIII (1965), p. 156.
26   W. B. Stephens, *The Seventeenth Century Customs Service Surveyed: William Culliford's Investigation of the Western Ports, 1682–84* (Farnham, 2012), pp. 35–54.
27   R. Stone, 'The Overseas Trade of Bristol in the Seventeenth Century' (unpublished PhD thesis, University of Bristol, 2012), pp. 153–6.

it for its own use; indeed, as the century progressed it was to become one of its main sources of income.[28] The first surviving Wharfage Book, in which the Society recorded its receipts from Wharfage, begins in May 1654, and provides a very detailed record of Bristol's trade. Indeed, as McGrath has noted, the Wharfage Books closely resemble the Port Books, but with the advantage that they survive in an unbroken series from 1654 to 1694.[29] They certainly record many of the same details as the Port Books; in addition to duty paid (at 8d. per ton) these included the name of the ship, where it came from, the type and volume of goods, and the name of the merchant importing them. Indeed, Jonathan Harlow has suggested that they were 'effectively duplicates of the Port Books', with both sets of records based on the same information, forming part of a continuous clearance process for the merchant.[30] Perhaps most crucially he has shown that 'a comparison with the Port Books for some arbitrarily selected cargoes shows the entries to be virtually identical in content and date' to those in the Wharfage Books.[31]

Harlow has perhaps slightly exaggerated the merits of the Wharfage Books. Although they did contain far more detail than was necessary for Wharfage purposes alone, the level of detail recorded declined slightly over time. The clerks were, for example, erratic as to whether they recorded the exact date of a shipment; indeed, this is largely omitted in the 1659/60 account, which simply states the month at the top of the page. More importantly, the port of origin is omitted after 1661, and by the 1670s the layout of the accounts had changed dramatically, making it increasingly difficult to tell exactly which vessel a consignment had come from. Rather than 'duplicates' of the Port Books, it might be better to see the Wharfage Books as separate records based on a similar model. When the Society of Merchant Venturers was deciding in 1654 how to record its Wharfage receipts, naturally they turned to the Port Books as an exemplar of what details to record and how they should be laid out. Over the years, however, the Wharfage Books developed independently, gradually removing extraneous details from the recording process. Nonetheless, they remain an invaluable record of Bristol's trade, all the more useful for surviving in a continuous series for a period where the Port Books are scant or even non-existent.

However, the amount of time it takes to input and process a year's Wharfage accounts means that it has not been possible to examine all of these in depth.

28   P. V. McGrath, *The Merchant Venturers of Bristol: A History of the Society of Merchant Venturers of the City of Bristol from Its Origin to the Present Day* (Bristol, 1975), pp. 71–2.
29   P. V. McGrath, *Records Relating to the Society of Merchant Venturers of the City of Bristol in the Seventeenth Century*, Bristol Record Society Vol. 17 (Bristol, 1951), p. liii.
30   J. A. S. Harlow, 'The Life and Times of Thomas Speed' (unpublished PhD thesis, University of the West of England, 2008), pp. 172–3.
31   *Ibid.*, p. 173.

Instead, three years of accounts, spaced at five-year intervals, were selected to give an impression of the state of trade in the crucial period where surviving Port Books are lacking. Although in some respects a limited sample, this still represents a considerable advance on any previous statistical surveys of trade in this period. The first year chosen was 1654/5, the first from which a Wharfage Book survives, and so the earliest chance to see any lasting impact of the Civil War on Bristol's trade, and how the American trades had developed in the sixteen years of statistical darkness.[32] A second year's accounts were selected from 1659/60, both to test the findings from 1654/5 and to show the state of Bristol's trade on the eve of the Restoration.[33] Although, as discussed, the declining level of detail in the Wharfage Books makes them harder to use after 1661, a third account from 1664/5 was also transcribed to trace the development of Bristol's trade after the Restoration. This required some additional measures to convert into a usable dataset, discussed separately below.

Valuing the Goods
Despite their many merits, the Wharfage Books do have one significant disadvantage compared to the Port Books: the Wharfage duty was based solely on the volume of goods being imported, and thus gives no account of their monetary value. With the help of a computer, however, it is relatively easy to create a similar set of data out of the Wharfage Books. Replicating the job of a seventeenth-century customs officer, it is possible to take the volumetric record of commodities from the Wharfage Books and, using the Book of Rates, assign a nominal value to each consignment. There are, however, a few difficulties that hamper this process. The most common is differences between the measures used in the Wharfage Books and the Book of Rates. In such cases it has usually proved possible to convert to the correct unit to value the goods, but where this was not achievable (for example with non-specific measures such as 'chests' of sugar or 'baggs' of wool), the Wharfage duty itself has been used to calculate the volume of goods, with 8d. of duty paid equating to a ton of goods. There are also a number of cases where the goods described in the Wharfage Book do not have a value listed in the Book of Rates. Even for a seventeenth-century customs officer this was not uncommon: there are certainly examples in the Port Books of the customs officer having to invent a value for non-listed

32 Unlike the Port Books that run from Christmas to Christmas, this Wharfage account only begins in May. In the interests of acquiring the earliest data possible, it was, therefore, decided to take the accounts for the year running from May 1654 to May 1655. May was a relatively quiet time in Bristol's trading calendar, so this is unlikely to have had any significant impact on the data. There does not appear to be any particularly consistent internal logic to the period covered by each set of Wharfage accounts, with summaries occurring at different quarters, usually Christmas or in September.
33 For 1659/60, the usual Christmas to Christmas year was adopted.

goods. Where possible, therefore, the rate used in previous Port Books has been adopted. Wool, for example, had ceased to incur duty by the Restoration, so the valuation in use in 1637/8 was adopted. Failing this, the rate for a similar commodity was substituted; for example, the rate for aquavita was used for 'spirrits', which does not appear in the Book of Rates.[34] Where no solution has been possible, such as the entries of 'several goods' on pages 17 and 62 of the 1659/60 account, entries have been omitted rather than corrupting the results with a guess. Adopting this methodology means that the figures cannot give a 100 per cent accurate set of data. On the other hand, however, errors are likely to be confined to individual consignments, and particularly to obscure goods rather than the main staples of Bristol's trade. Thus, the overall impact on the broad trends reflected is likely to be minimal. Cases in which it was not possible to assign a value made up just 1.23 per cent of imports in 1654/5 and 0.95 per cent in 1659/60.[35]

The 1664/5 Account

Unfortunately, unlike the Port Books and earlier Wharfage accounts, the 1664/5 Wharfage records do not usually list the port that the ship had come from, making analysis more difficult. It is, however, possible to determine the origin of a ship with a reasonable degree of accuracy based on the commodities it was carrying. Table 20 outlines the key commodities used to identify particular regions of origin.

The process of determining where ships had come from was aided by the few cases where the Wharfage Clerk had recorded the ship's origin. Via references to the same ship, it was possible to firmly identify the origin of 28 per cent of the trade. Conversely, in marginal cases where it is impossible to place exactly where a ship came from, again I have erred on the side of caution by leaving this blank, rather than guessing. Nonetheless, of 1,847 individual entries in the 1664/5 Wharfage Book it has been possible to identify the probable origin of all but fifty-three. In terms of value, the consignments for which origin could not be determined amounted to just £7,600, less than 2 per cent of total imports.

---

34   For a full list of commodities occurring in the Wharfage accounts, and the nominal valuations which have been ascribed to them, see Stone, 'Overseas Trade of Bristol in the Seventeenth Century', appendix 3.1.

35   These figures were calculated using the Wharfage duty paid on those consignments.

Table 20. Rules used to determine the origin of a ship based on the makeup of its cargo.

Region of origin	Commodity
American mainland	Predominantly tobacco
Baltic	Deal boards
France	Wine, aquavita/spirits, paper, canvas
Greece	Currants
Iberian Peninsula	Wine, dried fruit, olive oil
Ireland	Skins, tallow, frieze cloth, beef, grains
Netherlands	Mixed cargo, often including plates and ironware. Perhaps the most difficult to spot as similar to French trade, but also unlikely to have occurred to any great extent in 1664/5 due to the Anglo-Dutch War
West Indies	Mixed cargo of sugar, tobacco, occasionally other commodities such as ginger and indigo

Clearly, any analysis based on data from the 1664/5 account cannot be relied on to the same extent and cannot give the same level of detail as that based on fuller accounts. It is, for example, impossible to tell whether a ship carrying a superficially Iberian cargo came from Spain, Portugal or the Atlantic islands. Ships from Ireland may also present a problem, as analysis of earlier accounts shows that it was increasingly common for them to carry re-exports from the American and West Indian colonies. Unfortunately, the name of the ship has not been given with each consignment, and although it seems that Harlow's suggestion that subsequent entries were also carried on the previously listed ship is broadly accurate, the possibility of omission on the part of the Wharfage Clerk remains.[36] For example, some ships appear to have come from Ireland carrying significant quantities of commodities more characteristic of American or European trade. These may have been re-exports, the ship may have been on a multi-part voyage stopping off in Ireland on the way back from elsewhere, or the Wharfage Clerk may simply have neglected to note a change of ship. In such cases, unless it is clearly a single entry in the middle of a cargo entirely Irish in character (therefore likely to be a re-export), the origin has been left unknown.

36   Harlow, 'Life and Times', p. 172.

Bibliography

Primary Sources

Manuscript Sources
Particular Accounts
Bristol 'Particular' Customs Account, 1485/6 – Cabot Project dataset, forthcoming.
Bristol 'Particular' Customs Account, 1486/7 – Cabot Project dataset, forthcoming.
Bristol 'Particular' Customs Account, 1492/3 – Cabot Project dataset, forthcoming.
Bristol 'Particular' Customs Account, 1503/4 – http://hdl.handle.net/1983/1296.
Bristol 'Particular' Customs Account, 1516/17 – http://hdl.handle.net/1983/1297.
Bristol 'Particular' Customs Account, 1525/6 – http://hdl.handle.net/1983/1298.
Bristol 'Particular' Customs Account, 1541/2 – http://hdl.handle.net/1983/1299.
Bristol 'Particular' Customs Account, 1542/3 – http://hdl.handle.net/1983/1300.
Bristol 'Particular' Customs Account, 1545/6 – http://hdl.handle.net/1983/1301.
Bristol 'Particular' Customs Account, 1550/1 – http://hdl.handle.net/1983/1302.
Bristol 'Particular' Customs Account, Imports, 1563/4 – http://hdl.handle.net/1983/1303.
Bristol 'Particular' Customs Account, Exports, 1563/4 – http://hdl.handle.net/1983/1304.

Port Books
http://hdl.handle.net/1983/1305 – Bristol Port Book, Overseas Inwards, 1575/6.
http://hdl.handle.net/1983/1306 – Bristol Port Book, Overseas Outwards, 1575/6.
http://hdl.handle.net/1983/1307 – Bristol Port Book, Overseas, 1594/5.
http://hdl.handle.net/1983/1308 – Bristol Port Book, Overseas, 1600/1.
TNA PRO E190/1133/1 – Bristol Port Book, Controller, Overseas, 1601/2.
TNA PRO E190/1133/8 – Bristol Port Book, Controller, Overseas, 1608/9.
TNA PRO E190/1133/11 – Bristol Port Book, Customer, Overseas Outwards, 1611/12.

TNA PRO E190/1134/3 – Bristol Port Book, Customer, Overseas Inwards, 1612/13.

TNA PRO E190/1134/10 – Bristol Port Book, Controller, Overseas, 1620/1.

TNA PRO E190/1134/11 – Bristol Port Book, Customer, Overseas Outwards, 1620/1.

TNA PRO E190/1135/6 – Bristol Port Book, Controller, Overseas, 1624/5.

TNA PRO E190/1136/1 – Bristol Port Book, Customer, Overseas Outwards, 1628/9.

TNA PRO E190/1136/3 – Bristol Port Book, Customer, Overseas Outwards, 1618/19.

TNA PRO E190/1136/8 – Bristol Port Book, Customer, Overseas Outwards, 1636/7.

TNA PRO E190/1136/10 – Bristol Port Book, Customer, Overseas Inwards, 1637/8.

TNA PRO E190/1137/3 – Bristol Port Book, Customer, Overseas Inwards, 1670/1.

TNA PRO E190/1138/1 – Bristol Port Book, Controller, Overseas, 1671/2.

TNA PRO E190/1139/2 – Bristol Port Book, Customer, Overseas Inwards, 1677/8.

TNA PRO E190/1140/2 – Bristol Port Book, Customer, Overseas Outwards, 1678/9.

TNA PRO E190/1141/1 – Bristol Port Book, Controller, Overseas, 1679/80.

TNA PRO E190/1142/2 – Bristol Port Book, Customer and Controller, Overseas, 1680/1.

TNA PRO E190/1142/3 – Bristol Port Book, Controller, Overseas, 1680/1.

TNA PRO E190/1143/1 – Bristol Port Book, Customer, Overseas Outwards, 1681/2.

TNA PRO E190/1144/1 – Bristol Port Book, Controller, Overseas, 1681/2.

TNA PRO E190/1146/1 – Bristol Port Book, Controller, Overseas, 1682/3.

TNA PRO E190/1147/1 – Bristol Port Book, Customer, Overseas Outwards, 1683/4.

TNA PRO E190/1147/2 – Bristol Port Book, Customer, Overseas Outwards, 1684/5.

TNA PRO E190/1148/1 – Bristol Port Book, Controller, Overseas, Christmas 1686/7.

TNA PRO E190/1148/2 – Bristol Port Book, Customer, Overseas, Outwards, 1686/7.

TNA PRO E190/1149/1 – Bristol Port Book, Customer, Overseas Outwards, 1687/8.

TNA PRO E190/1240/6 – Bristol Port Book, Searcher, Overseas Outwards, 1661/2.

Adam Matthew Publications/University of Wolverhampton, 'The Gloucester Port Book Database, 1575–1765' (1998).

Other

TNA PRO E351/797-826 – New Impositions Returns, 1610–40.

TNA PRO E356/28-29 – Enrolled Accounts, 1560–1603.

BRO SMV/2/1/1/34 – Book of Trade, Society of Merchant Venturers of Bristol.

BRO 1374814 – William Adams's Bristol Chronicle (c. 1645).

BRO SMV/7/1/1/1 – Wharfage Book, 1654–59.

BRO SMV/7/1/1/2 – Wharfage Book, 1659–66.

BRO SMV/7/1/1/5 – Wharfage Book, 1672–74.

BRO 04220/1-2 – Register of Servants to Foreign Plantations. EXCEL Dataset created from: http://www.virtualjamestown.org/indentures/about_ indentures.html#Bristol.

Printed Primary Sources

Books of Rates

The Rates of Marchandises as they are set downe in the Books of Rates for the Custome and Subsidie of Poundage, and for the Custom and Subsidie of Clothes (London, 1604).

The Rates of Marchandises as they are set downe in the Books of Rates for the Custome and Subsidie of Poundage, and for the Custom and Subsidie of Clothes, Together with the Rates of Such Impositions as are Laide upon any Commodities, either brought into the Realme, or carried out of the same (London, 1608).

The Rates of Marchandises as they are set downe in the Books of Rates for the Custome and Subsidie of Poundage, and for the Custom and Subsidie of Clothes, Together with the Rates of Such Impositions as are Laide upon any Commodities, either brought into the Realme, or carried out of the same (London, 1612).

The Rates of Marchandises as they are set downe in the Books of Rates for the Custome and Subsidie of Poundage, and for the Custom and Subsidie of Clothes, Together with the Rates of Such Impositions as are Laide upon any Commodities, either brought into the Realme, or carried out of the same (London, 1635).

The Rates of Merchandises: That is to say, the Subsidie of Tonnage, the Subsidie of Poundage, and the Subsidie of Woollen, Cloathes, or old Drapery (London, 1642).

The Acts For: Tonnage and Poundage, Shipping and Navigation, Prevention of Fraud in His Majesties Customs, and the Book of Rates, together with an Abridgment of all the Statutes now in force, relating to the Customs (London, 1671).

The Act of Tonnage & Poundage, and Book of Rates, with several Statutes at large relating to the Customs (London, 1675).

Willan T. S. (ed.), *A Tudor Book of Rates* (Manchester, 1962).

Other

Evelyn J. (ed.), *Pomona, or, An appendix concerning fruit-trees in relation to cider the making and several ways of ordering it* (London, 1670).

Fox G., *Gospel Family-Order, Being a Short Discourse Concerning the Ordering of Families, Both of Whites, Blacks and Indians* (1676).

Worlidge J., *Vinetum Britannicum: Or a Treatise of Cider...* (London, 1678).

Secondary Sources

Andrews K., *Elizabethan Privateering* (Cambridge, 1964).

Ashworth W. J., *Customs and Excise: Trade, Production, and Consumption in England, 1640–1845* (Oxford, 2003).

Beckles H. McD., *The First Black Slave Society: Britain's 'Barbarity Time' in Barbados, 1636–1876* (Jamaica, 2016).

Blackburn R., *The Making of New World Slavery: From the Baroque to the Modern, 1492–1800* (London, 2010).

Bottigheimer K. S., 'Kingdom and Colony: Ireland in the Westward Enterprise, 1536–1660', in K. R. Andrews, N. P. Canny and P. E. H. Hair (eds), *The Westward Enterprise: English Activities in Ireland, the Atlantic and America 1480–1650* (Liverpool, 1978), pp. 45–64.

Bowly T., '"Herring of Sligo and Salmon of Bann": Bristol's Maritime Trade with Ireland in the Fifteenth Century', in R. Gorski (ed.), *Roles of the Sea in Medieval England* (Woodbridge, 2012), pp. 147–66.

Brenner R., *Merchants and Revolution: Commercial Change, Political Conflict, and London's Overseas Traders, 1550–1653* (London, 2003).

Broadberry S., Campbell B. M. S., Klein A., Overton M. and van Leeuwen B., *British Economic Growth, 1270–1870* (Cambridge, 2015).

Canny N., 'The Ideology of English Colonization: From Ireland to America', *The William and Mary Quarterly*, 30(4) (October 1973), pp. 575–98.

Canny N., *Kingdom and Colony: Ireland in the Atlantic World, 1560–1800* (London, 1988).

Canny N., 'England's New World and the Old', in N. Canny (ed.), *The Oxford History of the British Empire, Volume I: The Origins of Empire – British Overseas Enterprise to the Close of the Seventeenth Century* (Oxford, 1998), pp. 148–69.

Carus-Wilson E. M., 'The Overseas Trade of Bristol', in E. Power and M. M. Postan (eds), *Studies in English Trade in the Fifteenth Century* (London, 1933), pp. 183–246.

Carus-Wilson E. M., *Medieval Merchant Venturers* (London, 1967).

Carus Wilson E. M. and Coleman O., *England's Export Trade 1275–1574* (Oxford, 1963).

Cell G. T., *English Enterprise in Newfoundland, 1577–1660* (Toronto, 1969).

Cell G. T., *Newfoundland Discovered: English Attempts at Colonisation 1610–1630* (London, 1982).

Condon M. M. and Jones E. T., 'William Weston: Early Voyager to the New World', *Historical Research*, 91 (November 2018).

Cooper J., 'Social and Economic Policies under the Commonwealth', in G. E. Aylmer (ed.), *The Interregnum: The Quest for Settlement 1646–1660* (London, 1972), pp. 121–42.

Croft P., 'Fresh Light on Bate's Case', *The Historical Journal*, 30(3) (1987), pp. 523–39.

Croft P., 'The Rise of the English Stocking Export Trade', *Textile History*, 18(1) (1987), pp. 3–16.

Croft P., 'Trading with the Enemy 1585–1604', *The Historical Journal*, 32(2) (1989), pp. 281–302.

Cullen L. M., *Anglo-Irish Trade, 1660–1800* (Manchester, 1968).

Cullen L. M., 'Population Trends in Seventeenth-Century Ireland', *Economic and Social Review*, 6(2) (1975), pp. 149–65.

Davies K. G., *The Royal African Company* (London, 1957).

Davis R., 'England and the Mediterranean, 1570–1670', in F. J. Fisher (ed.), *Essays in the Economic and Social History of Tudor and Stuart England* (Cambridge, 1961), pp. 117–37.

Davis R., *A Commercial Revolution* (London, 1967).

Davis R., 'English Foreign Trade, 1660–1700', in W. E. Minchinton (ed.), *The Growth of English Overseas Trade in the 17th and 18th Centuries* (London, 1969), pp. 78–98.

Davis R., *The Rise of the English Shipping Industry in the 17th and 18th Centuries* (Newton Abbot, 1972).

Davis R., *English Overseas Trade 1500–1700* (London, 1973).

Davis R., *The Rise of the Atlantic Economies* (London, 1973).

Dejohn Anderson V., 'New England in the Seventeenth Century', in N. Canny (ed.), *The Oxford History of the British Empire, Volume I: The Origins of Empire, British Overseas Enterprise to the Close of the Seventeenth Century* (Oxford, 1998), pp. 193–217.

de Vries J., *The Industrious Revolution: Consumer Behaviour and the Household Economy 1650 to the Present* (Cambridge, 2008).

Donnan E., *Documents Illustrative of the History of the Slave Trade to America, Volume I: 1441–1700* (Washington, 1930).

Dresser M., *Slavery Obscured: The Social History of the Slave Trade in Bristol* (Bristol, 2001).

Dunlop R., 'A Note on the Export Trade of Ireland in 1641, 1665, and 1669', *English Historical Review*, 22(8) (1907), pp. 754–6.

Epstein M., *The English Levant Company: Its Foundation and Its History to 1640* (London, 1908).

Ewen M., *The Virginia Venture: American Colonisation and English Society, 1580–1660* (Philadelphia, 2022).

Fisher F. J., 'London's Export Trade in the Early Seventeenth Century', *Economic History Review*, 2nd ser., III(2) (1950), pp. 151–61.

Fisher F. J., 'The Sixteenth and Seventeenth Centuries: The Dark Ages in English Economic History', *Economica*, New Series, 24(93) (1957), pp. 2–18.

Flavin S., 'Consumption and Material Culture in Sixteenth-Century Ireland', *Economic History Review*, 64(4) (November 2011), pp. 1144–74.

Flavin S., *Consumption and Material Culture in Sixteenth-Century Ireland: Saffron, Stockings and Silk* (Woodbridge, 2014).

Flavin S. and Jones E. T. (eds), *Bristol's Trade with Ireland and the Continent, 1503–1601: The Evidence of the Exchequer Customs Accounts*, Bristol Record Society Vol. 61 (Dublin, 2009).

Friis A., *Alderman Cockayne's Project and the Cloth Trade: The Commercial Policy of England in Its Main Aspects, 1603–1625* (Copenhagen, 1927).

Geiter M. L., 'Penn, William', *Oxford Dictionary of National Biography* (Oxford, 2004).

Gillespie R., *The Transformation of the Irish Economy 1550–1700* (Dublin, 1998).

Gillespie R., 'Economic Life, 1550–1730', in J. Ohylmer (ed.), *The Cambridge History of Ireland, Volume II: 1550–1730* (Cambridge, 2018), pp. 531–54.

Grass N. S. B., *The Early English Customs System: A Documentary Study of the Institutional and Economic History of the Customs from the Thirteenth to the Sixteenth Century* (Cambridge, 1918).

Green C., *Severn Traders: The Westcountry Trows and Trowmen* (Gloucestershire, 1999).

Guidi Bruscoli, F., 'John Cabot and His Italian Financiers', *Historical Research*, 85 (2012), pp. 1–22.

Gwynn A., 'Medieval Bristol and Dublin', *Irish Historical Studies*, 5(20) (1947), pp. 275–86.

Hair P. E. and Law R., 'The English in Western Africa to 1700', in N. Canny (ed.), *The Oxford History of the British Empire, Volume I: The Origins of Empire – British Overseas Enterprise to the Close of the Seventeenth Century* (Oxford, 1998), pp. 241–63.

Hall I. V., 'Whitson Court Sugar House, Bristol, 1665–1824', *Transactions of the Bristol and Gloucestershire Archaeological Society*, 65 (1944), pp. 1–97.

Hall I. V., 'Bristol's Second Sugar House', *Transactions of the Bristol and Gloucestershire Archaeological Society*, 68 (1949), pp. 110–64.

Harlow J. A. S. (ed.), *The Ledger of Thomas Speed, 1681–1690*, Bristol Records Society Vol. 63 (Bristol, 2011).

Hinton R. W. K., *The Port Books of Boston 1601–1640*, Lincoln Record Society Vol. 50 (Hereford, 1956).

Hoon E. E., *The Organisation of the English Customs System 1696–1786* (Newton Abbot, 1968).

Hussey D., *Coastal and River Trade in Pre-Industrial England: Bristol and Its Region 1680–1730* (Ithaca, 2000).

Hutton R., *Debates in Stuart History* (Basingstoke, 2004).

Inikori J. E., 'Atlantic Slavery and the Rise of the Capitalist Global Economy', *Current Anthropology*, 61(supplement 22) (2020), pp. 159–71.

Ivinson J., '"To cleere the course scarse knowne": A Re-Evaluation of Richard Hakluyt's "Voyage of Master Hore" and the Development of English Atlantic Enterprise in the Early Sixteenth Century', *Historical Research*, 94(263) (2021), pp. 1–27.

João Soares M., 'The British Presence on the Cape Verdean Archipelago (Sixteenth to Eighteenth Centuries', *African Economic History*, 39 (2011), pp. 129–46.

Jenks S., *Robert Sturmy's Commercial Expedition to the Mediterranean (1457/8)*, Bristol Record Society Vol. 58 (Bristol, 2006).

Jennings J., 'Mid-Eighteenth-Century British Quakerism and the Response to the Problem of Slavery', *Quaker History*, 66(1) (1977), pp. 23–40.

Jones D., *Bristol's Sugar Trade and Refining Industry*, Bristol Historical Association Pamphlets no. 89 (Bristol, 2003).

Jones E. T., 'Bristol and Newfoundland, 1490–1570', in I. Bulgin (ed.), *Cabot and His World Symposium* (Newfoundland Historical Society, St. Johns, 1999), pp. 73–81.

Jones E. T., 'The *Matthew* of Bristol and the Financiers of John Cabot's 1497 Voyage to North America', *English Historical Review*, 121(492) (2006), pp. 778–95.

Jones E. T., 'Alwyn Ruddock: "John Cabot and the Discovery of America"', *Historical Research*, 81(212) (2007), pp. 224–54.

Jones E. T., 'Henry VII and the Bristol Expeditions to North America: The Condon Documents', *Historical Research*, 83(221) (2010), pp. 444–54.

Jones, E. T., *Inside the Illicit Economy: Reconstructing the Smugglers' Trade of Sixteenth Century Bristol* (Farnham, 2012).

Jones E. T., 'The Shipping Industry of the Severn Sea', in E. T. Jones and R. Stone (eds), *The World of the Newport Medieval Ship: Trade, Politics and Shipping in the Mid-Fifteenth Century* (Cardiff, 2018), pp. 135–59.

Jones E. T. and Condon M. M., *Cabot and Bristol's Age of Discovery* (Bristol, 2016).

Kaufman M., *Black Tudors: The Untold Story* (London, 2017).

Latimer J., *The Annals of Bristol in the Seventeenth Century* (Bristol, 1900).

Latimer J., *The History of the Society of Merchant Venturers of the City of Bristol, with Some Account of the Anterior Merchants' Guilds* (New York, 1970).

Leech R., Barry J., Brown A., Ferguson C. and Parkinson E. (eds), *The Bristol Hearth Tax, 1662–1763*, Bristol Record Society Vol. 70 (Bristol, 2018).

Lobel M. D. and Carus Wilson E. M., 'Bristol', in M. D. Lobel (ed.), *The Atlas of Historic Towns, Volume 2* (London, 1975), pp. 1–29.

Longfield A. K., *Anglo-Irish Trade in the Sixteenth Century* (London, 1929).

MacInnes C. M., *England and Slavery* (Bristol, 1934).

MacInnes C. M., *Bristol: A Gateway of Empire* (Bristol, 1939/Newton Abbot, 1968).

MacInnes C. M., *Bristol and the Slave Trade*, Bristol Historical Association Pamphlets (Bristol, 1963).

MacInnes C. M., *Ferdinando Gorges and New England* (Bristol, 1965).

Marshall I., *A History and Ethnography of the Beothuk* (Montreal, 1996).

McCusker J. J. and Menard R. R., *The Economy of British America, 1607–1789* (London, 1985).

McGrath P. V., *Records Relating to the Society of Merchant Venturers of the City of Bristol in the Seventeenth Century*, Bristol Record Society Vol. 17 (Bristol, 1952).

McGrath P. V., 'Merchant Shipping in the Seventeenth Century: The Evidence of the Bristol Deposition Books, Part I', *Mariner's Mirror*, XL (1954).

McGrath P. V., 'Merchant Shipping Part II', *Mariner's Mirror*, XLI (1955).

McGrath P. V.., *Merchants and Merchandise in Seventeenth-Century Bristol*, Bristol Record Society Vol. 19 (Bristol, 1955).

McGrath P. V., *The Merchant Venturers of Bristol* (Bristol, 1975).

McGrath P. V., 'Bristol and America, 1481–1631', in K. R. Andrews, N. P. Canny and P. E. H. Hair (eds), *The Westward Enterprise: English Activities in Ireland, the Atlantic and America 1480–1650* (Liverpool, 1978), pp. 81–102.

McNeill J., *The Life and Family of William Penn: 260 Years of Bloody Colonial History*, Bristol Radical Pamphleteer No. 18 (Bristol, 2012).

Meiksins Wood E., *The Origin of Capitalism: A Longer View* (London, 2017).

Menard R. R., 'From Servant to Freeholder: Status Mobility and Property Accumulation in Seventeenth-Century Maryland', *The William and Mary Quarterly*, 30(1) (1973), pp. 37–64.

Menard R. R., 'The Tobacco Industry in the Chesapeake Colonies, 1617–1730: An Interpretation', *Research in Economic History*, 5 (1980), pp. 109–77.

Minchinton W. E., 'Bristol, Metropolis of the West in the Eighteenth Century', *Transactions of the Royal Historical Society*, 5th ser., IV (1954), pp. 69–89.

Minchinton W. E. (ed.), *The Trade of Bristol in the Eighteenth Century*, Bristol Record Society Vol. 20 (Bristol, 1957).

Minchinton W. E. (ed.), *The Growth of English Overseas Trade in the Seventeenth and Eighteenth Centuries* (London, 1969).

Morgan K., *Bristol and the Atlantic Trade in the Eighteenth Century* (Cambridge, 1993).

Morgan K., 'The Economic Development of Bristol, 1700–1850', in M. Dresser and P. Ollerenshaw (eds), *The Making of Modern Bristol* (Bristol, 1996), pp. 48–75.

Morgan K., 'Sugar Refining in Bristol', in K. Bruland and P. O'Brien (eds), *From Family Firms to Corporate Capitalism: Essays in Business and Industrial History in Honour of Peter Mathias* (Oxford, 1998), pp. 139–69.

Morgan K., *Edward Colston and Bristol* (Bristol, 1999).

Morgan K., *Slavery, Atlantic Trade and the British Economy, 1660–1800* (Cambridge, 2000).

Morgan K., *Slavery and Servitude in North America, 1607–1800* (Edinburgh, 2000).

Morgan K., 'Colston, Edward', *Oxford Dictionary of National Biography* (Oxford, 2004).

Morgan K., *Slavery and the British Empire: From Africa to America* (Oxford, 2007).

Mortimer R. (ed.), *Minute Book of the Men's Meeting of the Society of Friends in Bristol 1667–1686*, Bristol Records Society Vol. XXVI (1971).

Nash R. C., 'The English and Scottish Tobacco Trades in the Seventeenth and Eighteenth Centuries: Legal and Illegal Trade', *Economic History Review*, 33(2) (1982), pp. 354–72.

Nash R. C., 'Irish Atlantic Trade in the Seventeenth and Eighteenth Centuries', *The William and Mary Quarterly*, 42(3) (1985), pp. 329–56.

Nef J. U., 'The Progress of Technology and the Growth of Large-Scale Industry in Great Britain, 1540–1640', *Economic History Review*, 5(1) (1934), pp. 3–24.

Nott H. E. (ed.), *The Deposition Books of Bristol, Volume I: 1643–1647*, Bristol Record Society Vol. 6 (Bristol, 1935).

O'Brien P., 'European Economic Development: The Contribution of the Periphery', *Economic History Review*, 35(1) (1982), pp. 1–18.

O'Flanagan P., *Port Cities of Atlantic Iberia, c. 1500–1900* (Aldershot, 2008).

Pelteret D., 'Slave Raiding and Slave Trading in Early England', *Anglo-Saxon England*, 9 (1981), pp. 99–114.

Pike R., 'Sevillian Society in the Sixteenth Century; Slaves and Freedmen', *The Hispanic American Historical Review*, 47(3) (1967), pp. 344–59.

Pomeranz K., *The Great Divergence: China, Europe, and the Making of the Modern World Economy* (Princeton, 2000).

Pope P. E., *Fish into Wine: The Newfoundland Plantation in the Seventeenth Century* (Chapel Hill, NC, 2004).

Power E. and Postan M. M. (eds), *Studies in English Trade in the Fifteenth Century* (London, 1933).

Price R., *Bristol Burgesses: 1525–1557, Calendared from the Corporation's Great Audit Books* (Bristol, 2010).

Ramsay G. D., *English Overseas Trade during the Centuries of Emergence: Studies in Some Modern Origins of the English-Speaking World* (London, 1957).

Richardson D., *The Bristol Slave Traders: A Collective Portrait* (Bristol, 1985).

Richardson D., *Bristol, Africa, and the Eighteenth-Century Slave Trade to America, Volume 1: The Years of Expansion, 1698–1729*, Bristol Record Society Vol. 38 (Bristol, 1986).

Richardson D., 'The Eighteenth-Century British Slave Trade: Estimates of Its Volume and Coastal Distribution in Africa', *Research in Economic History*, 12 (1989), pp. 151–95.

Richardson D., 'Cape Verde, Madeira and Britain's Trade to Africa, 1698–1740', *The Journal of Imperial and Commonwealth History*, 22(1) (1994), pp. 1–15.

Richardson D., 'The British Empire and the Atlantic Slave Trade, 1660–1807', in P. J. Marshall (ed.), *The Oxford History of the British Empire, Volume II: The Eighteenth Century* (Oxford, 1998), pp. 440–64.

Richardson D., 'Slavery and Bristol's "Golden Age"', *Slavery and Abolition*, 26(1) (2005), pp. 35–54.

Rodney W., 'Portuguese Attempts at Monopoly on the Upper Guinea Coast, 1580–1650', *The Journal of African History*, 6(3) (1965), pp. 307–22.

Rogers J. E. T., *A History of Agriculture and Prices in England, Volume 5* (Oxford, 1887).

Ruddock A. A., *Italian Merchants and Shipping in Southampton, 1270–1600* (Southampton, 1951).

Sacks D. H., *The Widening Gate: Bristol and the Atlantic Economy, 1450–1700* (London, 1993).

Shammas C., *The Pre-Industrial Consumer in England and America* (Los Angeles, 2008).

Sherborne J. W., *The Port of Bristol in the Middle Ages* (Bristol, 1965).

Smith B., 'Late Medieval Ireland and the English Connection: Waterford and Bristol c.1360–c.1460', *Journal of British Studies*, 50(3) (2011), pp. 546–65.

Smith E., *Merchants: The Community That Shaped England's Trade and Empire* (London, 2021).

Smith E., 'The Social Networks of Investment in Early Modern England', *The Historical Journal*, 64(4) (2021), pp. 912–39.

Souden D., '"Rogues, Whores and Vagabonds"? Indentured Servant Emigrants to North America, and the Case of Mid-Seventeenth-Century Bristol', *Social History*, 3(1) (1978), pp. 23–41.

Steeds M. and Ball R., *From Wulfstan to Colston: Severing the Sinews of Slavery in Bristol* (Bristol, 2020).

Stephens W. B., *Seventeenth-Century Exeter: A Study of Industrial and Commercial Development, 1625–1688* (Exeter, 1958).

Stephens W. B., 'The Cloth Exports of the Provincial Ports, 1600–1640', *Economic History Review*, 22 (1969), pp. 228–48.

Stephens W. B., 'Trade Trends at Bristol, 1600–1700', *Transactions of the Bristol and Gloucestershire Archaeological Society* (1974), pp. 156–61.

Stephens W. B., *The Seventeenth-Century Customs Service Surveyed: William Culliford's Investigation of the Western Ports, 1682–84* (Farnham, 2012).

Stone R., 'The Overseas Trade of Bristol before the Civil War', *The International Journal of Maritime History*, 23(2) (2011), pp. 211–39.

Stone R., 'Bristol's Overseas Trade in the Later Fifteenth Century: The Evidence of the "Particular" Customs Accounts', in E. T. Jones and R. Stone (eds), *The World of the Newport Medieval Ship: Trade, Politics, and Shipping in the Mid-Fifteenth Century* (Cardiff, 2018), pp. 183–203.

Supple B. E., *Commercial Crisis and Change, 1600–1642: A Study in the Instability of a Mercantile Economy* (Cambridge, 1949).

Tinniswood A., *Pirates of Barbary* (London, 2011).

Turner E. R., 'Slavery in Colonial Pennsylvania', *The Pennsylvania Magazine of History and Biography*, 25(2) (1911), pp. 141–51.

Vanes J. M. (ed.), *The Ledger of John Smythe, 1538–1550*, Bristol Records Society Vol. 28 (Bristol, 1975).

Vanes J. M., *The Port of Bristol in the Sixteenth Century*, Bristol Historical Association Pamphlets no. 39 (Bristol, 1977).

Vanes J. M., *Documents Illustrating the Overseas Trade of Bristol in the Sixteenth Century*, Bristol Record Society Vol. 31 (Bristol, 1979).

Wallerstein I., *The Modern World-System II: Mercantilism and the Consolidation of the European World-Economy, 1600–1750* (London, 2011).

Walvin J., *Slaves and Slavery: The British Colonial Experience* (Manchester, 1992).

Willan T. S. (ed.), *A Tudor Book of Rates* (Manchester, 1962).

Williams A. F. (edited by G. Hancock and C. W. Sanger), *John Guy of Bristol and Newfoundland* (St. Johns, 2010).

Williams E., *Capitalism and Slavery* (London, 1964).

Williams J., *Food and Religious Identities in Spain, 1400–1600* (London, 2017).

Williams N., *Contraband Cargoes: Seven Centuries of Smuggling* (London, 1959).

Wilson C., *Profit and Power – A Study of England and the Dutch Wars* (London, 1957).

Wilson C., *England's Apprenticeship, 1603–1763* (London, 1965).

Wilson S. S., *Descriptive List of Exchequer, Queen's Remembrancer, Port Books, Part 1 – 1565 to 1700* (London, 1960).

Woodward D. M., 'The Overseas Trade of Chester, 1600–1650', *Transactions of the Historic Society of Lancashire and Cheshire*, CXXII (1970), pp. 25–42.

Woodward D. M., *The Trade of Elizabethan Chester* (Hull, 1970).

Woodward D. M., 'The Anglo-Irish Livestock Trade of the Seventeenth Century', *Irish Historical Studies*, 18(72) (1973), pp. 489–523.

Zahedieh N., 'Trade, Plunder, and Economic Development in Early English Jamaica, 1655–89', *Economic History Review*, 32(2) (1986), pp. 205–22.

Zahedieh N., 'Overseas Expansion and Trade in the Seventeenth Century', in N. Canny (ed.), *The Oxford History of the British Empire, Volume I: The Origins of Empire – British Overseas Enterprise to the Close of the Seventeenth Century* (Oxford, 1998), pp. 398–422.

Zahedieh N., 'Morgan, Sir Henry c. 1635–1688', *Oxford Dictionary of National Biography* (Oxford, 2008).

Zahedieh N., *The Capital and the Colonies: London and the Atlantic Economy, 1660–1700* (Cambridge, 2010).

Zahedieh N., 'Colonies, Copper, and the Market for Inventive Activity in England and Wales, 1680–1730', *Economic History Review*, 66(3) (2013), pp. 805–25.

Zahedieh N., 'Britain's Atlantic Slave Economy, the Market for Knowledge and Skills, and Early Industrialisation: A Response to Joel Mokyr's "Holy Land of Industrialism"', *Journal of the British Academy*, 9 (2021), pp. 283–93.

Zahedieh N., 'Eric Williams and William Forbes: Copper, Colonial Markets, and Commercial Capitalism', *Economic History Review*, 74(3) (2021), pp. 784–808.

Unpublished Theses

Harlow J. A. S., 'The Life and Times of Thomas Speed' (University of the West of England, 2008).

Heal C., 'The Felt Hat Industry of Bristol and South Gloucestershire, 1530–1909' (University of Bristol, 2012).

Millard A. M., 'The Import Trade of London, 1600–1640' (University of London, 1956).

Stone R., 'The Overseas Trade of Bristol in the Seventeenth Century' (University of Bristol, 2012).

Tyack N. C. P., 'The Trade Relations of Bristol with Virginia during the 17th Century' (University of Bristol, 1930).

Tyack N. C. P., 'Bristol Merchants, Shipwrights, Ship-Carpenters, Sailmakers, Anchorsmiths, Seamen, Tobacco-Cutters, Tobacco-Rollers, Tobacconists, Tobacco Pipe-Makers. A Transcript Chronologically Arranged, from the Bristol Burgess Books: 1607–1700' (unpublished transcript, University of Bristol, 1930).

Index

Please note that individual people appear as headings in their own right, with the exception of Bristol's merchants (*see* Bristol, merchants of). Scholars appear only when their work is engaged with in a substantial and sustained way. Page numbers in bold refer the reader to images. Finally, we have taken the view that, even though enslaved people were generally regarded as commodities throughout this period, they should not be indexed as such (*see* slavery, transatlantic).